Focus on Educating for Sustainability

Focus on Educating for Sustainability: Toolkit for Academic Libraries

Edited by Maria Anna Jankowska

Library Juice Press
Sacramento, CA

Published in 2014 by Library Juice Press

PO Box 188784
Sacramento, CA 95822

http://libraryjuicepress.com/

This book is printed on acid-free, sustainably-sourced paper.

Library of Congress Cataloging-in-Publication Data

　　Focus on educating for sustainability : toolkit for academic libraries / edited by Maria Anna Jankowska.
　　　　pages cm
　　Summary: "Compiles best practices, case studies, and activities ready for implementation within academic libraries to advance a mission of education for environmental sustainability"--Provided by publisher.
　　Includes bibliographical references and index.
　　ISBN 978-1-936117-61-1 (alk. paper)
　　1. Academic libraries--Relations with faculty and curriculum. 2. Academic libraries--Environmental aspects. 3. Libraries--Special collections--Sustainability. 4. Libraries--Special collections--Sustainable development. 5. Sustainability--Study and teaching (Higher) 6. Sustainable development--Study and teaching (Higher) 7. Environmental literacy--Study and teaching (Higher) 8. Environmental education. 9. Academic libraries--United States--Case studies. 10. Libraries and colleges--United States--Case studies. I. Jankowska, Maria Anna, editor of compilation.
　　Z675.U5F63 2014
　　027.7--dc23

　　　　　　　　　　2013047672

Table of Contents

Table of Contents

Acknowledgments

This volume would not be possible without the support of many individuals including my family, the contributing authors and all librarians who have inspired the book editor over the course of many years to undertake this effort. This book is dedicated to all of them.

Introduction

The contextual idea of sustainability dates back to the mid-nineteenth century conservation movement and the twentieth century environmental movement. Thomas R. Wellock (2007) named three schools of thought that influenced both movements: natural resource management and conservation (championed by Gifford Pinchot), wilderness preservation (John Muir), and urban quality of life issues related to environment (Edwin Chadwick). Higher education's commitment to sustainability started in the late eighties and was influenced by many historical events and documents, but two of them need to be mentioned here. The first is the Report of the World Commission on Environment and Development (WCED) from December 11, 1987 known as the Brundtland Report, *Our Common Future*. It addressed the Commission's concerns "about the accelerating deterioration of the human environment and natural resources and the consequences of that deterioration for economic and social development," and defined sustainability as a balance between economic vitality, social equity, and the ecological integrity to meet "...the needs of the present without compromising the ability of future generations to meet their own needs" (WCED, 1987, p. 43).

The second is the 1990 *Talloires Declaration* signed by the University Leaders for Sustainable Future (USLF) from all over the world. The declaration stated that: "Universities bear profound responsibility to increase the awareness, knowledge, technologies and tools to create an environmentally sustainable future" (USLF, 2001). The Talloires Declaration spurred the academic move-

1

ment, supported by national organizations, aiming to strengthen the campus environment (Campus Ecology), university efforts toward sustainable teaching and research (Second Nature), and in 2006 the Association for the Advancement of Sustainability in Higher Education (AASHE), which serves as the first professional higher education association for the campus sustainability community.

For the editor of this book, it was Manfred Max-Neef (1992) and his "barefoot economics" theory that sparked her interest in sustainability, and desire to inform others about sustainability issues. This Chilean economist and ecological visionary is an expert on poverty and a strong believer in balanced economic growth having its limits. After reaching the maximum sustainable level, economic growth becomes dangerous due to a disregard of an even distribution of economic benefits, social equity, and environmental impacts. As a library student, she helped collect and send books to countries where sustainability awareness was low or non-existent, and when this became too difficult to continue, in 1992 she started the *Green Library Journal: Environmental Topics in the Information World*. In 1994 it became the *Electronic Green Journal*, the first open access journal published by an academic library and the first electronic journal focused on environmental justice, literacy, social equity, sustainability topics. The importance of the journal for the library profession was underscored in the following quote: "The creation of the *Electronic Green Journal* not only demonstrates entrepreneurial librarianship, but also marks an important milestone in sustainability research and publication" (Krautter, Lock & Scanlon, 2012, p.184).

Chairing the ALA's Task Force on the Environment for more than ten years and being active as a council member of the ALA's Social Responsibility Round Table provided crucial experience for the editor to start thinking about the active participation of libraries in the university sustainability movement. This was an exciting time for libraries and sustainability, and the concept of libraries becoming active participants in university efforts crystalized and gained momentum after the 2007 Presidents' Climate Commitment. Through this Commitment university presidents and chancellors dedicated their institutions to finding new solutions to environmental, economic, and social issues through their teaching, research, and service operations.

Academic libraries responded by shifting their focus from "greening" libraries to becoming active partners in advancing education and research for sustainability. In discussions about future development of academic libraries, sustainability has become the most important attribute to strategic planning and assessment practice both in design and content. Sustainability indicates how libraries contribute to the future improvements in social, economic, and environmental conditions of the university community, the public, and beyond.

As David Owen (2009) emphasized:

"The crucial fact about sustainability is that it is not a micro phenomenon: there can be no such things as a "sustainable" house, office building, or household appliance, for the same reason that there can be no such things as a one-person democracy or single-company economy. …
[I]t's the network, not the individual constituents, on which our future depends." (p. 40)

Two recycling bins or one isolated sustainability program does not make a sustainable library. A single library promoting sustainability practices does not matter in the absence of a network of academic libraries working collectively toward advancing sustainability. This book emphasizes Owen's point by contributing a unique mix of interests, services, collaboration and programs created in the network of American academic libraries. All presented initiatives have one common goal: strengthening institutional focus on educating for sustainability.

In this volume sustainability is defined in many ways. As Melanie DuPuis and Tamara Ball (2013) note: "Defining sustainability is not taken as a problem that needs to be 'solved', but an opportunity to raise new ways of thinking about the world" (p.66). In this regard this volume presents an opportunity to raise a new way of thinking in and about academic libraries. For example Burt stresses: "sustainability discussions must balance questions such as whether fracking delivers the right balance of cheap and environmentally safe energy, or if increasing the minimum wage would benefit the country as a whole.

Amy Brunvand, Alison Regan, Joshua Lenart, Jessica Breiman, and Emily Bullough define sustainability as "an interdisciplinary and transdisciplinary area of study."

Goals and Outline of the Book

This collection strives to capture the current status and future direction of libraries' and librarians' commitment to advance sustainability education. The book emphasizes a new role for academic libraries, infusing sustainability content into information literacy, collection development, scholarly publishing and communication, services, actions, and the education of future leaders. Its goal is to serve as a toolkit offering a wide range of best practices, case studies, and activities ready for implementation within academic libraries and the library profession.

The volume is divided into four sections. Section 1: *Integrating Sustainability Literacy Into Information Literacy and University Courses* includes seven chapters focused on integrating sustainability literacy into the first-year composition curriculum, interior design, humanities, information literacy sessions, and teaching by doing. The first chapter, "Legitimizing the Local: Integrating Sustainability Into Information Literacy Instruction and First-Year Composition" is submitted by Kathleen Ryan, a Professor of Rhetoric and Composition at Montana State University and Megan Stark, an Undergraduate Services Librarian and Assistant Professor at University of Montana. In this chapter the authors describe how the university library and composition program at the University of Montana developed strong sustainability-focused research instruction for their first-year composition curriculum. The next chapter by Alessia Zanin-Yost from Hunter Library at Western Carolina University is titled, "Three for One: Teaching Sustainable Education, Information Literacy, and Visual Literacy with the Inventory Compilation Assignment." In this chapter Zanin-Yost argues that students, specifically those studying interior design, can greatly benefit from learning the interconnectivity between sustainability and their profession.

In chapter three, Toni M. Carter and Gregory J. Schmidt contribute "Sustainability Literacy and Information Literacy: Leveraging Librarian Expertise." The authors examine three avenues by which librarians at Auburn University integrate sustainability literacy into information literacy sessions. Amy Pajewski from the West Texas A&M University Library contributes chapter four, "Teaching Sustainable Information Literacy: A Collaborative Endeavor in the Humanities." In this chapter Pajewski provides tools to start a collaborative effort to promote lifelong critical thinking in sustainability that can be adapted to a broad range of disciplines. Laura Burt-Nicholas from the College of DuPage Library contributes chapter five, "Making Research Real: Focusing on Community-Based Sustainability", which examines how using problem-based learning focused on local sustainability issues inspired students to complete complex research projects.

Mary G. Scanlon, Peter A. Romanov, and Mary Beth Lock from the Z. Smith Reynolds Library at Wake Forest University contribute chapter six, "Teaching by Doing: Sustainability Education and Practice in a Student-Services Program." The authors present a successful case study on teaching students by practicing sustainable solutions during a finals week. The final chapter of the section, "Library Showcase: Modeling Sustainability across Campus" is by Dawn Emsellem from the McKillop Library, Salve Regina University and Jameson F. Chace, an Associate Professor of Biology and coordinator of the Environmental Studies program at Salve Regina University. This chapter reports on new strategic directives for the library that spun off several initiatives, including a formal library commitment to sustainability, the formation of a staff/faculty environmental group, a building-wide recycling and donation program, and online research guides highlighting the library's environmental science resources.

4

Section 2: *Building Collection Supporting Sustainability Curriculum* begins with teamwork contribution by Amy Brunvand, Alison Regan, Joshua Lenart, Jessica Breiman, and Emily Bullough from the J. Willard Marriott Library at University of Utah. In their chapter, "Building an Academic Library Collection to Support Sustainability," the authors present how to develop collections that would help in teaching and research on sustainability. The next chapter is contributed by Kasia Leousis and Greg Schmidt from the Auburn University Library. In their chapter, "Interdisciplinary Collaboration for Collection Development in Sustainability: Starting from Scratch," the authors present how collaboration among librarians and faculty across multiple disciplines helped create a core sustainability collection.

Section 3: *Sustainable Scholarship* includes three chapters. The first chapter, "Connecting Journal Articles with Their Underlying Data: Encouraging Sustainable Scholarship through the Public Knowledge Project (PKP) - Dataverse Network Integration Project," is by Eleni Castro from Harvard Dataverse Network. The author presents collaboration between academic institutions and publishers for scholarly output to be shared and preserved in a sustainable manner. This collaboration focuses on connecting journal publications with their underlying data through the integration of two well-established open source systems: PKP's Open Journal Systems (OJS) and Harvard's Dataverse Network web application. Barbara DeFelice from the Dartmouth College Library contributes the next chapter, "Library Publishing Services for Sustainability." In this chapter the author makes a case for providing new publishing opportunities for faculty and students interested in sustainability. The third chapter, "Community Archiving and Sustainability: Denison University's Homestead," contributed by Joshua Finnell from the Denison University, provides an overview of creating a digital archive documenting the cultural impact of the pioneering experiment on the campus.

Section 4: *The Landscape for Changes* consists of seven chapters. It is filled with examples of best practices, initiatives, solutions, activities, and literature to inspire readers in their work and daily life. Section four opens with a teamwork contribution by Anne Marie Casey from the Hunt Library at Embry-Riddle Aeronautical University, Jon E. Cawthorne from the Florida State University Libraries, Kathleen DeLong from the University of Alberta Libraries, Irene M. H. Herold from the University of Hawaii Library, and Adriene Lim from the Oakland University Libraries in Michigan. The first chapter, "The Triple Bottom Line Accounting (TBLA): Portable Applications and Best Practices for Sustainability in Academic Libraries," presents a TBLA method of measuring the economic, environmental, and community service impacts of an organization rather than the traditional practice of measuring just the financial bottom line. It concludes with ideas for the implementation of TBLA in libraries.

The next chapter, "Becoming Sustainability Leaders: A Professional Development Experience for Librarians" is contributed by Madeleine Charney from University of Massachusetts Amherst Libraries. In this chapter Madeleine describes her work as an instructor during a two-week course on sustainability for library professionals. The third chapter, "Academic Libraries as Sustainability Leaders" is contributed by Karren Nichols from the J. Willard Marriott Library, University of Utah. In this chapter readers will discover how academic libraries could become living laboratories where students, faculty and staff can easily connect to find the space and resources to explore environmental sustainability and enhance the learning experience. The next chapter by Kim Kane and Annelise Sklar titled, "Greening the Mothership: Growing the Environmental Sustainability Group at the University California San Diego Library," describes sustainability projects undertaken by the library staff at the authors' library. This chapter is aimed at libraries starting to plan environmental sustainability activities, and in Appendix I of this chapter the readers will find advice on creating sustainability groups at their library.

Chapter five presents "Sustainability: Putting Principles into Practice at a Catholic University Library" by Ted Bergfelt and Allison Brungard from the Gumberg Library at Duquesne University. This chapter examines Duquesne University sustainability initiatives and the Gumberg Library's role in them, relating these to the larger context of Catholic Social Thought. Chapter six, "Seed Libraries: Growing a New Library Service" by René Tanner from the Arizona State University Libraries describes the efforts made by libraries as well as various institutions to preserve seed diversity and encourage gardening. The chapter also delves into the main reasons why seed preservation is important and the benefits seed libraries can have to promote diverse food ecosystems. The last chapter in section four, "Sustainability and the Increasing Energy Demand to Access Library Resources" by Mara M. J. Egherman from the Central College Library in Pella reports on how librarians in higher education are taking a leadership role in reducing energy demands to access library resources.

Overall, this volume presents several inspiring solutions ready to be implemented by librarians to make academic libraries network more sustainable for the future users. Ideas presented in these chapters should provide a strong platform for discussion about the integrated library network focused on advancing learning for sustainability.

References

DuPuis, M. & Ball, T. (2013). How not what: Teaching sustainability as process. *Sustainability: Science, Practice, & Policy*, 9(1), 64-74.

Krautter, M., Lock M. B., & Scanlon, M. G. (2012). *The entrepreneurial librarian: Essays on the infusion of private-business dynamism into professional service*. Jefferson, NC: McFarland & Company, Inc., Publishers.

Max-Neef, M. A. (1992). *From the outside looking in: Experiences in "barefoot economics"*. London: Zed Books.

Owen, D. (2009). *Green metropolis. Why living smaller, living closer, and driving less are the keys to sustainability*. New York: Riverhead Books.

Wellock, T.R. (2007). *Preserving the nation: The conservation and environmental movements, 1870-2000*. Wheeling, IL: Harlan Davidson, Inc.

World Commission on Environment and Development (WCED) (1987). *Our common future*. Oxford: Oxford University Press.

University Leaders for Sustainable Future (USLF). (2001). *Talloires Declaration*. Retrieved from http://www.ulsf.org/programs_talloires_report.html

Section One

Integrating Sustainability Literacy into Information Literacy

Legitimizing the Local: Integrating Sustainability into Information Literacy Instruction and First-Year Composition

Kathleen J. Ryan and Megan Stark

Abstract

This chapter describes how the university library and composition program at the University of Montana (UM) developed strong sustainability-focused research instruction for the first-year composition curriculum. The authors discuss best practices for translating national information literacy standards meaningfully to local environments in the context of specific course and assignment design.

Introduction

Collaboration between composition or first-year writing programs and academic libraries is commonplace. Boyd-Byrnes and McDermott (2006) examined the interaction between academic libraries and first-year instruction, including the integration of Association of College and Research Libraries (ACRL) standards, and found that sixty percent of the libraries surveyed deliver library instruction in English composition (p. 8), and a large majority of librarians incorporate ACRL information literacy standards in some way into instruction (p. 12). Librarians have continually learned new strategies for developing effective information literacy programs from participation within first-year instruction.

Library instruction programs have learned that building robust collaboration depends upon librarians and instructors working together to design research-based writing assignments (Barratt, et. al., 2009). The authors have learned to refine specific tasks like "research logs" (Brady, et. al., 2009) to better connect to the course content and minimize their perception, by students, as "busy work" and unnecessarily "detailed record keeping" (Corbett, 2010, p. 274). Also, the authors have learned that asking students to reflect critically on their pursuit of sources must be done thoughtfully, carefully (Deitering and Jameson, 2008, p. 68; Corbett, 2010, p. 274).

Finally, and most significantly for integrating sustainability into information literacy instruction, the authors have learned that composition instructors are more focused on how a source is used than where a source is from (Barratt, et. al., 2009, p. 54)—that the so-called objective qualities of scholarly material are less important for source evaluation than a student's ability to effectively position sources around a topic. As Peter Goggin and Zach Waggoner noticed, "the concept of sustainability assumes confluence of pragmatism, activism, and critical awareness conceived within the complex realm of social context" (p. 52). A source gains meaning and value based on how it is used by a student researcher. Deitering and Jameson (2008) focused on the "epistemological dimension [of] critical thinking" (p. 59) by encouraging students to recognize that knowledge—and organized information—is a construct and not a set of definitive answers waiting to be discovered.

Theoretical Rationale

Academic libraries have encouraged students to objectively interact with information in at least two major ways. First, collection development across institutions is so similar that the content held by academic libraries has tremendous overlap. This includes monographs, media and, database holdings. Information that makes our collections unique is frequently relegated to Archives and/or Special Collections, is difficult to access, challenging to cite, and rarely included in information literacy instruction outside departments requiring a focus on primary material.

Second, academic librarians have aligned information literacy instruction so rigidly with national ACRL standards that librarians seem to believe that college students achieve the same information literacy performance indicators regardless of any influence of their local environment. This practice contributes to students' perception that finding and evaluating information always follows the same research path, and that "good" information has intrinsic qualities that are discoverable by "good" researchers – that what counts as "good" is not context dependent. This assumption may seem harmless, but it means librarians teach students to interact with information as consumers tasked only with revealing the intrinsic, objective qualities of information instead of as meaning makers (Berthoff, 1981).

Librarians should be developing information literacy skills that motivate students to question the ways information is constructed and valued by academic libraries and teaching them that finding and evaluating sources does not depend upon an external, objective value system. Integrating sustainability into information literacy instruction presents an opportunity to re-establish local, contextual meaning to the ways librarians teach students to find and engage sources. Translating national, abstract standards to a local context restructures how to teach students to engage research and encourage students to, "develop as sustainable thinkers...capable of investigating information and applying their research in ways that inherently link sustainability to their scholarly practices" (Stark, 2011). To that end, this case study describes how the university library and composition program at the University of Montana (UM) developed strong sustainability-focused research instruction for the first-year composition curriculum. In particular, the authors discuss best practices for translating national information literacy standards meaningfully to local environments in the context of specific course and assignment design. Integrating sustainability into information literacy instruction invigorates our thinking by challenging the traditional use of sources in academic libraries and the way library research supports student writing.

Course Description

The authors work together builds on a long-term collaborative relationship between the university's library and first-year composition program. In "The Learning Environment: First-Year Students, Teaching Assistants, and Information Literacy," Sue Samson and Michelle S. Millet (2002) describe ways in which information literacy is embedded in first-year composition and public speaking courses. Since 1998, instruction librarians have collaborated with program directors to help teaching assistants bring appropriate information literacy concepts into the curriculum. This approach is a "carefully developed plan of teaching the teachers who then provide the information literacy instruction within the framework of their classes" (Samson & Millet, p. 86). Since 2010, the authors have developed this collaboration in two ways: extended the amount and kind of teaching of teachers and focused on ways to incorporate sustainability research, including local research, into the first-year composition curriculum. These program revisions are a response to the authors' personal and professional commitment to, on the one hand, focus on inquiry into sustainability as a framework for teaching research to encourage students to explore "fundamental interconnections between culture, survival, body, and place" (Owens, 2001, p. xiii). Also on the other, to develop the ways the authors teach teachers to more effectively help instructors (graduate students) help their students find, evaluate, and use sources.

The authors began this work by participating in a cross-disciplinary faculty development workshop, called Green Thread, on ways to integrate sustainability into undergraduate courses (http://www2.umt.edu/urelations/nf/archive/020209.html#article7). As educators at an institution with a strong commitment to sustainability (UM offers minors in climate change and wilderness and civilization, nationally recognized College of Forestry and Conservation and Environmental Studies Program, and the university president signed the American College and University Presidents Climate Commitment in 2007), the authors are well-positioned to speculate on how life place curricula may function for our students.

In Spring 2009, the first-year composition curriculum was revised to focus on inquiry into sustainability following participation in this workshop. Through this collaboration and research into ecocomposition, a subfield of rhetoric and composition, the authors realized that sustainability is a productive way to shape first-year composition on our campus for students and teachers. Ecocomposition, as "the study of the relationships between environments (natural, constructed, and even imagined places) and discourse (speaking, writing, and thinking)" (Dobrin and Weisser, 2002, p. 6), offers a powerful way to encourage students and teachers to inhabit where they live, work, and study in the context of learning what it means to recognize writing as an ecology. The authors emphasize an ecological literacy approach to ecocomposition, where aspects of sustainability—from town/gown tensions to the "greenwashing" of the term itself—are subjects of inquiry, but also one that enacts what Dobrin and Weisser call a discursive ecology approach by encouraging students to "see writing as an activity of relationships" (p. 584). This second focus means students learn to conduct research as a means of entering academic discourse through the lens of a scholarly conversation.

The authors brought an emphasis on restructuring the research process to the curriculum. Based on analysis and reflection on the topic of sustainability and information literacy standards operative at UM, the authors have taken up the critical argument that, "[e]ncouraging students to pursue the value of local knowledge is a fundamental step in fusing sustainability into information literacy practices" (Stark, 2011, p. 6). That is, inquiry into sustainability brings together abstract information literacy standards and local knowledge and practices. The authors have further developed our instructional collaboration because of two challenges: first, inquiry into sustainability is unfamiliar for teachers and second, research that focuses on sustainability and local sources disrupts the way information has been traditionally valued and organized by academic libraries.

Adapting the Library Instruction and Material

The changes to the library research program involved the complex task of mapping national standards to local practices. Translating national information literacy standards meaningfully to a local environment and within the context of the first-year composition curricula required us to rethink a number of pedagogical practices. First, students needed assistance finding sources outside the academic library collection. This effort involved creating a custom library guide (http://libguides.lib.umt.edu/writ101) specifically for the course rather than using the library homepage as a central starting page. The library guide includes links to the online catalog and key, pre-selected databases that contain material related to sustainability. It also includes links to local material not represented in the library's holdings. These links include online, regional news sources and links to state government reports, watershed organizations, university documents, etc. The guide also includes a space for students and teachers to submit their own sources; these diverse sources serve as an ongoing space for students to build a valuable—and valued—information repository. The authors have been pleased by the use of this information; in fact, usage statistics show that the students view these resources at a level that rivals the academic databases.

Next, students needed help developing a different framework for evaluating sources—one that developed their skills assessing whether the source was appropriate for their intended use. Like many academic libraries and composition collaborations, the authors designed a research journal (http://lgdata.s3-website-us-east-1.amazonaws.com/docs/71/684924/WRIT101_Research_Journal_Sustainability_Version.pdf) to guide students through library research. The journal was refocused in significant ways. Unlike the libraries responding to Boyd-Byrnes and McDermott's (2006) survey that reported the "relative infrequent use" of using ACRL standards to "develop tools for evaluation" (p. 15), the Mansfield Library had already established a strong outcome related to source analysis. However, the source analysis framework was generic and encouraged students to examine all sources using a singular, objective method. The information literacy rubric was modified to include "impact" among the other assessment criteria (bias, timeliness, authorship, credibility, etc.) and created a list of questions to prompt students in these categories. This list appears in the research journal and students are required to examine their sources using these questions. The research journal also draws heavily from the course texts, Bruce Ballenger's *The Curious Writer* and Andrea Lunsford's *The Everyday Writer,* and asks students, both at the beginning of the research stage and for each source, to inquire more deeply into their evolving understanding of their research.

Adapting the Composition Training

The authors had previously designed multiple instructional opportunities during the Teaching Assistant (TA) orientation, coursework embedded in the TA pedagogy course, and individual mentoring meetings for TAs needing additional support in teaching research. By doing so, it creates a composition program that acknowledges "the complexity, the difficulty, and the centrality of information literacy within contemporary writing environments" since the authors agree that doing so "counteract[s] the skills mindset" (Artman, Friscicaro-Pawlowski, and Monge, 2010, p. 97) characteristic of one-shot library instruction. Conducting a one-shot model of teaching teachers how to teach information literacy is no better than doing so with first-year students. It is not sustainable.

During the weeklong TA summer orientation, an afternoon is dedicated to meeting in the library instruction classroom and teaching TAs the information literacy instruction priorities for first-year composition. This introduction includes explaining to TAs their role in teaching information literacy at the 100 level and the librarian's role in supporting them, as well as a general introduction to the library website and the course library guide. The instructions situate this introduction in the context of working through the first major unit of the class, a personal academic research essay. The assignment asks students to, "focus on two moves: first, you'll work on defining sustainability (as a class and individually) and developing a researchable question about sustainability to pursue that both interests you and affects you and your audience" (https://sites.google.com/site/writ101fa2012/personalacademicessay).

The genre of this research assignment invites students to consider their relationship to their research, so they are encouraged to think about how their perspective and knowledge informs their research and to conduct local research and to consider local perspectives. More specifically, there is a focus on teaching teachers how, in a few class meetings, to help their students move from developing research questions related to the broad topic of sustainability to creating effective keyword searches while beginning to track their searches and evaluate their findings in a research journal. To do this, TAs collaborate to develop keywords for a sample research question, and then move to their individual computers to conduct searches in some of the databases appropriate for first-year students, using the research journal to help them track and reflect on their sources as they gather them. Doing so models the moves the teachers need to make with their students and enables them to see the potential challenges their students may face in, for example, coming up with related terms for a complex term like sustainability, or in navigating library databases, perhaps for the first time, when the subject cuts across traditional Library of Congress subject headings or may require local research that is harder to trace. The day concludes with a written reflection of teaching library research, in order to gauge the TAs' comfort levels and concerns with teaching research and better plan for a class meeting during their graduate course on composition pedagogy.

During the fall class meeting, which is co-facilitated and which takes place around the fourth week of the semester, their earlier work is further explored by asking TAs to share their experiences teaching first-year composition students keyword searches, evaluation of sources, and the library research journal to problem-solve difficulties and share successes. In addition, TAs read scholarship to help them refine their own thinking on these topics and to develop additional ways to help students over the semester. In the past, the authors have emphasized how students might use Wikipedia and Google searches, using articles like James Purdy's (2010) "Wikipedia is good for you!?" This past year, the focus shifted to supporting TA's efforts to teach students how to *use* sources, which seems to be an area of difficulty with a gap between finding sources and citing them that teachers struggle to bridge with students. TAs read "Reading games: strategies for reading scholarly sources," by Karen Rosenberg (2011), which emphasizes rhetorical reading and offers different strategies for doing so, from analyzing the ideal audience of a text to learning how to read abstracts and introductions. They also read Joseph Bizup's (2008) "BEAM: A rhetorical vocabulary for teaching research-based writing," which offers a new way of treating sources. Bizup offers BEAM (background, exhibit, argument, and method) as a way to classify source use instead of labeling sources with the terms "primary" and "secondary." Learning to read rhetorically helps students learn to use sources to further their line of inquiry. In addition, moving away from thinking about sources as primary or secondary requires students learn to use sources for a purpose. That means a student might be able to use a method source to apply an article about restoration in one community to talk about prospects of restoration locally or to identify key terms for her research. BEAM's orientation towards context provides a valuable way to emphasize local meaning making. Throughout the orientation and academic year, the librarian also meets individually with teachers to help them develop their plans, integrate information literacy into other assignments effectively, or simply troubleshoot difficulties they faced in this work to apply to a future assignment or semester.

Critical Reflection

The authors encountered both challenges and new opportunities that influenced their thinking during this collaboration. The biggest challenge for the first-year writing program involved encouraging and supporting TAs who are often intimidated at the prospect of teaching research. The biggest challenge for the library involved overcoming traditional library perceptions about the value of local, non-scholarly sourced material. The students were eager to engage this information—and surprised to see it discussed as valid and worthy of inclusion in scholarly pursuits. It is heartening to see this work not only revalues community and students' experiences, but also disrupts metrocentric thinking or anti-rural prejudices (Heldke, 2006). Another challenge was encouraging students to evaluate information in a new way; rather than focusing on whether the source was objective and scholarly (i.e., from a library database, peer-reviewed, etc.), students were required to examine whether the source was appropriate for their intended use. Once students understood that the value of information came from the way they crafted a scholarly conversation, they seemed much more engaged with trying to position their sources meaningfully around a line of inquiry while simultaneously developing their own perspectives and voices.

New Directions

A number of new, and sometimes unexpected, directions arose from this collaboration. The design of this course contributed to building a complementary information literacy instruction program across first-year curricula. Now, students enrolled in the first year at the university encounter sustainability-focused information literacy instruction in several classes, including freshman seminar, introduction to public speaking, global leadership seminar, and introduction to honors, rather than simply composition. This approach results in the opportunity for first-year students to further develop and practice new habits of mind regarding their interactions with information.

Through the work of highlighting the value of local sources, the library also found a new, unexpected connection with university service learning courses. The model established in the composition classroom was easily recognized by service learning instructors as a missing piece in the type of information literacy instruction offered in that program. A program devoted to helping students see the connection between theoretical, abstract information and information in the real world was designed and the library is now fully integrated into the university's service learning program (http://libguides.lib.umt.edu/servicelearning).

The most significant, and perhaps most exciting, result was that moving toward sustainability requires a new epistemology for librarians and the programs wherein librarians collaborate to offer information literacy instruction. Librarians can no longer accept that there is a standard, national way of thinking about or interacting with information. The current understanding of how information is organized, accessed, and evaluated does not accommodate, and will not produce, critical thinkers prepared to encounter the serious challenges of our time. Librarians must re-evaluate professional standards (including instruction, cataloging, and access) to build more robust lifelong learners equipped to competently interact in highly specific, local environments. Eric Zencey (1996) has cautioned against professors who are, as he states, "supposed to belong to the boundless world of books and ideas and eternal truths, not the infinitely particular world of watersheds, growing seasons, and ecological niches" (p. 72). The authors have found that embracing a focus on sustainability effectively "roots" our collaborative curriculum and better positions students as savvy researchers and writers. Ultimately, librarians are training the next generation of information consumers and creators, and a focus on sustainability in information literacy prepares them for the complexities they will encounter as they move into new, or familiar, landscapes.

References

Artman, M., Frisicaro-Pawlowski, E., & Monge, R. (2010). Not just one-shot: Extending the dialogue about information literacy in composition classes. *Composition Studies, 38*(2), 93-110.

Ballenger, B. (2011). *The curious writer.* New York: Pearson Longman.

Barratt, C., Nielsen, K., Desmet, C., & Balthazor, R. (2008). Collaboration is key: Librarians and composition instructors analyze student research and writing. *Portal: Libraries and the Academy, 9*(1), 37-56.

Berthoff, A. (1981). *Making of meaning: Metaphors, models, and maxims for writing teachers.* Montclair, N.J.: Boynton/Cook Publishers.

Bizup, J. (2008). BEAM: A rhetorical vocabulary for teaching research-based writing. *Rhetoric Review, 27*(1), 72-86.

Boyd-Byrnes, M., & McDermott, D. (2006). Reaching first-year college students: Current practices in instructional programs. *Public Services Quarterly, 2*(4), 1-22.

Brady, L., Singh-Corcoran, N., Dadisman, J. A., & Diamond, K. (2009). A collaborative approach to information literacy: First-year composition, writing center, and library partnerships at West Virginia University. *Composition Forum, 19*, 1-18.

Corbett, P. (2010). What about the "Google effect"? Improving the library research habits of first-year composition students. *Teaching English in the Two Year College, 37*(3), 265-277.

Deitering, A., & Jameson, S. (2008). Step-by-step through the scholarly conversation: A collaborative library/writing faculty project to embed information literacy and promote critical thinking in first year composition at Oregon State University. *College & Undergraduate Libraries, 15*(1), 57-79.

Dobrin, S., & Weisser, C. (2002). *Natural discourse: Toward ecocomposition.* Albany, N.Y.: State University of New York Press.

Goggin, P., & Waggoner, Z. (2005). Sustainable development: Thinking globally and acting locally in the writing classroom. *Composition Studies, 33*(2), 45-67.

Heldke, L. (2006). Farming made her stupid. *Hypatia, 21*(3), 151-165.

Lunsford, A. (2009). *The everyday writer 4th edition. UM edition.* Bedford St. Martin's.

Owens, D. (2001). *Composition and sustainability: Teaching for a threatened generation.* Urbana, I.L.: National Council of Teachers of English.

Purdy, J. (2010). Wikipedia is good for you?! In C. Lowe, & P. Zemliansky (Eds.), *Writing spaces: Readings on writing, volume 1.* Parlor Press.

Rosenberg, K. (2011). Reading games: Strategies for reading scholarly sources. In C. Lowe, & P. Zemliansky (Eds.), *Writing spaces: Readings on writing, volume 2.* Parlor Press.

Samson, S., & Millet, M. (2003). The learning environment: First-year students, teaching assistants, and information literacy. *Research Strategies, 19*(2), 84-98.

Stark, M. (2011). Information in place: Integrating sustainability into information literacy instruction. *Electronic Green Journal, 1*(32), 1-16.

University of Montana. Mansfield Library. (n.d.). *Library Research Journal WRIT 101.* Retrieved from http://lgdata.s3-website-us-east-1.amazonaws.com/docs/71/684924/WRIT101_Research_Journal_Sustainability_Version.pdf

Zencey, E. (1996). The rootless professors. In W. Vitek, & W. Jackson (Eds.), *Rooted in the land: Essays on community and place* (pp. 15-19). New Haven, C.T.: Yale University Press.

Three for One: Teaching Sustainable Education, Information Literacy, and Visual Literacy with the Inventory Compilation Assignment

Alessia Zanin-Yost

Abstract

This chapter argues that students, specifically interior design students, can greatly benefit from learning the interconnectivity between sustainability and their profession. Through a common assignment given in the interior design curriculum, the students can learn various research techniques that enhance both their knowledge of sustainability and related topics, as well as aid their future design careers.

Introduction

In recent years, more and more interior design firms are specifying designs that are Leadership in Energy and Environmental Design (LEED) certified. Because of this demand, the issue of sustainability has also been introduced in the interior design curriculum. To be successful designers, interior design students need to think critically about what type of information to use and where to find it. They also need to learn that their future profession is truly interdisciplinary; thus, they need to know how to find, access, and use resources from environmental studies, business, and urban planning, among other disciplines. The purpose of the chapter is to provide information to other instructional librarians on how to integrate information and visual literacy resources about sustainability in a common research project to satisfy the future research needs of interior design students. The chapter focuses on how the Inventory Compilation Assignment, a component of the Life Cycle Analysis, in a foundation course in interior design can be used to integrate the Association of Colleges and Research Libraries (ACRL) information and visual literacy competencies as well as the Art Libraries Society of North America (ARLIS/NA) "Information Competencies for Students in Design Discipline." The ideas reported here can help librarians propel assignments that will teach students valuable research skills to be used long after graduation.

Sustainability Design

Sustainability is not a new concept. Throughout *human* history, societies have created objects to ensure prosperity and promote social and economic growth. Portable dwellings, for example, were designed by nomadic people to take advantage of local recources: animal hides and wood; nature was seen as a provider of life. The Industrial Revolution in the 19th Century changed all of this. Led by the technology of the time, tools were designed to manufacture something in large quantities and quickly. The idea of creating objects that were both beautiful and durable was later adopted by the Bauhaus (1913-1933). By the mid-1900s, technology had advanced so rapidly it was used to create mass production projects. In the late 1960s, environmentalists opposed mass material production and voiced concerns about its environmental impact (Papanek, 1971). In 1972, the UN Summit on Human Environment was the first conference to discuss global environmental problems and by 1989, global awareness of how ecological and social problems are interconnected continued to grow (Fowkes & Fowkes, 2009).

Today sustainability is a globally recognized concept, but the absence of a widespread definition for sustainability often causes confusion. In the Brundtland Report (1987), sustainability is defined as: "development that meets the needs of the present without compromising the ability of future generations to meet their own needs" (United Nations, 1987). Sustainability means finding a balance between using available natural resources and meeting present and future needs. Although the Brundtland Report's definition is the most widely accepted, the term sustainability is still broadly defined.

Sustainability has become synonymous with green design, ecological design, sustainable design, environmentally conscious design, and environmentally responsible design. Some authors note a subtle difference among the terms (Jones, 2008); some emphasize the interconnectivity of sustainability between culture and business (Shedroff, 2009) while others like Yeang and Woo (2010) combine all of the terms under the term "ecodesign." Jason McLennan (2004), one of the green building movement's most influential personalities, states that the term "sustainable design" is not wrong, but it does not reflect the multiplicity of ideas and practices and perhaps, "better words could have been chosen such as **restorative design** to imply the challenge ahead, or **ecological design** to highlight the main focus of the philosophy," (pp. 2-3).

Sustainability Education

Sustainable education, however, is an emerging concept. In 2002, the United Nations declared 2005-2014 as the Decade of Education for Sustainable Development (UNESCO, 2005). While initiatives on how to apply green practices on school campuses have flourished (Maragakis and van den Dobbelsteen, 2013; Betts, 2001; Ghosh, 2011; Kissel, 2010), little attention has been devoted to teaching sustainability (Chase & Rowland, 2004; Nasr, 2013; Segalas, Ferrer-Bals & Mulder, 2010; Cotton, Bailey, Warren & Bissell, 2009; de le Harpe & Thomas, 2009). The problem, as articulated by David Orr almost 20 years ago, is that sustainability cannot be taught in one class but needs to be integrated in a variety of disciplines so students may be exposed to different points of view because it is better to, "reshape ourselves to fit a finite planet than to attempt to reshape the planet to fit our infinite wants" (1994, p. 9). Research, regardless of topic or level, is essential to form thoughtful ideas. In order to conduct research, students need to be exposed frequently to the methods of research (Zanin-Yost & Tapley, 2008). Through research, students learn to compare and contrast facts and develop their own points of view. To grow intellectually, students always benefit from a multidisciplinary approach to research.

The National Council for Interior Design Qualification (NCIDQ) emphasizes that interior design is a multi-faceted profession and the designer "follows a systematic and coordinated methodology, including research, analysis and integration of knowledge into the creative process" (2012, para.1). Interior design students do not just study design. They use information from other disciplines to provide the best solutions to their clients. For example, in designing a child care center, designers need to be aware of regulations, the needs of adults and children, and safety concerns regarding pollutants emitted by materials. Interior design students need to learn and understand, according to Blackmer "how information can be used to come to conclusions or take action. It includes knowing the boundaries within which factual information can be applied when problem solving" (Blackmer, 2005, p. vii). Kuhlthau (1995) noted that when students are not shown how to conduct research and investigate other possibilities, they tend to settle for the first answer they find. With today's plethora of online information, this is truer than ever. Students need to learn how to conduct research so they can develop critical thinking skills about information. The librarian becomes an integral partner in teaching students the mechanics of how to conduct research and collaborating with faculty to develop assignments and assess course outcomes.

The Life Cycle Analysis Assignment

The 2011 Professional Standards of the Council for Interior Design Accreditation (CIDA) note that students must demonstrate, "understanding of the concepts, principles, and theories of sustainability as they pertain to building methods, materials, system and occupants" (p. 13) and they also need to have "awareness of sustainability guidelines" (p. 22). Like information literacy, the concept of sustainability is, "a lifelong journey requiring continual education and vigilance" (Stieg, 2006, p. xx). Sustainability in design is addressed throughout the curriculum with a variety of assignments, papers, and projects, one of which is the Life Cycle Analysis (LCA), also known as cradle-to-cradle.

The LCA is a complex research method which, according to the U.S. Environmental Protection Agency (EPA), is "a technique to assess the environmental aspects and potential impacts associated with a product, process, or service" (Curran, 2006, p.2). The framework that defines the LCA is set by the International Organization for Standardization (ISO). The ISO standards that oversee sustainability were first published in 1997 and then revised in 2006. The ISO 14040:2006 series outlines the LCA requirements and guidelines (Ballast, 2006, p. 441). An LCA is composed of the following four parts (Rebitzer et. al., 2004):

1) *Goal & Scope Definition.* This phase determines the product to be assessed, the purpose of the assessment, what type and quantity of information needs to be collected, what parts of the inventory analysis can be skipped, and the type of measurement units to be used to make a comparison with another product.

2) *Inventory Compilation.* This is the most time consuming phase because both inputs and outputs need to be considered. Elements to consider might include how much and what type of energy is used, amount and type of pollution generated, and waste.

3) *Impact Assessment.* In the third phase, the consumption and emission of the resources listed in the inventory compilation are evaluated using the ISO 14040:2006.

4) *Interpretation.* The last stage of the LCA consists of the evaluation of and recommendations for the product.

The experience of the author with this assignment has been at the foundation level, one of the first courses interior designers take. In the foundation class, students do not cover the whole LCA, only the second phase, the Inventory Compilation (IC). They do not conduct a comparison between two products, but become experts on one product. The IC assignment is the optimal tool to teach interior design students how to develop both information and visual literacy skills. Instilling good research habits in students must begin with their first classes. The expectations of early assignments and projects set the tone for later works. To complete the inventory compilation of the LCA, students need to find and use information from a variety of resources and disciplines and think critically about how the information can support their product, a practice that interior designers are expected to apply in their profession.

The Inventory Compilation Assignment

The IC of the LAC is time consuming and complex, requiring students to understand where to find different types of information. Students need to learn how to find online and print resources in disciplines foreign to them such as chemistry, business, and technology. Looking for information outside their comfort zone can be intimidating. A librarian could show students how the same skills used to search for information about design can be applied to other disciplines.

The IC is made of four steps—raw materials; manufacturing (which includes processing, refining, assembly); use; and disposal—each requiring students to find different types of information. At each stage, the research must include what type of energy and how much water is used (input), and what type of pollution and amount of water are produced (outputs) as showed in Figure 1.

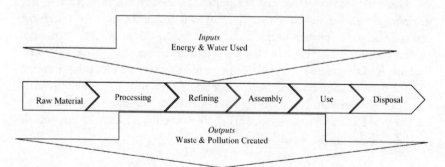

Figure 1. The Inventory Compilation (IC) Process

This figure illustrates the four steps of the IC. Raw materials are manufactured (process, refine, assembly), used and disposed. The inputs and outputs of each step require a different amount of energy and water.

The IC process

Collaboration between librarians and instructors is essential to ensure students learn the skills they need to succeed. Having a specific assignment makes the inclusion of information and visual literacy goals easier to understand and concretizes the skills. Establishing assignment parameters is important because the objectives need to match the ACRL Information Literacy Competency (ACRL, 2000) and Visual Literacy Competencies (ACRL, 2011) as well as the Art Libraries Society of North America (ARLIS/NA) "Information Competencies for Students in Design Discipline" (Brown et. al., 2006). Before thinking about how to integrate the standards, both librarian and faculty need to have a clear idea of what they expect the students to learn. It is important to define the purpose of the assignment from the beginning. Some questions to consider include:

- Do the students need to learn how to find current information or historical information as well?
- Do they need to find proprietary information?
- How much detail is needed?
- What online resources can be used?
- Do the students need to compare products?
- Do images or graphs need to be included?

Once the framework of the assignment is established, students will need guidance for each research phase. Guiding students through the research process is especially important at the foundation levels--this might be the first time students are introduced to the library's resources and services. One way to ease students into the research process is to provide them with a chart that has starting questions as shown in Figure 2. Depending on how much time is available for the library session, the librarian can conduct this brainstorming in class or ask the instructor to have the students come to the library instruction with this component already prepared.

IC Process Cheat Sheet

1. Raw Material	3. Use
• Where does the raw material come from? • How is the material extracted? • How is the raw material transported and where (how far)?	• What types of wastes are created? • What type of maintenance is needed? • What is the life span of your product?
2. Manufacturing Steps: processing, refining, and assembly. Consider: • For each step, does the product need to travel to another location? • What type of energy is used at every step? • How much pollution is generated at every step?	4. Disposal • How much energy is used? • What parts are recyclable? • What is the rate of decomposition? • What types of pollutants are generated?

The research for each step of the IC Process can be facilitated through a series of questions.

Guiding the IC Research

With the IC assignment, students explore materials used in their profession and many times they come up with impressive products, such as engineered quartz or coconut wood composite tiles. To best support the students' ingenuity, the librarian should conduct a preliminary study of what is available in the collection, create a list of suggested material topics, and place a selection of resources in the course reserve. As time goes by, the librarian should keep track of what topics the students select and purchase resources in preparation for future classes. In doing so, the collection will grow and meet learning and teaching needs (see Appendix A for a list of resources).

Integrating the Competencies in the IC Assignment

To provide a seamless incorporation of the ACRL Information and Visual Literacy Competencies as well as the ARLIS/NA "Information Competencies for Students in Design Discipline," the librarian needs to use the course objectives as the starting point. In collaboration with the instructor, the librarian needs to determine what skills the students need to learn. One excellent way to do this is by using a rubric. The rubric will not only keep both faculty and librarian organized, but it will also outline expectations for the students. The rubric also shows the faculty how the standards can be easily incorporated into existing objectives. Once the objectives are determined, both librarian and faculty need to decide which competencies to include. It is important to recognize that not all of the competencies need to be addressed; only those that will help students complete the task. What follows is an example of the development and incorporation of the competencies.

Step 1. Determine the goal: Students will learn how to conduct research by completing the IC for one material. The assignment requires them to write a 10 page paper.

Step 2. Two main objectives for the library instruction are identified:
Objective 1. Must use at least four scholarly resources. Encyclopedias are fine. Must include, in addition to the four resources, at least one governmental resource.
Objective 2. Include one color image of the selected material.

Step 3. Determine which competencies best accomplish the objectives.
Objective 1. Use of scholarly resource and identify different types of resources. In the right column of Figure 3 the ARLIS/NA Competencies are identified, in parenthesis the corresponding sections in the handbook.
Objective 2. Select and include in the assignment one image. For this objective, the ACRL Visual Literacy Competencies need to be included (see Figure 4).

Task to be completed	ACRL Information Literacy Competencies	ARLIS/NA Information Competencies Handbook
Know how to explore general sources	Explores general information sources to increase familiarity with the topic (1.1.c) and identifies the value and differences of potential resources in a variety of formats (1.2.c)	Match sources to information need (pg.12)
Identify scholarly information	Identifies the purpose and audience of potential resources (1.2.d) and examines and compares information from various sources in order to evaluate reliability, validity, accuracy, authority, timeliness, and point of view or bias (3.2.a)	Evaluate information and sources by such criteria as relevance and coverage, authority, accuracy, objectivity, currency and peer review process (pg.13)
Determine if the quality and quantity of the information obtained is enough	Determines the availability of needed information and make decisions on broadening the information seeking process (1.3.a)	Determine whether the information satisfied the research or information need (pg.14)
Cite the information properly	Selects an appropriate documentation style and uses it consistently to cite sources (5.3.a)	Properly assign credit for the source of information and ideas (pg.13)

Figure 3. Alignment of Task and ARLIS/NA Competencies without the Use of Images.

If the objective of the instruction is to teach students about scholarly resources and different types of resources the librarian will identify specific tasks (on the left). These tasks are then aligned with the both the ACRL and ARLIS//NA.

When images are part of the assignment, the librarian will need to align the ACRL Visual Literacy Competencies to both the ACRL information literacy and ARLIS/NA competencies to demonstrate a correlation of skills.

From the information in the figures above, the librarian can determine what skills the students need to learn to successfully complete the IC. The skills for this example include the following:

1) Understand how to explore general sources.
2) Determine if the quality and quantity of the information obtained is enough.
3) Identify scholarly information.
4) Understand how to cite information properly.
5) Know how to find an appropriate image.
6) Know how to manipulate the image (transfer, copy, and crop).

ACRL Visual Literacy Competencies	ACRL Information Literacy Competencies	ARLIS/NA Information Competencies Handbook
Selects the most appropriate image for the scope (5.1.b)	Uses prior knowledge to find images (4.1.d)	Find images illustrating fundamentals of visual perception and design (Pg.13)
Knows how to properly cite the image (7.3.a, b, c)	Knows how to properly cite the image (5.3.a)	Properly assign credit for the source of information and ideas (Pg.13)
Determines what type of image is needed (size, color, etc. (5.2.b) and knows how to properly edit the image (5.2.c)		Manipulate digital text, images and data transferring appropriately to a new context (Pg.14)

Figure 4. Alignment of the ACRL and ARLIS/NA Competencies when Using Images.

Step 5. Developing the library instruction is the last component. The library instruction should cover the six identified skills that students need to master. Assuming that the librarian has 50 minutes of time available, the library instruction might look like this:

1) _Understand how to explore general sources._

- Provide an overview of the type of materials and where they are located. For example, general collection vs. reference collection.

- Show how to search using the library catalog and one database.
- Explain how to use any local borrowing services the library might have and how to request the material from another library.

2) *Determine if the quality and quantity of the information obtained is sufficient.*

- Discuss with students the different types of resources; for example, trade magazines, scholarly journals, and books. Pass around different resources for the students to look at.
- Show students how to formulate questions that will help them determine what type of information is needed (Figure 2). Remind them to check the guidelines about how much detail is needed for the assignment.
- Teach students where the different pieces of information can be found and how to read a library record. For example, to find out what nylon is made of, sources in chemistry and technology are most likely to have the information needed.
- Emphasize the importance of using synonyms or related concepts. For example, when searching for information about energy-efficient windows, terms such as day-lighting, fenestration, and glazing can be used. It's also helpful for the students to know that common synonyms for sustainable include environmental, green, ecological, and so forth.

3) *Identify scholarly information*

- Divide the students into groups and give each group a different source (book, trade article, microfilm, government pamphlet, Web page etc.). Ask them to determine if the resource is or is not scholarly material.
- Move on to discuss how scholarly information differs from other resources. Show how it is possible to limit the search of scholarly articles in the database.

4) *Understand how to cite information properly*

- Check the assignment guidelines to determine which citation style to use.
- Ask students what type of information needs to be cited and why.

- Show where the Writing Center page is located, and direct students to those resources.
- Demonstrate how to cite an image in text and in the bibliography.

5)*Know how to find an appropriate image. For the IC assignment, the best images are found online. Keeping this in mind:*

- If the library subscribes to an image database, show the students what type of images they can find and let them determine if this will be the best approach or not.
- Show how to search for images using Google Image and the advanced function.
- Demonstrate how different keywords will produce different images. Ask the students to make a list of possible keywords for their material and have them search online.

6)*Know how to manipulate the image (transfer, copy, and crop).*

- Do not assume that students know how to do this. Show them how to do it and then ask them to do the same to search for their material.

The faculty-librarian partnership starts with the development of outcomes, but it does not end with library instruction. As the assignment is modified and resources/needs change, the librarian can provide continuous support to both faculty and students. Accreditation agencies expect faculty and librarians to collaborate so students can, "use library resources as a part of the learning process" (Thompson, 2002, p. 221). By learning how to research information, "with guidance, support, and direction from experts" (Bhavnagri & Bielat, 2005, p. 126) students learn to question the issues connected to their research and become both information and visually literate in the process.

Conclusion

The interdisciplinary nature of interior design invites the librarian to teach students an array of skills, demonstrating how research can be transferable from one field to another. The inventory compilation assignment is just one component of the life cycle analysis, but it offers many opportunities to teach students lifelong skills about sustainability, information literacy, and visual literacy. The integration of the competencies cannot happen in isolation. Competencies and course outcome must be combined seamlessly and provide the opportunity for students to complete an assignment with clear learning goals. Imbedding competencies from the ACRL information and visual literacy as well as the ARLIS/NA competencies for design students, the curriculum demonstrates it follows national practices and at the same time meets accreditation requirements.

As LEED certification becomes the norm and green materials are more readily available, knowledge of sustainability research will become a professional necessity for interior design students. By teaching how to find information and make environmentally conscious decisions, both librarians and faculty are preparing future designers to play a leading role in the global sustainability movement.

References

ACRL. (2000). Information literacy competency standards for higher education. [Brochure]. Chicago: Association of College & Research Libraries.

ACRL. (2011). Visual competency standards for higher education. Retrieved from http://www.ala.org/acrl/standards/visualliteracy

Ballast, D. (2006). Interior design reference manual. Belmont, CA: Professional Publications.

Betts, K.S. (2001). Greening the campus. Environmental Science & Technology, 35(9), 198A-202A.

Bhavnagri, Navaz, & Veronica Bielat. (2005). Faculty-librarian collaboration to teach research skills: electronic symbiosis. Reference Librarian, 43(89), 121–138.

Blackmer, B.E. (2005). Knowledge on knowledge. Journal of Interior Design 31(1), vii–xii.

Brown, J., Carlin, J., Caswell, T., Crowe, E., Gervits, M., Lewis, S.,…, Parker, J. (2006). Information competencies for students in design disciplines. Art Libraries of North America. Retrieved from http://www.arlisna.org/resources/onlinepubs/informationcomp.pdf

Chase, G., & Rowland, D. (2004). The Ponderosa Project: Infusing sustainability into the curriculum. In P. Barlett & G. Chase (Eds.), Sustainability on campus: Stories and strategies for change (pp. 91–105). Cambridge, MA: MIT Press.

CIDA Professional Standards. (2011). Retrieved from http://accredit-id.org/professional-standards

Cotton, D., Bailey, I., Warren, M., & Bissell, S. (2009). Revolutions and second-best solutions: Education for sustainable development in higher education. Studies in Higher Education, 34(7), 719-733.

Curran, M.A. (2006). Life Cycle Assessment: Principles and practice. U.S. Environmental Protection Agency. Retrieved from http://www.epa.gov/nrmrl/std/lca/pdfs/chapter1_frontmatter_lca101.pdf

de le Harpe, B. & Thomas, I. (2009). Curriculum change in universities: Conditions that facilitate education for sustainable development. Journal of Education for Sustainable Development, 3(1), 75-85.

Fowkes, M, & Fowkes, R. (2009). Planetary forecast: The roots of sustainability in the radical art of the 1970s. Third Text 100, 23(5), 669-674.

Ghosh, S. (2011). Participation in the green power - Partnership. An analysis of higher education institutions as partners in the program. International Journal of Sustainability in Higher Education, 12(4), 306-321.

Jones, L. (2008). Environmentally responsible design: Green and sustainable design for interior designers. Hoboken, N.J.: Wiley.

Kissel, A. (2010). Under the green thumb: Totalitarian sustainability on campus. Academic Questions, 23(1), 57-69.

Kuhlthau, C. C. (1995). The process of learning from information. School Libraries Worldwide, 1(1), 1-12.

Maragakis, A., van den Dobblesteen, A. (2013). Higher education: Features, trends and needs in relation to sustainability. *Journal of Sustainability Education*, 4 (Jan). Retrieved from http://www.jsedimensions.org/wordpress/content/higher-education-features-trends-and-needs-in-relation-to-sustainability_2013_02/

McLennan, J.F. (2004). *The philosophy of sustainable design: The future of architecture.* Kansas City, Mo: Ecotone LLC.

Nasr, N. (2013). Sustainability education comes of age. *Industrial Engineer: IE*, 45(3), 24-24.

NCIDQ. (2012.). *NCIDQ Board Approves New Definition of Interior Design.* Retrieved from: http://www.ncidq.org/AboutUs/AboutNCIDQ/News/NewDefinitionofInteriorDesign.aspx

Orr, D.W. (1994). *Earth in mind: On education, environment, and the human prospect.* Washington D.C.: Island Press.

Papanek, V. (1971). *Design for the real world.* New York: Pantheon Books.

Rebitzer, G., Ekwall, T., Frischnecht, R., Hunkeler, D, Norris, G.Rydberg, T.,... Pennington, D.. (2004). Life cycle assessment Part 1: Framework, goal and scope definition, inventory analysis, and applications. *Environment International, 30*(5), 701-720.

Segalas, J.J., Ferrer-Bals, D.D., & Mulder, K.F. (2010). What do engineering students learn in sustainability courses? The effect of the pedagogical approach. *Journal of Cleaner Production, 18*(3), 275-284.

Shedroff, N. (2009). *Design is the problem: The future of design must be sustainable*. Rosenfield Media: New York.

Stieg, C. (2006). The sustainability gap. *Journal of Interior Design. 32*(1), vii-xxi.

Thompson, G. B. (2002). Information literacy accreditation mandates: What they mean for faculty and librarians. *Library Trends, 51*:218–41.

Yeang, K., & Woo, L. (2010). *Dictionary of ecodesign*. New York: Routledge.

UNESCO. (2005). *The UN decade of education and sustainable development (DESD 2005-2014)*. Retrieved from http://unesdoc.unesco.org/images/0015/001540/154093e.pdf

United Nations (1987). *Report of the world commission on environment and development*. Retrieved from http://www.un.org/documents/ga/res/42/ares42-187.htm

Zanin-Yost, A., & Tapley, E. (2008). Learning in the art classroom: Making the connection between research and art. *Art Documentation, 27*(2), 40-45.

Appendix A

Background Information

Print

Ashby, M.F. (2009). *Materials and the environment: Eco-informed material choice*. Boston: Butterworth- Heinemann.

Selection, production and use of materials and the environmental consequences.

Bonda, P. & Sosnowchik, K. (2007). *Sustainable commercial interiors*. Hoboken, N.J.: Wiley.

Features examples of sustainable commercial interiors, green design tools, and materials.

Fernandez, J. (2006). *Material architecture: emergent materials for innovative buildings and ecological construction.* Burlington, MA: Architectural Press.

Provides information on how to evaluate and select architectural materials.

Godsey, L. (2012). *Interior design materials and specifications.* Fairchild Publications.

Information on how to evaluate, select and specify materials, taking into account code compliance, building standards, and sustainability guidelines.

Means, R.M. (2006). *Green building: Project planning & cost estimating.* Kingston, MA: R.S. Means.

Woolley, T. (2006). *Natural building: A guide to materials and techniques.* Wiltshire: Crowood.

Analyzes the principles of green building and the issues involved in planning.

Websites

American Society of Interior Designers Position on Sustainable Design. http://www.asid.org/content/asid-position-sustainable-design

Designing Products and Services with Sustainable Attributes: An Internal Assessment Tool for Product Developers. http://nbis.org/nbisresources/product_design/designing_products%20_sustainable_attributes.pdf

Describes the environmental impact matrix developed by the Design Work Group of the West Michigan Sustainable Business Forum.

Whole Building Design Guide http://www.wbdg.org/

Resources and design guidance organized by building use types. Included are standards, technologies and emerging issues.

World Green Building Council http://www.worldgbc.org/

Resources include case studies, bibliography, e-newsletter, and statistical reports.

Materials

Print

Farrelly, D. (1984). *The book of bamboo: A comprehensive guide to this remarkable plant, its uses, and its history.* San Francisco: Sierra Club Books.

Comprehensive sourcebook on proprieties and uses.

Höland, W., Beall, G. (2012). *Glass ceramic technology.* Hoboken, NJ: American Ceramic Society.

Covers the various types of glass-ceramic materials, the methods of their development, and their applications.

Lacinski, P., Bergeron, M. (2000). *Serious straw bale: A home construction guide for all climates.* White River Junction, Vt.: Chelsea Green Pub. Co..

Use of straw bale building in extreme climates.

Nielson, K. (2007). *Interior textiles: fabrics, application, and historic.* New York: Wiley.

Covers the process of textile specifications, properties, selection, installation and sustainable design issues are also considered.

Rubin, I. (1990). Handbook of plastic materials and technology. New York: Wiley.

Properties, processes, and industry practices and additional useful information and tables.

Walker, A. (2005). The Encyclopedia of wood: A tree-by-tree guide to the world's most versatile resource. New York: Facts on File.

Explains tree anatomy, tree growth, wood grain, logging practices, conservation, and the various processes for seasoning and preservation of wood.

Websites

Ebuild http://www.ebuild.com/

Directory of building products and manufacturers.

Oikos http://oikos.com/

Serves professionals whose work promotes sustainable design and construction. Includes a product directory.

Certifications, Exams & Continuing Education

Print

Ballast, D. (2006). *Interior design reference manual: A guide to the NCIDQ exam.* Belmont, CA: Professional Publications.

Essential guide to take the National Council for Interior Design Qualification (NCIDQ) exam with examples and test preparation samples.

Kubba, S. (2010). *LEED practice, certification, and accreditation handbook.* Burlington, MA: Butterworth-Heinemann.

Provides examples and information to achieve LEED personal certification or project certification.

Cottrell, M. (2012). *Guide to the LEED AP interior design and construction (ID+C) exam.* Hoboken, N.J.: Wiley

A guide to understand the exam. Ideal for interior designers, architects, engineering and contractors seeking the certification.

Websites

U.S. Green Building Council http://new.usgbc.org/

An essential resource for LEED certification information, register for workshops, webinars, and online courses. Also contains project case studies.

Chemicals, Pollution and Waste

Websites

EPA Measuring Greenhouse Gas Emissions from Waste. http://www.epa.gov/
climatechange/waste/measureghg.html

TOXMAP http://toxmap.nlm.nih.gov

> From the National Library of Medicine an easy to use map that shows on-site toxic chemical releases and hazardous waste sites.

Energy

Websites

American Solar Energy Society (ASES) http://www.ases.org/

> ASES is the United States Section of the International Solar Energy Society.

Energy Design Resources http://www.energydesignresources.com/

> Valuable resources on integrated energy design, lighting technology, building types, links to standards and case studies.

EPA Water Sense. http://www.epa.gov/watersense/

> Information on water-efficiency and calculate water savings.

Green Business Guide. http://www.sba.gov/

> This government website provides resources for energy-efficient design and construction.

Healthy Building Network. http://www.healthybuilding.net/

> Updated information on life cycle analysis, products, and economics that impact green design.

Green Government Database. http://www.naco.org/

> A searchable database of green programs, policies, and plans worldwide.

U.S. EPA Energy Star. http://www.energystar.gov/

Provides the national standard for energy efficiency rankings. Overviews on sustainable product design.

U.S. Department of Energy. http://energy.gov/

Renewable energy, sustainable building and design.

Sustainability and Designers

Print

Chick, A., & Micklethwaite, P. (2011). *Design for sustainable change: How design and designers can drive the sustainability agenda.* La Vergne, TN: Ingram Publisher Services.

Explore how design can be used to support sustainability. Includes ethics of design profession.

Shedoff, N. (2009). *Design is the problem: The future of design must be sustainable.* Brooklyn, N.Y.: Rosenfeld Media.

Valuable practical tips for designing more sustainable products

Thorpe, A. (2007). *The designer's atlas of sustainability.* Washington, DC: Island Press.

Covers the basic principles of concepts and practices of sustainable design.

Vezzoli, C, & Manzini, E. (2010). *Design for Environmental Sustainability.* London: Springer.

Provides a comprehensive framework and a practical tool to support the design process.

Walker, S. (2006). *Sustainable by design: Explorations in theory and practice.* Sterling, VA: Earthscan.

Covers the design process in the context of sustainability.

Yeang, K., & Woo, L. (2010). Dictionary of Ecodesign: An illustrated reference. New York: Routledge.

Covers the terminology of sustainable design.

Sustainability Literacy and Information Literacy: Leveraging Librarian Expertise

Toni M. Carter and Gregory J. Schmidt

Abstract

This chapter examines three avenues by which librarians at Auburn University integrate sustainability literacy into information literacy sessions: 1) English composition courses; 2) courses offered through the sustainability studies program; and 3) upper-level departmental sustainability electives. The authors highlight differing pedagogical approaches that Auburn's librarians apply toward each type of course and the impact of these efforts on the University's academic sustainability initiative. By focusing on sustainability literacy within the context of information literacy, librarians at Auburn University have leveraged their expertise to promote the larger institution's academic sustainability goals. The support offered by librarians to the emerging sustainability studies program at Auburn University will provide readers with ideas to explore within their own libraries and institutions.

Introduction

Information literacy, "a set of abilities requiring individuals to recognize when information is needed and have the ability to locate, evaluate, and use effectively the needed information" (ACRL, 2000) became a general education goal for Auburn University in 2007. Dedicated to producing information literate graduates, librarians at Auburn University Libraries (AUL) impart these skills in various settings, including reference desk encounters, one-on-one consultations, and course-integrated library instruction sessions. The instruction sessions are supported by an active and well-respected library instruction program, and offer the most consistency in students' exposure to information literacy concepts and skills. The Information Literacy Competency Standards for Higher Education (ACRL, 2000) provides the basis for the University's general education goal and serves as the framework for librarians' lesson plans. Where the Libraries have embraced information literacy instruction, the University as an institution has similarly embraced sustainability in instruction, research, and outreach. This chapter will examine three avenues by which librarians at Auburn University Libraries integrate sustainability literacy into information literacy sessions and the impact of these efforts on the sustainability goals of the University. These avenues include: 1) English composition courses; 2) courses offered through the sustainability studies program; and 3) upper-level departmental courses with sustainability components.

Background

Auburn University is a public institution located in Alabama with an enrollment of over 25,000 students. As a land-grant institution, its history includes agricultural and engineering research, such as crop rotation and low-impact tillage that would now fall under the rubric of sustainability. In fall 2004, the Auburn University Sustainability Initiative was founded to integrate sustainability into the three missions of the University: instruction, research, and outreach and to demonstrate the viability and practicality of sustainable practices by using the campus as a sustainability laboratory. In 2008, it became the Office of Sustainability, an officially recognized campus unit. The mission of the Office is, "to develop an ethic, practice, and culture of sustainability throughout Auburn University, and to serve as a sustainability education and training resource for individuals and organizations within the University and in local, regional, national, and international communities" (Office of Sustainability, 2013). Also that year, the University added a minor in Sustainability Studies. This minor exposes students to topics such as natural capitalism, the interdependence of economics, environment and social equity, systems thinking, climate change and the future of energy, and biomimicry in human engineered systems (Office of Sustainability, 2013).

The Sustainability Office is organized into two divisions: Campus Sustainability Operations and Academic Sustainability Programs. The former division concerns itself with the way the University conducts itself as a sustainable organization. This includes contributing to University decisions on construction, landscaping, energy and resource conservation, waste reduction, and purchasing. The latter office focuses on training students in the concepts and application of sustainability, expanding the incorporation of sustainability into the curriculum through faculty training workshops, and fostering interdisciplinary sustainability research (Office of Sustainability, 2013). Sustainability education may occur in courses from freshman-through senior-level. In 2010, AUL assigned a librarian to be liaison to the academic program. The liaison, in addition to performing collection development, was charged with providing library instruction to sustainability courses as requested.

Literature Review

Both information literacy and sustainability literacy are common topics in higher education. Literature combining both topics is limited but growing. Increasingly, researchers and practitioners point to competence in information literacy as an essential skill set for student success in sustainability literacy. Megan R. Stark (2011) of the University of Montana, Missoula states that "little has been written on the connections between library instruction and sustainability" (p. 2). She argues that despite the acceptance of green library practices, library professionals have yet to fully explore their potential involvement on campus by integrating sustainability into information literacy instruction – a task she urges librarians to take on. An "information literacy framework" and rubric provided by the author illustrate the mapping of these standards across the University of Montana's curriculum. Stark (2011) identifies the missing component for Montana and possibly other libraries grappling with this issue: "a clear connection between critical thinking and applying these skills in a sustainable world" (p. 6). She discusses ways in which sustainability could be embedded into information literacy instruction and views the integration of sustainability into the information literacy rubric as librarians' "next-step" (Stark, 2011, p.15). Stark's (2011) conclusion shares commonality with Lugg and Hodgson's (2009) study which found students relied too heavily on the Web for source material in a first year environmental literacy course. The authors stress the importance of information literacy as a "precursor" (p.12) to student achievement in environmental literacy and critical thinking. Although examining reference interviews rather than information literacy classes, Hare, Moreton, Jo, Stamm, & Winter (2011) explore the use of evidence-based practice at the reference desk, incorporating information literacy concepts to assist students in locating and evaluating sustainability information. This is done in an effort to increase the science literacy of students with no background in science.

Case studies detailing efforts to integrate information literacy and sustainability literacy have begun to appear in the literature. One such study examines Newcastle University's initiative to integrate information literacy into its environmental sciences curriculum (Bent & Stockdale, 2009). The authors stress the importance of assessment, promoting self-reflective activities for students as one method of evaluation (Bent & Stockdale, 2009). Kutner (2000) explores specific challenges with imparting information literacy to interdisciplinary majors, using the environmental program at the University of Vermont as an example. She finds that the lag time in the Library of Congress's creation of subject headings for new areas of study is one such obstacle in teaching successful research strategies. She follows up with a book chapter (Kutner & Danks, 2007, pp.183-190) going into greater detail regarding the collaboration between a librarian and the environmental program faculty, as well as her thoughts on what has made this project a success. The University of North Carolina at Greensboro's library experimented with an online ten-module research tutorial for information literacy, using recycling as the example topic. The author argues that through this process students became more environmentally literate, although assessment of "the usefulness of embedding the green message" (para. 12) had yet to be done (Filar Williams, 2011). Students can get a head start for college in programs such as Learn, Explore, Navigate, Solve program, at Wake Forest University. During the summers of 2010 and 2011, high school students participated in this three-week academic program in which each student worked on a, "community-action proposal outlining how he/she might work with others to solve a sustainability-related issue in their home town" (Johnston, et al., 2012, p. 245). The student learning outcomes for the program included: 1) Sustainability literacy (ecological, social, and economic); 2) Problem-based learning; 3) College-level writing proficiency; and 4) Information literacy (necessary for students to research their community-action proposals). The authors explain the expectations for students in each of these categories. For the information literacy learning outcome, librarians provided an instruction session that introduced students to searching the library catalog and databases for sources on sustainability. Lastly, although not focused on embedding sustainability into information literacy, librarians Gauder and Jenkins (2012) state that their development of a research methods course for International Studies (INS250), "will serve as a model of how to build a credit-based course with application to other fields such as political science, sustainability, human rights, and international business" (p. 277). Because of the interdisciplinary structure of INS250, students need exposure to and proficiency in using a variety of subject-specific databases. The authors describe the course and offer examples of classroom activities mapped to the ACRL standards (ACRL, 2000) along with student feedback from end-of-the-course evaluations. While listing the benefits and advantages of teaching such a class, Gauder and Jenkins (2012) point to the time commitment and manpower needed for this type of interdisciplinary undertaking.

Integration of information literacy into sustainability literacy without the assistance of librarians is not uncommon. Walton and Archer (2004) report on an engineering class in which students completed projects related to sustainable rural development. The instructors, who specialize in education and writing, apply a scaffolding approach to information literacy instruction and focus on outcomes related to finding and evaluating web sources (Walton & Archer, 2004). Another study examines improving students' information literacy in science through a climate change and human history course (Nam & Ito, 2011). The authors note that for this interdisciplinary class, course instructors helped students find appropriate resources for their research (p.236). In her phenomenographic study of an environmental studies course, Lupton (2008) does not mention the role of librarians in first-year students' understanding of information literacy, but does state that the study holds significance for them.

Similar to the literature reviewed above, Auburn University Libraries' involvement with the academic sustainability program on campus offers additional insight into interdisciplinary topics and information literacy. Librarians at Auburn University are actively involved in advancing ACRL information literacy standards. At the same time, the Libraries has recognized the institutional commitment to sustainability and has endeavored to embrace both organizational and academic sustainability. Auburn's strength in information literacy instruction has helped inform its approach to academic sustainability instruction. This chapter will serve to add an additional case study to the growing literature on libraries and the challenge of meeting university academic sustainability commitments.

English Composition

Assessment of student learning in information literacy occurs mainly in English composition, a mandatory course at Auburn. All sections of composition attend two to three library instruction sessions, with each session corresponding to one of three sequential assignments. Composition instructors and librarians meet prior to class to determine what skills and concepts students need to complete their assignments. Librarians address only one to two ACRL (2000) outcomes per session – foundational outcomes that will be built upon in discipline-specific course instruction – and all classes contain an active learning component.

During 2007, the same year the University adopted information literacy as a general education goal, the English department revamped the composition curriculum, adding course themes, "to reflect students' academic interest, but they were also intended to allow for discussion of the major social, ethical, legal, and economic implications of these fields" (English Department, Auburn University, 2007, p.4). Now, when registering for composition classes, students may choose from the themes of sustainability, business, liberal arts, cultural diversity, health and medicine, and science and technology. As a result, AUL librarians incorporate the appropriate themes into their instruction classes. Through research, students gain familiarity with at least one issue within these broader topics. For instance, in a sustainability-themed instruction session librarians may cover 1) narrowing large sustainability themes to specific research questions; 2) selecting keywords and synonyms to search; 3) using search strategies with sustainability resources; 4) and evaluating the enormous amount of information available on sustainability in both library databases and on the Web. The following discussion highlights these four outcomes and shares strategies used at Auburn to integrate sustainability literacy into information literacy sessions aimed at English composition students.

Topic Development

Although English composition instructors advise students to develop topics for their papers prior to the library sessions, students often arrive with only broad, unworkable ideas for research. Examples of these vague topics include fossil fuels, global warming, sustainable architecture, and sustainable farming. The librarian leads students through the process of exploring the nuances of their topics, with the goal of developing narrow and realistic research questions or topic proposals. In one effective lesson plan, the librarian shows a short video on a general sustainability topic, for instance wind farms. The students are asked to list the important concepts covered in the video and collaborate to generate a specific research question on the topic of wind farms. Students then brainstorm on their own topics. Brainstorming may take the form of concept mapping or mind mapping, in which students diagram or "map" the relationships between concepts relevant to potential topics. As students complete this activity, librarians encourage them to search online for possible subtopics in hopes this will assist them in narrowing their research questions. Through this process, students begin to uncover vocabulary and jargon related to their sustainability topics.

AUL is currently experimenting with online modules that composition students complete prior to library instruction classes. The modules include videos on mind mapping and developing research questions, directing students to complete these tasks before the instruction sessions.

Keywords and Synonyms

To locate sources for their papers, whether in library databases or on the Web, students must first identify the important words, or search terms and phrases, within their research questions. Librarians at Auburn refer to this process as "keywording." Using the example of wind farms, a research question could be "The cleanliness of wind farms outweighs the impact on wildlife, such as bird and bat fatalities caused by the turbines." Students who identify only "wind farms" as a main key phrase may miss important sources without also conducting searches for windmills, wind turbines, wind power, and/or wind energy. Therefore, students also develop synonyms and related terms for the main keywords or phrases in case their first choices fail to yield sufficient or relevant results. To complete this activity, students are provided with worksheets to write their research questions, keywords, and synonyms/related terms. Librarians often supplement the teaching of this outcome by comparing keywords to the use of tags on the photo-sharing website Flickr (Noe, 2009, pp. 180-181), using images related to sustainability as examples. By identifying keywords and synonyms/related terms, students continue to build upon their familiarity with the vocabulary and jargon used in sustainability literature.

General Databases and Subject Databases

Though students may find sufficient information about their sustainability research on the Web, composition instructors usually require the use of at least a few scholarly and/or peer-reviewed articles. Library databases of scholarly articles, not often available online for free, remain the students' best source for these types of resources. Librarians explain the differences between the Web and library database search strategies. Students learn that databases do not respond well to questions or sentences, but instead require properly selected keywords (confirming the need for the "keywording" exercise). A general database that covers all topics, such as Academic Search Premier, allows students to practice the development of search strategies, evaluation of results, and securing of full-text sources. After students seem comfortable with a general database, librarians may introduce a subject database related to the class focus. An introduction to business, sociology, or other applicable subject databases teaches students that sustainability encompasses not only the environment, but also economic and social components as well.

Evaluating Sources

Although composition instructors follow a prescribed curriculum, librarians have noticed a slight change in the types of sources they require students to use in their assignments. While just a few years ago instructors frowned upon Web sources, they now allow students to use some online sources. This may reflect a growing trust on the instructors' part in the quality of information available on the Web. Changes in the vocabulary used by instructors from "scholarly" and "popular" to "credible, reliable, dependable, and/or reputable" illustrate this subtle shift. Instructors appear to no longer consider print as inherently more reliable than electronic or a popular magazine as automatically more credible than a popular online news blog. Regardless of the types of sources used, students must be taught to identify evaluative factors such as bias and authority. While some English composition instructors still request two separate library sessions on source evaluation – one on scholarly vs. popular literature and another on websites – there is a movement (at least at Auburn) to abandon this traditional sequence and teach source evaluation in one class. Librarians approach this in a variety of ways, but most include examples of sustainability websites, online magazines, and journals related to sustainability topics, and printed articles on sustainability from library databases. Although some instructors may not require scholarly sources, librarians discuss the publication timeline and the intended increase in reliability when review processes are in place. Students, by locating peer-reviewed sustainability articles covering decades of research, discover that the field is not a fad but a legitimate academic pursuit.

Sustainability Studies Program

While the ENGL1120 information literacy instruction series is intended to reach a vast majority of Auburn students in their first year, additional information literacy instruction during students' time enrolled in Auburn is not guaranteed. Additional sessions are often oriented toward specific disciplinary information needs and only occur with the course instructor's decision to incorporate library instruction into the course syllabus. Library instruction will still cover information literacy outcomes, but it is much more in the context of fulfilling the disciplinary objective of the course and using academic resources specific to the discipline. Academic courses in sustainability, allowing for interdisciplinary studies, can be a challenge in a library instruction setting. As such, library instruction for Courses in the Sustainability Minor courses occupies something of a middle ground between foundational ENGL1120 training and highly-specialized library instruction for sustainability-related, discipline-specific courses in engineering, architecture, agriculture, and wildlife sciences, among others.

When Auburn began offering a minor in Sustainability Studies fall semester of 2008, the program was intended to provide students with knowledge of sustainability they could apply to their field of study and in their future careers. Sustainability courses are denoted with the prefix SUST and, while focused on the broad interdisciplinary topic of sustainability, allow students to craft their research projects in ways that relate to their intended academic majors. To receive a minor in Sustainability Studies, a student must take the introduction to sustainability course, SUST2000, 9 hours of approved electives, and the capstone sustainability course, SUST5000. The 9 hours of electives can come from 41 courses offered through 19 different academic units on campus. For the first two years of its existence, the program had no library liaison assigned to instruction and collection development. The appointment of a sustainability liaison in 2010 allowed the libraries to engage the program directly.

In a series of emails sent through the Sustainability Office's mailing list, the newly appointed librarian liaison contacted SUST course instructors and explained library instruction services and objectives. Instructors for SUST courses were receptive to library instruction oriented toward student research papers. SUST2000 (and its Honors College equivalent HONR1037) are the sophomore-level courses for the Introduction to Sustainability. Instructors for these courses concluded that, while most students enrolled had prior exposure to information literacy concepts from the ENGL1120 series, they could still benefit from a refresher on accessing and evaluating potential research material. Those students who had not completed a sustainability-themed English composition class not only needed a review in the core concepts of information literacy, but also needed an introduction to sustainability information resources.

Since 2011, library instruction has been incorporated into SUST2000/HONR1037 courses. As faculty in sustainability expressed a need for both refresher information literacy instruction and more-specific sustainability literacy instruction, the weekly class schedule accommodates a 2-day library instruction series. The first class takes place in an auditorium with approximately 80-100 students, while the second consists of smaller 'breakout' sessions with 15-20 students. The first instruction session is designed to reinforce students' information literacy outcomes from their English composition classes; namely the core skills and strategies needed to get the most from library research. Over a single

40 minute session, the sustainability liaison explains topic development, key-wording, and source evaluation for sustainability, and reviews both the library catalog and the general article databases students used in ENGL1120 courses. The librarian also reasserts the availability of help on the library website and through in-person visits to reference librarians for individual and group research consultations. The information literacy outcomes for this session are very similar to those from English composition, but are condensed into one session with the expectation that the instruction is serving to reinforce rather than introduce the students to the foundations of information literacy.

The second meeting for SUST2000/HONR1037 students takes place in a library instruction classroom and is designed to introduce students to sustainability-specific resources in both print and electronic format. Students attending the second library instruction session should leave with a broader knowledge of sustainability information and an improved understanding of the key concepts and terms useful for their research effort. The 70 minute class is organized into an initial lecture by the librarian followed by 30-40 minutes of supervised individual and group exploration of information resources. Special emphasis is placed on the use of keywording strategies from the first SUST instruction session as applied to subject-specific databases in social sciences, business, sciences and engineering. The individual and group exploration component allows the librarian to circulate through the class while students attempt, often for the first time, to use these subject-specific article databases. The librarian guides the students in the selection of subject databases relevant to their chosen topics. The subject databases may be oriented toward the subject of sustainability in a particular field of study, such as GreenFile or BuildingGreen Suite for architecture and building science disciplines. In most cases though, students will use a subject database oriented toward the discipline as a whole and not necessarily just the sustainability aspects of the discipline. For example, a student researching a topic relating to sustainable farming would be directed to an agriculture database, such as AGRICOLA, or a student with a topic relating to the economics of sustainable business practices would be directed to a business-specific database. As the SUST2000/HONR1037 courses are sophomore-level, these instruction sessions may be the students' first exposure to subject databases.

Upper-Level Departmental Courses

While library instruction for sustainability courses focuses on subject databases and discipline-specific information resources, instruction for students in upper-level sustainability electives marks a natural progression in information literacy expectations. Where the English composition emphasis on information literacy fundamentals led to the Introduction to Sustainability's emphasis on sustainability resources, sustainability elective instruction gives students an opportunity to begin mastering self-directed learning in their chosen field of study. Students at the junior and senior levels should have taken part in several library instruction sessions prior to these courses and are generally expected to be comfortable with the core information literacy competencies of topic development, keywording, and source evaluation.

Since 2010 and the appointment of a sustainability liaison, Auburn has averaged 12 instruction sessions per year in sustainability elective courses. As the 9 hours of required electives can come from 41 courses offered through 19 different academic units on campus, the subject specialist for the academic unit, rather than the sustainability liaison, usually conducts instruction for sustainability electives. These elective courses, though they have a strong component of sustainability studies at their core, are not restricted to students in the sustainability minor. Elective courses that have taken advantage of library instruction include Food, Agriculture, and Society, Sociology of Natural Resources and the Environment, Global Consumer Culture, and Urban Geography.

Auburn's experience with Urban Geography (GEOG 5010) instruction provides an example of the opportunity librarians have with upper-level courses to support both sustainability programs and information literacy outcomes. The Geography Department's description for Urban Geography states the course's focus as "Analysis of urban patterns and the processes creating them" (Geology & Geography, 2013). This broad description has allowed the course instructor, in collaboration with the sustainability liaison, to design course projects that require research in engineering, building science, and urban planning databases. The instructor encourages students in Urban Geography to focus their class projects on one sustainability issue specific to the University and the City of Auburn. To complete their projects, students may also need to access archival resources and maps from University and City archives.

Students in Urban Geography attend one 50-minute library instruction session, prior to which they select a topic and have it approved by their instructor. Though students' topics may still need some refinement, this step allows the session to focus more on advanced information resources and less on fundamental information literacy objectives. After only a brief refresher on keywording and source evaluation, the sustainability librarian and geography instructor lead the instruction session in tandem. The librarian instructs students in archival access to planning documents and maps held in University and City offices and emphasizes that these resources may be available electronically, in print, or in microfilm formats. This is often the first exposure students have with archival research and access, and represents a notable progression in their information literacy skillset. U.S. Census research is another area covered that may be unfamiliar to most students. The librarian instructs students on electronic access to Census data and leads them through a short series of Census queries to familiarize them with both current Census and historic Census Web interfaces. The geography instructor assists in the session with a brief introduction to the databases most useful to their research, including Engineering Village and Web of Science. The librarian and instructor dedicate the remainder of the session to assisting students with using the U.S Census Web portal and the databases the geography instructor discussed earlier. Given the breadth and complexity of the information resources that could be needed by Urban Geography students for this assignment, the librarian emphasizes throughout the session the availability of research consultations, reference desk assistance, and guidance with archival access. The librarian also reminds students that the general databases they have used throughout their time at Auburn University may also provide them with relevant, usable results. What they learn in this library session is meant to build upon their knowledge of library resources, not supplant it.

Conclusion

Universities' engagement with sustainability as a practice and a discipline manifests itself in various ways. This may occur through mission statements and directives, or more organically, through collaboration with teaching faculty. In addition to the traditional imperative of collection development, libraries can contribute to institutional sustainability goals with their expertise in information literacy training. At Auburn University, the sustainability librarian has begun speaking at sustainability curriculum development workshops, allowing for engagement with faculty teaching sustainability-related courses outside of the sustainability minor program. This marks a significant step toward fully engaging with sustainability research and teaching across the institution.

Sustainability efforts at Auburn University Libraries began just a few years ago and continue to mature. The appointment of a sustainability liaison with funds for discretionary materials purchases marked the first step toward engagement with the discipline. The second step, one that appears to offer the greatest opportunity for growth, was the adaptation of library instruction to orient information literacy classes toward sustainability information and resources. While sustainability-related materials acquisition budgets at Auburn University Libraries have remained steady or declined in purchasing power, interest in sustainability course instruction has gained momentum.

For academic libraries to fully integrate information literacy into sustainability literacy, an agreed-upon definition of the latter term is necessary. An agreed-upon definition of sustainability literacy could pave the way for the inclusion of sustainability into ACRL (2000) information literacy standards. Once embedded into the standards, classroom assessment methods already in place for information literacy could be adjusted to measure student growth in sustainability literacy. This could provide helpful statistics and feedback to both academic programs in sustainability and to the libraries serving them, in turn helping institutions to meet the commitments they have made to develop the emerging discipline.

References

Association of College and Research Libraries. (2000). Information literacy competency standards for higher education. Retrieved from http://www. ala.org/acrl/standards/informationliteracycompetency

Auburn University Office of Sustainability. (2013). In Auburn Sustainability. Retrieved from http://www.auburn.edu/projects/sustainability/website/ our_office/our_office.php

Bent, M. & Stockdale, E. (2009). Integrating information literacy as a habit of learning-assessing the impact of a golden thread of IL in the curriculum. Journal of Information Literacy, 3(1), 42-57. http://dx.doi. org/10.11645/3.1.212

English Department, Auburn University (2008). Orientation, ENGL1120 Curriculum (internal print document).

Filar Williams, B. (2011). Embedding your green message through asynchronous learning. Electronic Green Journal, 1(32). Retrieved from http:// www.escholarship.org/uc/item/4vt250k7

Gauder, H., & Jenkins, F. (2012). Engaging undergraduates in discipline-based research. Reference Services Review, 40(2), 277-294. doi:10.1108/00907321211228327

Geology & Geography, Auburn University College of Sciences and Mathematics. (2013). In Courses in Geography. Retrieved from http://www.auburn. edu/academic/cosam/departments/geology/academics/GeographCourses. htm

Hare, R.G., Moreton, E., Jo, J., Stamm, A., & Winter, D. (2011). Identifying and understanding valid sustainability information: the crossroad of evidence-based practice, science literacy, and information literacy. Issues in Science and Technology Librarianship, 67. doi: 10.5062/F47P8W90

Johnston, L., Collins, B. L., Boyle, A., & Womack, H. D. (2012). Looking at sustainability through a different LENS. Sustainability: The Journal of Record, 5(4), 244-247. doi:10.1089/sus.2012.9943

Kutner, L.A. (2000). Library instruction in an interdisciplinary environmental studies program: Challenges, opportunities, and reflections. Issues in Science and Technology Librarianship, 28. Retrieved from http://www.istl. org/00-fall/article2.html

Kutner, L.A. & Danks, C. (2007). Collaborating on the core curriculum: Transformation of an environmental studies course. In T.E. Jacobson & T.P. Mackey (Eds.), Information Literacy Collaborations that Work. New York: Neal-Schuman Publishers, Inc.

Lugg, A. & Hodgson, L. (2009). How should we teach environmental literacy? Critical reflection on virtual teaching and learning experiences. Paper presented at "Outdoor Education Research and Theory: Critical Reflections, New Directions," the Fourth International Outdoor Education Research Conference, La Trobe University, Beechworth, Victoria, Australia. Retrieved from http://www.latrobe.edu.au/education/downloads/2009_conference_lugg_hodgson.pdf

Lupton, M. (2008). Evidence, argument and social responsibility: First-year students' experiences of information literacy when researching an essay. Higher Education Research & Development, 27(4), 399-414. doi: 10.1080/07294360802406858

Nam, Y. & Ito, E. (2011). A climate change course for undergraduate students. Journal of Geoscience Education, 59, 229-241. Retrieved from http://nagt-jge.org/doi/pdf/10.5408/1.3651405

Noe, N. (2009). Toasting tags and cubing keywords with flickr photos: Flickr keywording/tagging exercise. In R.L. Sittler & D. Cook (Eds.), The library instruction cookbook. Chicago: Association of College and Research Libraries.

Stark, Megan R. (2011). Information in place: Integrating sustainability into information literacy instruction. *Electronic Green Journal*, 1(32). Retrieved from http://www.escholarship.org/uc/item/1fz2w70p

Walton, M. & Archer, A. (2004). The web and information literacy: Scaffolding the use of web sources in a project-based curriculum. British Journal of Educational Technology, 35(2), 173-186. Retrieved from http://www.cet.uct.ac.za/files/KnowledgeBase/2004ResearchOutput/bjet_4_Walton_Archer.pdf

Teaching Sustainable Information Literacy: A Collaborative Endeavor in the Humanities

Amy Pajewski

Abstract

The author argues that sustainability topics should be easily integrated into information literacy classes. All examples identify information literacy and research classes primarily related to literary topics at West Texas A&M University. This chapter provides teaching faculty and academic librarians the tools to start a collaborative effort to promote lifelong critical thinking in sustainability that can be adapted and fused to a broad range of disciplines.

Introduction

Academic librarians ought to become active partners in advancing and integrating sustainable literacy into instruction through collaborative teaching across disciplines. Embedding a librarian into a classroom in collaboration with faculty ensures Association of College and Research Libraries (ACRL) standards will be adapted appropriately to the culture, economy, local history, and ecology of West Texas A&M University. It will also promote the importance of sustainability and the impact of student research to the future. This chapter outlines a collaborative effort in the humanities, specifically studies in the Western Memoir, and blends ecocriticism, the West, place and identity, and synthesizes the impact of information and research through an ecological, economic, and social lens. As Otto and Wohlpart's stated the "...struggle has been to infuse education for sustainability into the curriculum across all colleges," and isolated courses "...rarely allow for a full transformation of perspectives or understanding" (2009). Librarians have the unique position on campus to reach a vast array of students from multiple disciplines either in one-shot information literacy classes or through faculty collaboration.

The humanities in particular, where students are exposed to a wide variety of disciplines and perspectives including the study of language and literature, is easily disposed to shake values and beliefs and effect change in university culture. Librarians inhabit a space in the university to build, preserve, and provide access to information and it is the library's role to provide information literacy across the curriculum to foster critical thinking skills and life-long learning. Until this point, librarians have not fully reached their potential in integrating sustainability education into the information literacy process.

Information Literacy and Sustainability

Even though the United Nations declared 2005-2014 to be the "Decade of Education for Sustainable Development," higher education has not proven well equipped to fulfill their goal (UNESCO, 2005). DuPuis and Ball argue that librarians must look at a fresh characterization of "sustainable knowing" and shift to a more collaborative and dialogic process (2013). In other words, librarians must move from didactic knowledge of sustainability to a more conceptualized and relational model found through meaningful connections and collaboration. As stewards, librarians are capable of guiding students to create knowledge that can be applied through "interpretation, experience, and practice" (DuPuis & Ball, 2013).

Embedding sustainability into information literacy through collaborating ultimately gives students the tools to think critically about sustainability and how research and information engages with the real world. According to the ACRL, information literacy is defined as

"a set of abilities requiring individuals to recognize when information is needed and have the ability to locate, evaluate, and use effectively the needed information. ... Academic librarians coordinate the evaluation and selection of intellectual resources for programs and services; organize, and maintain collections and many points of access to information; and provide instruction to students and faculty who seek information." (ALA, 2000, p. 2)

According to Stark, there are five strong standards for information literacy with clear performance indicators and outcomes:

1) The information literate student determines the nature and extent of the information needed.
2) The information literate student accesses needed information effectively and efficiently.
3) The information literate student evaluates information and its sources critically and incorporates selected information into his or her knowledge base and value system.
4) The information literate student, individually or as a member of a group, uses information effectively to accomplish a specific purpose.
5) The information literate student understands many of the economic, legal, and social issues surrounding the use of information access and uses information ethically and legally (2011).

Librarians are tasked with adhering to these standards when shaping and integrating information literacy in the classroom, but the standards fail to evaluate how students perceive place and local knowledge. Often times, students are unaware of how their research impacts their local communities and how that information can benefit the preservation of the local histories in their inhabited space.

Collaboration and Local Knowledge

In order to create a more comprehensive curriculum to advance sustainability, librarians and faculty crafted a collaborative course in Western Memoir. This class blends ecocriticism, the West, place and identity, and synthesizes the impact of information and research through an ecological, economic, and social lens. Students engage with western memoirs and use ecocriticism as a lens to further investigate their texts. In the process, students are introduced to the idea of Western identity and place and the impact of critical regionalism in scholarship. Integrating sustainability education and information literacy into the curriculum provides students the ability to shift their perspective to investigate, critique, and evaluate their use of information in a global sense. In this collaborative endeavor, students conduct primary source inquiries in the local community with faculty guidance while the librarian promotes the use of open access content to secondary scholarly research in order to cultivate a breadth of information. The synthesis of primary and secondary scholarship leads students to think critically about the local consequence, application, and manifestation of information. This research and primary oral histories are then preserved by the library where students can recognize the significance of their research for the future, therefore fostering and promoting the importance of sustainability. Students leave the course with a better understanding of how knowledge and information can impact local culture and traditions and understand the fusion of critical thinking and sustainable thinking as inherently necessary.

The class is set up in such a way that students will consider the verity and the consequences of Wendell Berry's remark quoted by Stegner "if you don't know where you are, you don't know who you are" (1992, p. 199). There is an emphasis to consider the differences between wild places and domesticated or worked ones and ask what varying models of self and experience emerge. Students are required to read the following literary works that provide an ethical framework that includes ecological integrity, nonviolence, and peace further expanding our idea of sustainability:

1) Wallace Stegner, *The Wilderness Letter*
2) Rick Bass, *Winter: Notes from Montana*
3) Barry Lopez, *Arctic Dreams*
4) Mark Spragg, *Where Rivers Change Direction*
5) Terry Tempest Williams, *Refuge*
6) Gretel Ehrlich, *The Solace of Open Spaces*
7) Edward Abbey, *Desert Solitaire*

The librarian role in the class is to demonstrate and frame the following capabilities for secondary research based on Stark's criteria explicitly articulated according to the national ACRL standards:

1) Identify and explain discourse communities
2) Identify research questions; translate to keywords
3) Recognize different information resources and explain the value and differences between them (i.e. finding aids, library catalog, databases, etc.)
4) Construct in-text citations and a bibliography, inclusive of all source types and formats (i.e. articles, images, music, etc.)
5) Explain the importance of citing research sources and academic honesty
6) Describe how information is produced and organized
7) Recognize ethical, legal, and social issues surrounding the use of information
8) Access the reliability, validity, accuracy, authority, timeliness, and point of view or bias of information sources (2011).

The librarian also serves to teach students the value of primary research. Based on outcomes and requirements during class, students learn the importance of place-based studies. To belong to the landscape, one must get to know the stories of the place. Students are required to seek out locals of the area because primary sources garner sustainable authenticity. A sense of place makes it possible for those seeking self-discovery, and a true sense of place combines geography and the human spirit. Students then synthesize primary and secondary scholarship and develop a better understanding in thinking critically about the local consequence, application, and manifestation of information. DuPuis and Ball claim "knowledge is gained through practical action [and] is fundamental to human understanding" (2013). Students who participate in practice-based research take away practical sustainability knowledge that allows them to apply it to everyday endeavors. Overall, students obtain a sense of ownership in their research and recognize the importance of sustainability and keeping local histories intact as an essential component of protecting place.

Preservation and Perspective

Research means nothing to the students unless it is protected and preserved, so it is essential the library put in policies and procedures for featuring regional stories. In today's information-driven world, digitizing these local histories along with photographs of the region could make an interesting collection. Weekly, librarians promoted student research via social media outlets with an accompanying interview with the student to gain perspective.

After the project is completed, students are required to answer exit questions to discover what they expected in their research and how the assignment integrated into their preexisting knowledge:

1) What did you find most challenging about this assignment?
2) What did you find most interesting?
3) What do you already know about the history of the Texas Panhandle?
4) Coming into the class, what perspectives did you hold about land and place?
5) What did this assignment mean to you? How do you think your perspective has shifted regarding place after interviewing your local?

Conclusion

The above questions sparked discussion about students' responsibility as authors to forge a new story of the West. To inhabit a space as an outsider or student, and give it a sense of home unlike the sense of ownership, but rather where students and librarians share what they have– a place of mutuality, a place endured for the sake of others, of belonging. "Home" could also be read as a metaphor for wholeness, centeredness, and connection, and students internalize being grounded to place. This project shows the need for stories that will inspire action and teach students about protecting their land and place where they live. Stories cannot be lost so long as the land remains sacred to the people who have worked to preserve it. These local histories, sought after by students, hold authenticity of place and foster a sense of responsibility to protect and think critically about land and establish a foundation for life-long learning.

References

American Library Association (ALA). Association of College and Research Libraries. (2000). *Information literacy competency standards for higher education*. Retrieve from http://www.ala.org/ala/mgrps/divs/acrl/standards/standards.pdf

DuPuis, M. E., & Ball, T. (2013). How not what: teaching sustainability as process. *Sustainability: Science, Practice, & Policy, 9*(1), 64-75.

Otto, E., & James, W. (2009). Creating a culture of sustainability. *Journal of Education for Sustainable Development, 3*(2), 231-235.

Stark, M. R. (2011). Information in place: Integrating sustainability into information literacy instruction. *Electronic Green Journal, 1*(32), 1-16. doi: uclalib_egj_10926

Stegner, W. (1992). *Where the bluebird sings to the lemonade springs: Living and writing in the West*. New York, NY: Random House.

United Nations Educational, Social, and Cultural Organization (UNESCO). 2005. *UNESCO and Sustainable Development*. Retrieved from http://www.unesco.org/new/en/education/themes/leading-the-international-agenda/education-for-sustainable-development/

Making Research Real: Focusing on Community-Based Sustainability

Laura Burt-Nicholas

Abstract

Sustainability is an important topic for students to research and understand, but they can feel daunted by the complexity of global issues. This chapter examines how using problem-based learning to focus on local sustainability issues inspired students to complete complex research projects. Students were able to describe practical changes that could be made in the community in order to alleviate existing sustainability problems.

Introduction

When the United Nations General Assembly voted to name 2005-2014 the Decade of Education for Sustainable Development, they hoped that this action would spur significant changes in the way we approached sustainability, not only in higher education, but in life. However, five years after the Decade officially began, UNESCO created the Bonn Declaration at the Conference for Education for Sustainable Development, which reaffirmed the importance of sustainability and admitted that progress on the issue of education and sustainable development "remains unevenly distributed and requires different approaches in different contexts" (2009). One of the reasons that sustainability education poses such a problem may be its complexity: while we often focus on environmental sustainability, the Environmental Protection Agency website stresses that sustainability is built upon "three pillars": environment, society and economy (2008). Therefore, sustainability discussions must balance questions such as whether fracking delivers the right balance of cheap and environmentally safe energy, or if increasing the minimum wage would benefit the country as a whole. As these questions become increasingly important to our future as well as increasingly complicated, it is clear that higher education needs to address these questions through student education.

This complexity of definition and situation offers incredible opportunities both for higher education and for librarians. In "Moving Beyond Green: Sustainable Development Toward Healthy Environments, Social Justice, and Strong Economies," Keith Edwards (2012) argues that higher education often places too much emphasis on the environmental aspect of sustainability and that campus environments provide a perfect testing ground to model sustainability decisions for students (p. 20). While Edwards' argument to involve students in the decision process for topics such as whether to offer plastic cups in the cafeteria is intriguing, it should be expanded to include student research projects rooted in information literacy principles. These research projects will make the principles of sustainability real to all students.

Currently, academic literature on libraries and sustainability rarely focuses on information literacy. For example, Vivian-Elizabeth Zazzau (2006) addresses environmental problems due to our consumption of technology—e-waste, recycling, etc.—but her solution to the problem is primarily legislative and personal. She does ask librarians to discuss information and environmental ethics in library sessions but does not call for working specifically to create assignments with faculty that flesh these problems out (p. 104). In response to this trend, in "Information in Place: Integrating Sustainability into Information Literacy Instruction," Megan Stark (2011) highlights the lack of literature connecting sustainability and information literacy and calls for adapting the current information literacy standards to include sustainability outcomes (p. 2-4).

This chapter deals with an attempt to answer these questions. For three years the author taught a section of a required general education course at her university that focused on consumption and sustainability. In this research and writing course, the author worked to expand students' definition of sustainability and to create a research project that forced them to think about systemic injustice through the lens of one local situation. The author used the Association of College and Research Libraries (ACRL) standards to ensure that their research projects were informed by local data and reflected the complexity of the real world. In that time, the author found the best pedagogical design to be at the intersection of sustainability, problem-based learning, and our local community. Asking students to pose solutions to concrete local problems inspired students to thoughtfully consider problems of sustainability in our society. This approach led to engaged students who felt invested in city problems and approached them as informed citizens. This chapter describes the evolution of the course, from the way the author adapted the course topic to the changing teaching strategies, as well as depicts the overall student response.

Background

All sophomores at North Park University must take Dialogue 2, a semester-long cross-disciplinary introduction to research, writing, and ethics. The author has worked with Dialogue 2 in two capacities: as a reference librarian, by helping other faculty in the program to design their research assignments and offering library sessions for their students. She also taught a section of the course, to understand how students approached the research and writing processes. For the last three years, the course focused on consumption: how what we buy impacts our personalities, societies, and the environment. In addition to assigned readings, students had to research a consumption "problem" and propose a solution to it. Many wrote about topics like coffee farms and rainforest destruction, the impact of the choice between organic agriculture and industrial agriculture on starvation or the environment, chocolate consumption and child slavery, and the link between fashion trends, textile productions, and landfills.

After two years teaching the course, the author became dissatisfied with the results. The complexity of the research projects were too hard for most students to manage. Too many students were focusing on large consumption problems that involved international law, global trade patterns, and foreign cultures that students had little familiarity with. It was unfair to ask them to become experts on all of these topics in one semester, and their papers reflected a weak understanding of the problems involved. Many students would propose solutions which were nearly impossible to implement. Despite the prompts, many focused on "should" statements in their solution papers, such as "corporations should not allow slavery on the plantations from which they buy cacao," or "people should not buy non-shade grown coffees." As these proposals assumed a common ethical standard not all people ascribe to, they were useless as solution papers. Furthermore, students often ended the semester discouraged; believing no true solution to these complex problems existed.

The author decided to refocus the course, paying special attention to Information Literacy Standard Three: "The information literate student evaluates information and its sources critically and incorporates selected information into his or her knowledge base and value system," and Four: "The information literate student, individually or as a member of a group, uses information effectively to accomplish a specific purpose" (ACRL, 2000). She theorized that she could redirect students to focus on creating solutions for problems they were familiar with, which would allow them to research—and communicate—from informed perspectives. As North Park University is also a Christian liberal arts university whose mission is preparing students for "lives of significance and service," the author was particularly interested in getting students to act upon the ethical conclusions that they formed; she thought that swapping from a focus on an amorphous problem—consumption—to a concrete solution—sustainability—would help students to achieve this goal (North Park University, 1999).

Methodology

To help revitalize the course, the author turned to the strategy of problem-based learning, a system wherein students are asked to articulate a problem, analyze its causes, and propose a solution while working collaboratively in groups. Research has stated that problem-based learning could encourage higher-level research thinking in students and increase student engagement (Kenney, 2008, Spence, 2004, Summerlee and Murray, 2010). Michael Pelikan (2004) described how Penn State University had integrated problem-based learning into the general education program, by moving students from a scattershot approach to research to the ability to clearly articulate research needs and then begin to search for information to answer them (p. 510-11). Pelikan asked students to craft a "problem statement" of their own, which evolved into a research question as he worked to help the students understand what they didn't know (p. 516). Furthermore, problem-based learning could be combined with a community focus: librarians Martin Kesselman and Adria Sherman (2009) at Rutgers created a team-based research project where student groups worked with local businesses to complete projects such as suggesting new food additives (p. 308). They found not only did students feel satisfied with their relationships with faculty in this project, but industry partners were pleased with the results of the research project and student work (p. 312-3). While the author's first courses had many of the elements of problem-based learning, she concluded that when students struggled to define the extent of the problem, this was due to the scope of the project which made it unmanageable.

To fit the problem-based learning strategy, the author decided to change the student research projects to focus on sustainability rather than consumption. The lens of sustainability also gave students an automatic framework within which to ask their research question. Rather than merely asking if a topic was ethical, they could ask if it was sustainable. They found this to be an easier question to manage. Therefore; students were required to pick a sustainability topic, either environmental (such as public transportation, or green energy) or human (such as food access or health care access). The author tried to restrict the large categories to topics that immediately affected students either as Chicago residents or as future professionals so that students would be innately interested in their research.

The author required students to focus their research on Chicago and describe, through a combination of their own experience, popular articles, government data and academic research, the extent of the problem facing the city. She also took advantage of the huge amounts of government data related to the city of Chicago. Through its website and an online data portal, the city provides a vast array of information about citizen health, education, city finances, and the services the city provides. Once students knew that this data existed, they could use it to describe the extent of the problem within the city, or in some cases, within one neighborhood. The class then discussed how to use academic research articles to place this data in context and how they could draw comparisons between different neighborhoods, or how other cities exhibited these problems, or even how earlier proposed solutions to the problems had failed.

The local focus helped the students come up with creative solutions to their problems as well. The author emphasized looking at nonprofits or community organizations currently working in similar neighborhoods or on similar programs. They then proposed a solution that worked in partnership with local nonprofit organizations or community groups, and showed how existing programs might be changed or broadened to better impact city residents. Students were also encouraged to discuss how existing city laws could be changed to either ameliorate the problem described or fund potential solutions to it.

The author also tried to make the group approach to research in problem-based learning add to the educational impact of my course. Educational research has shown that students who learn collaboratively have higher impact learning, including higher grades and better knowledge retention (Oakley et. al, 2004, p. 9). The author took guidance from performance indicator six for Information Literacy Standard Three: "The information literate student validates understanding and interpretation of the information through discourse with other individuals, subject-area experts, and/or practitioners." To encourage discourse among experts and to encourage the problem-based focus on the collective wisdom of groups, the author created permanent small groups in the class. Student groups worked together throughout the semester to analyze class readings and respond to in-class assignments. This allowed groups to work out problems with group dynamics early on, through no-cost assignments, so that students knew how to collaborate together prior to the high stakes assignments. For their final sustainability research project, each small group focused on one broad sustainability topic together (such as "public transportation" or "health care access"). Not only did the small groups work together to discover sources and share research, but they had to do a group class presentation that forced them to synthesize their research and look for common problems. They also proofread each other's work, from thesis statements to draft papers, and the author regularly tried to save class time so the small groups could discuss their research together.

The redesigned course required a more strategic approach to research instruction. The author had two separate research sessions with students, one focused on academic research and literature reviews, and one on gathering government data. While the first session was offered to everyone in the course, for the second session on government data, she met individually with the research groups to discuss the research problems they were encountering and suggested some reports and websites they could use to better understand their sustainability problem.

The redesigned course required the author to meet with students outside of class more frequently, either one-on-one or with their small groups, to make sure that they were on the right track. These meetings helped to produce more enthusiastic students who were dedicated to the promise of sustainability rather than students overwhelmed by what they perceived as insurmountable problems. For the first time, the author heard students lecturing one another on whether urban sprawl was sustainable or how living in a food desert—a location without easy access to grocery stores--affected public health. The class also benefited from the increased energy that came with invested students, as the author could bring in newspaper headlines and have the students analyze them through a window of their current research and class readings. When an economics article focused on incentives was the assigned reading, during class students read a *Chicago Tribune* article that discussed how elementary school children were throwing out the newly provided oranges and apples that came with their subsidized school lunches. Students used the article to both analyze how the intended solution of encouraging healthy eating habits among school children had backfired, and then other students working food sustainability topics could discuss how other groups had tackled this problem, such as in school gardens.

Conclusion

After this experience with sustainability-focused problem-based learning, the author has encouraged other professors at the university to adopt similar pedagogical methods. Having engaged, thoughtful students tackling local issues of sustainability resulted in complex research projects created by students who truly understood sustainability in at least one context. The project also modeled a good research process for future civic problems students might want to address. The author is currently working on a math/chemistry project on recycling and plastics that uses data from industry reports and Chicago data on recycling. Using the city data set to identify the environmental ramifications of our sporadic city-wide recycling program has increased student understanding of this real, global problem.

Mixing local problem-based learning and sustainability created an engaged community of learners as well. Student groups grew to work together and rely on their partners' research and expertise, forging a bond between professor and student as well. One future change would be to have students officially collaborate with community partners in the class. This would allow students to see how community organizations work to handle sustainability initiatives while facing political, financial, and geographical limitations.

References

ACRL. (2000). *Information literacy competency standards for higher education.* Retrieved from http://www.ala.org/acrl/standards/informationliteracycom petency#stan

Bonn Declaration. (2009). UNESCO. Retrieved from http://www.esd-world-conference-2009.org/fileadmin/download/ESD2009_BonnDeclara-tion080409.pdf

Edwards, K. E. (2012). Moving beyond green: Sustainable development toward healthy environments, social justice, and strong economies. *New Directions for Student Services,* (137), 19–28.

Environmental Protection Agency. Sustainability at the EPA (2008). Retrieved from http://www.epa.gov/sustainability/

Kenney, B. F. (2008). Revitalizing the one-shot instruction session using prob-lem-based learning. *Reference & User Services Quarterly, 47*(4), 386–391.

Kesselman, M. A., & Sherman, A. (2009). Linking information to real-life problems: An interdisciplinary collaboration of librarians, departments, and food businesses. *Journal of Agricultural & Food Information, 10*(4), 300–318.

North Park University. (1999). *Our promise.* Retrieved from http://www. northpark.edu/Admissions/Undergraduate-Admissions/Explore/Our-Promise

Oakley, B., Brent, R., Felder, R. M., & Ethajj, I. (2004). Turning student groups into effective teams. *Journal of Student Centered Learning, 2*(1), 9–31.

Pelikan, M. (2004). Problem-based learning in the library: Evolving a realistic approach. *Portal: Libraries and the Academy, 4*(4), 509–520.

Spence, L. (2004). The usual doesn't work: Why we need problem-based learning. *Portal: Libraries and the Academy, 4*(4), 485–493. doi:10.1353/ pla.2004.0072

Stark, M. R. (2011). Information in place: Integrating sustainability into in-formation literacy instruction. *Electronic Green Journal, 1*(32), 1–16. doi: uclalib_egj_10926

Summerlee, A., & Murray, J. (2010). The impact of enquiry-based learning on academic performance and student engagement. *Canadian Journal of Higher Education, 40*(2), 78–94.

UNESCO. (1998-2010). Education for sustainable development (ESD). *United Nations Educational Scientific and Cultural Organization*. Retrieved from http://www.unesco.org/new/en/education/themes/leading-the-international-agenda/education-for-sustainable-development/

United Nations. (2008). About ESD. *Decade of education for sustainable development*. Retrieved from http://www.desd.org/About%20ESD.htm

United States Environmental Protection Agency. (n.d.). *Sustainability at the EPA*. Retrieved from http://www.epa.gov/sustainability/

Zazzau, V. E. (2006). Becoming information literate about information technology and the ethics of toxic waste. *Portal: Libraries and the Academy*, 6(1), 99–107. doi:10.1353/pla.2006.0014

Teaching by Doing: Sustainability Education and Practice in a Student-Services Program

Mary G. Scanlon, Peter A. Romanov, and Mary Beth Lock

Abstract

The authors describe the sustainable efforts made by librarians and staff during a finals week event. The library chose to implement gradual changes to mitigate the program's environmental impact while still serving a large student population. Some of the efforts included: eliminating Styrofoam, encouraging reusable drink ware, and providing space for student-made sustainable art. The librarians from Wake Forest University are using an incremental approach to making this event more sustainable.

Introduction

Since 2006, the Z. Smith Reynolds Library (ZSR) at Wake Forest University has hosted an event during final exams called *Wake the Library* (*WTL*). During this event, the library stays open around the clock for eight days, serves free coffee continuously, and sponsors activities that provide study breaks. Of all the elements of *WTL*, students most appreciate the food the staff serves each night at midnight. Though highly valued, feeding 300 to 350 students every night creates a great deal of waste, much of it not recyclable. Three years ago the library's Sustainability Committee began a campaign to make *WTL* more sustainable.

The campaign's primary focus has been twofold: to decrease the total amount of waste generated and to increase the relative proportion of recyclable materials. The university's Office of Sustainability has been an essential partner in this effort. In the course of the campaign, the library's committee has tried to demonstrate more sustainable behaviors in the hope that students will adopt them beyond the eight days of *WTL*. Education efforts on sustainable practices have focused on two groups: students who consume the food and beverages, and the library's administration which manages the event. The two groups have required very different approaches to change. The students are interested in the variety and quantity of food, while the administration is concerned with costs and student satisfaction.

In this article, the library's Sustainability Committee reports on its goals and accomplishments as well as the challenges it faced and overcame. It concludes with a statement of its goals for further waste reduction and increased education efforts surrounding the event.

Wake the Library Event

ZSR's leadership, aware of students' all night study habits, realized there were no overnight study spaces on campus. In the spring semester of 2006, our new director responded to this void by keeping the library open 24 hours a day

Figure 1. Students line up for food at *Wake the Library*. Credit: Susan S. Smith

during the week of final exams. Staff volunteered to take overnight shifts in exchange for their regular day shifts.

Library management recognized that even if the library stayed open, many
other campus facilities (most notably food service) would not be open all night.
Thus, library staff recommended serving food at midnight. *WTL* staff solicited
donations of money and food from campus departments and corporate sponsors
to support the program. The final step in *WTL*'s evolution was the addition of
free coffee, which is served around the clock in the center of the library known
as the atrium, where students naturally congregate.

Through every exam week since it began, the program has changed in some
way, while staying true to the original idea. The library now runs on a 24/5
schedule, so *WTL* operates with fewer volunteers. In addition, *WTL* has its own
standing committee to organize the food and coffee while soliciting nightly

Figure 2. WFU marching band playing on library balcony. Credit: Susan S. Smith

volunteers to serve it. In addition, funding for the program now comes from
the Provost's office, instead of solicitation efforts. Students regard the food at
midnight as a study break and other campus groups use that time to create additional events. In recent *WTL*s, the student council has organized boisterous
dance parties known as raves, student dance groups have performed, and the
Wake Forest University marching band has played.

For most of its duration, the *WTL* menu has consisted of fast food, fruit,
and bottled water. These items are easy to serve under sanitary conditions, and
students move quickly and efficiently as though they are in a cafeteria line. The

original intent was to provide as much food as our small budget would allow. The initial tactic of buying individually packaged fast food met the need for expediency, but generated a lot of trash - an unintended consequence. In the early days, no one spoke up about the impacts of serving coffee in Styrofoam cups nor snacks individually packaged on Styrofoam plates.

Benefits and Impact of *WTL*

The impact of *WTL* cannot be understated. Students immediately recognized that the library administration and staff were interested in their point of view, and willing to work hard to meet their needs. Of all the library's programs, *Wake the Library* has become the most popular. Further, it has helped change Wake Forest culture by expanding hours of operation of many other essential services on campus, such as opening study spaces that had previously been locked after 5pm. While the implementation, promotion, and operation of *WTL* brought attention to students' need for late-night study space, the environmental impacts were not given top priority.

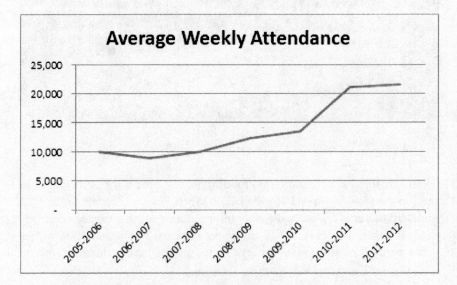

Figure 3. ZSR Average Weekly Attendance 2005-2012. Source: ZSR gate counts, 2005 - 2012

Partly as a result of *WTL*'s success, overall use of the library has increased dramatically.

Collaborating with the Office of Sustainability

The Office of Sustainability has been a valuable partner in implementing sustainable practices within the library. Its mission is to, "encourage and facilitate the collaborative efforts of faculty, students, and staff to generate knowledge, acquire skills, develop values, and initiate practices that contribute to a sustainable, high quality of life on campus, in the Triad, and across the globe" (Wake Forest University, 2013). One of its very popular accomplishments was the installation of a water bottle filling station inside the library. What was once just a water fountain is now a filtered water dispenser and water fountain where library patrons can effortlessly refill their reusable drink ware. A "Choose to Reuse" sign is affixed prominently to the station and a digital counter tells users how many disposable bottles have been avoided. In addition to providing the library with recycling bins and the filling station, the Office of Sustainability often collaborates with the library's Sustainability Committee to educate library patrons on sustainable practices. Co-sponsoring film screenings has been an effective means of bringing students together in the library to learn about social responsibility and environmental issues such as fracking and the environmental impacts of drinking water from disposable bottles.

Sustainable changes to *Wake the Library*

Since its inception in 2009, the library's Sustainability Committee has brought about significant, sustainable changes to *WTL*. During its first year, the committee worked with the university's Office of Sustainability to acquire new recycling bins for the library as part of its plan to place bins all over campus. Participation in recycling improved because of the bins' consistent color scheme, (black for trash, green for recycling), and customized shapes: round holes for bottles, rectangular slots for paper. Following the bins' placement, the university saw a marked decrease in recycling contamination, (defined as 30% or more of non-recyclables in each bag of recycled material). The library was given enough bins to distribute throughout the building, when before, bins had only been placed in a few high-traffic areas. The presence of these larger, well-marked bins throughout the library building contributes to higher use in general and a significant reduction in waste during *WTL*.

In 2010, the committee further reduced the library's waste stream by initiating a mug giveaway which encouraged students to choose a reusable mug rather than a Styrofoam cup. The goal was to break the cycle of using an item once and throwing it away. Library staff contributed unwanted mugs and the Office of Sustainability purchased additional ones from Goodwill, all of which were washed and sterilized in the dining hall's dishwashers. Student volunteers from the Office of Sustainability staffed a table in the library and handed them out to students and a sign on the table reminded students to use the mugs for *WTL* coffee. Having the table staffed by students rather than librarians introduced an element of peer influence. The program was such a success that the library continues to give away mugs during the spring and fall semesters a few days before the first exams (see Figure 4).

During *WTL* 2011, the Sustainability Committee convinced the WTL Committee to replace Styrofoam cups with paper cups. In addition, the cups were kept behind the Circulation Desk so students had to ask for them, an obstacle which encouraged them to use their own mugs. So many students embraced the concept during the 2012 spring and fall *WTL* periods, that disposable cup usage declined dramatically. For the spring 2013 semester, the library continued to promote environmental responsibility by providing reusable mugs and supplementing, when requested, with paper cups.

Having succeeded in eliminating Styrofoam from the event, in the spring of 2011, the committee established a new goal: eliminating disposable plastic water bottles. Consistent with prior changes, the committee took an incremental approach, encouraging the *WTL* Committee to purchase smaller water bottles. The committee reasoned that while the event would still generate plastic waste, it would generate less waste since the bottles were smaller. Unfortunately, the smaller bottles had the opposite effect because students took multiple bottles. In light of student response to the smaller bottles, the Sustainability Committee revised its tactics the following semester by encouraging students to rely on reusable water bottles. By this time, the Office of Sustainability had installed a water bottle filling station in the library which was an essential element in moving toward the committee's goal. It has become very popular with students and reusable water bottles are now a common sight in the library. In its first year, students refilled enough reusable water bottles to keep 12,000 disposable water bottles out of circulation.

To further promote the use of reusable water bottles, in the fall of 2012 the committee placed a water dispenser on the beverage table with the disposable water bottles; its presence was intended as a reminder that students should refill/reuse their own drink ware. The dispenser held chilled, filtered water from the water bottle refilling station. As the Sustainability Committee drives toward its

Figure 4. Students from the Office of Sustainability hand out mugs during *Wake the Library*. Credit: Susan S. Smith

goal of eliminating disposable water bottles from *WTL*, it will strive to make the water dispenser a permanent addition to *WTL*.

Education

The committee has taught by doing, but plans to teach more overtly at future *WTL* events. To educate students on the importance of following sustainable practices during the event, the committee and library staff will use a broad range of tactics such as posting signage during the event and promoting best practices through social media. The main purpose will be to raise awareness of sustainable practices in a way that will grab students' attention.

Signage will play an important role; placing eye-catching and interesting signs on the serving tables is one tactic, and utilizing the library's electronic signage is another. Placing table tents on the atrium tables where many students eat will serve as another means of educating students. Social media will play an important role, as well. On the library's Facebook page, the committee will remind students to bring their reusable mugs and water bottles to *WTL*, and the library's Twitter feed will reinforce these messages. Posts to both networks will stress "reduce, reuse, recycle". The ceramic mugs, the water bottle filling station, and the presence of recycling bins will reinforce this message. In addition to statements promoting conservation and recycling, trivia questions and recycling facts will be tweeted on *WTL* nights or posted on Facebook.

The library staff has observed that student-led initiatives are more effective than staff-led initiatives, so the Sustainability Committee has invited student groups to join its efforts. For example, students from the Office of Sustainability give away the ceramic mugs, providing peer influence at the point of use.

Another form of peer influence consists of student-created art installations which raise awareness about the consequences of consumption. One semester, students created a tree out of discarded coffee cups (see Figure 5.); the students wanted to make their peers aware of just how much waste is generated by dis-

Figure 5. Student art installation made from plastic cups. Credit: Susan S. Smith

carded cups. Another year, students constructed an American flag using recycled bottles, again providing a visible symbol of our consuming habits. These installations convey a visual message which has more impact than the printed word.

Challenges

To make "reduce, reuse, recycle" a reality during *WTL*, the committee has had to convince two groups to change: students and the library's administration. As student use of the library continues to grow, both recyclable and non-recyclable trash volumes will grow. When *WTL* started in 2006, it was the library's only source of food-related waste. The committee noticed an increase in trash during the event, but since it lasted only two weeks a year, little attention was paid to managing it. Students are now allowed to eat and drink in the library year-round. *WTL* generates a waste stream on top of the normal daily volume, which doubles the amount of food-related waste during *WTL*. Our challenges are two-fold: first to reduce the volume of waste by changing the inputs to *WTL* and second, to insure that all waste is properly recycled or discarded. The committee is addressing the problem at the front and back ends of the event, managing inputs and outputs appropriately.

The education efforts with the library's administration have focused on highlighting the environmental impact of the program, showing how small changes diminish its impact and save money, and demonstrating student acceptance of the changes. The administration has been open to suggestions from the committee, but slow to make changes, out of concern for the students' acceptance.

Conclusion

In recent years, ZSR's Sustainability Committee has focused on the inputs and outputs of a very successful program to decrease its environmental impact. A program that used to generate mountains of trash produces far less today. Among the inputs the committee has influenced is the elimination of Styrofoam plates and cups, the distribution and promotion of re-usable drink ware, and a current effort to eliminate disposable plastic water bottles. The output has been improved by the addition of more recycling bins placed in more conspicuous locations, which are consistent in appearance and labeling across the entire campus leading to a higher rate of use. Less waste is generated and students are recycling more of it.

The committee has been able to make small but consistent changes in each iteration of *Wake the Library*. It has been a slower process than the committee would wish for two reasons. The committee has had only indirect influence over the program which is operated by a different committee; and the library's administration is very careful in making changes to a highly successful program.

Up to the present time, the committee has taught by example, modeling the behaviors it wants students to adopt. At the next WTL, the committee will employ multiple tactics to teach students more directly: to create awareness of environmental challenges, and to present sustainable practices that address the challenges.

References

Wake Forest University. Office of Sustainability. (2013). *Mission and Guiding Principles*. Retrieved from http://sustainability.wfu.edu/about/mission-and-guiding-principles/

Further Reading

Anderson, E. S., & Lennox, A. (2009). The Leicester model of interprofessional education: developing, delivering and learning from student voices for 10 years. *Journal of Interprofessional Care, 23*, 557–573. doi: 10.3109/13561820903051451

Eagan, D. J. (1992). Campus environmental stewardship. *New Directions for Higher Education, 77*, 65–76. doi: 10.1002/he.36919927709

Fien, J. (2002). Advancing sustainability in higher education: issues and opportunities for research. *International Journal of Sustainability in Higher Education, 3*, 243–253. doi: 10.1108/14676370210434705

Jones, P., Colin J. T., and Richards, J. (2008). Embedding education for sustainable development in higher education: a case study examining common challenges and opportunities for undergraduate programmes. *International Journal of Educational Research, 47*, 341–350. doi: http://dx.doi.org/10.1016/j.ijer.2008.11.001

Tolley, S. G., Everham, E. M., McDonald, M.R., & Savarese, M. (2002). The campus ecosystem model: Teaching students environmental stewardship. *Journal of College Science Teaching, 31*, 364–69.

Library Showcase: Modeling Sustainability across Campus

Dawn Emsellem Wichowski
and Jameson F. Chace

Abstract

In this chapter, the authors describe how an instructional collaboration between environmental studies faculty and library staff resulted in expanded awareness of environmental issues across campus. An undergraduate class was provided with unlimited access to the library building and staff to conduct an analysis of the library's carbon footprint. Over the semester, students and library staff learned more about the impact of their daily activities on the environment. As a result of student recommendations, staff made many changes to their workflow, multiple environmental sustainability initiatives spun off from those changes, and new efforts to integrate environmental sustainability research into the library's education programs have begun. The authors situate this project in the context of environmental sustainability initiatives on campuses nationwide.

Introduction

At Salve Regina University's McKillop Library, library staff and biological sciences faculty modeled a vision of the library as a promoter of campus sustainability through a student-centered, hands-on learning experience: mapping the library's carbon footprint. The students produced a detailed, carefully researched final report, which was publicly presented and submitted to the institutional repository (http://digitalcommons.salve.edu/bio_proj/).

91

The student report informed new strategic directives for the library and spun off several initiatives, including a formal library commitment to sustainability, the formation of a staff/faculty environmental group, a building-wide recycling and donation program, and online research guides highlighting the library's environmental science resources. These activities provide a model for library/faculty collaboration and sustainability leadership on campus.

Salve Regina University (SRU) is a small liberal arts institution in an historic setting in Newport, Rhode Island with an undergraduate population of 2,000. Salve Regina undergraduates major primarily in business studies, teaching, nursing, administration of justice and liberal arts. Founded and administered by the Sisters of Mercy, the university has a mission that incorporates a commitment to environmental sustainability: "...recognizing that all people are stewards of God's creation, the University encourages students to work for a world that is harmonious, just and merciful" (Salve Regina's Mission, 2013). Following this commitment to stewardship, in 2006 the Board of Trustees agreed to a university environmental sustainability policy that balanced the economic, social, and ecological practices and operation of the university (About Sustainability at Salve, 2013). At Salve Regina University, the library has become a center of active environmental stewardship and fulfillment of university commitments made with the Sustainability Policy.

This chapter highlights a symbiotic collaboration between the university library and biological sciences department, in which the library became a part of students' semester-long assignment to assess the library's carbon footprint, present the findings, and make recommendations. The authors first describe the collaboration between library staff and the students and faculty of a general education course on a project to determine the library's environmental impact. The authors then describe the effect that this project has had on the students, library staff, and university, ending with perspectives on the challenges that may face libraries and institutions of higher learning interested in leading the way to a sustainable future.

The Project

BIO 140: Humans and Their Environment is a general education course that considers the interdependence and tension between humans and their environment. Discussions of contemporary, social, economic, and ecological concerns such as population growth, world hunger, pollution, and resource utilization provide students with the general knowledge necessary for consideration of environmental ethics. During the fall 2009 semester, one section of the course had 24 students who, for their research project, were invited by the McKillop

Library director to evaluate the library's impact on the environment to determine how well the library was meeting the stewardship mission and sustainability policy of the university.

Educational Goals

Faculty and library staff worked together to integrate the library's mission to promote information literacy with science educators' mission to spread scientific literacy. The university library and the university's biological sciences department planned the project in accordance with American Association for the Advancement of Science (AAAS) Project 2061 recommendations. According to recommendation 2061 (AAAS, 1993), scientifically literate students should be aware that science has both strengths and limitations and is an interdependent enterprise with math, technology and society; students should be able to use scientific ways of thinking and knowledge for individual and social purpose and be competent in communication and collaboration.

In general education science courses, key learning objectives typically include an ability to understand the scientific method, gaining a foundational level of scientific literacy, demonstrating an ability to qualitatively and quantitatively analyze data to answer a research question, and being able to provide a logical application of scientifically gained information to a problem (AAAS, 1989). This concept of scientific literacy melds well with the Association of College and Research Libraries' (ACRL) Information Literacy Competency Standards for Higher Education (ACRL, 2013). In the course of the collaboration between the faculty of the biological sciences department and the library, students completed hands-on learning activities and found tools to evaluate the library's environmental impact, quality sources to support their findings, and used these resources in creating their recommendations for action. It is clear from their final presentations they synthesized the findings from their research and the sources they used into their knowledge base about environmental science, suggesting that the project was successful both from a scientific and information literacy perspective.

The structure for the research project was modeled on an environmental science pathway to knowledge using a modified environmental impact assessment protocol (Eccleston 2011; Glasson et al. 2005). Students met with the director of the library. She outlined the scope of the problem and introduced the students to key department heads. Department heads toured the students through the library, describing environmental issues as they encountered them and addressing student questions. Following this meeting and tour, the students brainstormed key aspects of the library's carbon footprint and divided into teams based on a self-assessment of skills, a modified version of Bordeau & Arnold (2009). Duties, responsibilities, and key deadlines for completion were self-determined for each team. Teams decided to focus on (1) heating and cooling of the building, (2) electricity use in the building, (3) solid waste and, separately, (4) paper waste generated by the building, and (5) transportation of materials and staff. Each member of the class was also assigned to an additional team by the instructor to enhance synthesis, communication, and cohesion among the teams and for the final report. These synthesis teams focused on: editing the drafts and final report (http://digitalcommons.salve.edu/bio_proj/), producing a PowerPoint presentation for the library, creating a team leader executive committee, and a group of members who would report weekly to the class on group findings and problems encountered.

Analysis

Each team set out to estimate, quantitatively and qualitatively, the direct and indirect impacts of library practices on climate change through carbon dioxide emissions. The heating and cooling team examined building insulation, the HVAC system, and the roof to estimate impacts and make recommendations. Using temperature and humidity data loggers and infrared thermometers the students found inefficiencies in the 71,000 square foot, three floor library. Temperature and humidity fluctuated highly, a concern for librarians and patrons alike, which was most apparently connected to an outdated HVAC system. The highly isolative quality of the windows and building materials was a positive but the degree of solar heating via the windows was not regulated. In total, the students were able to approximate that the library was consuming 47,250 Ccf of natural gas, an equivalent of nearly 280 short tons of carbon dioxide emissions.

Using information from National Grid, the local electricity provider, the university's facilities department on lighting, and direct measures of electrical devices using Kill-A-Watt meters, the electricity team was able to quantify the library's carbon dioxide production and make specific carbon saving recommendations. The library consumed 1,134 megawatts of energy in the last year, based on the sources of electrical energy at that time, resulting in an equivalent of 965 pounds of released carbon dioxide. The local energy provider offers a "Greenstart" program encouraging customers to switch to low carbon sources of energy, primarily hydropower and wind in the university's region. If the library were to adopt such a program, electricity cost would increase for a significant reduction in carbon dioxide (840 pounds/megawatt).

The solid waste team found that ink cartridges, DVD plastic cases, and plastic packaging were significant contributors to the library's solid waste stream, having both direct and indirect impacts on the library's carbon footprint. The cost of printing was economically unsustainable at nearly $10,000/year for ink cartridges. Students located cartridge recyclers that would, if the campus purchased recycled toner in return, reduce the cost by 50% or more. The new library "Red-Tag" system for DVDs meant that, in one year, 600 #7 plastic cases were thrown away. Recyclers for this carbon-based waste could not be found; however, moving to online movie use would eliminate the red-tag system and allow the library to retain the use of the non-recyclable DVD cases. Interlibrary loan and shipment of new book orders result in significant solid waste due to plastic inside the recyclable cardboard boxes. Recognizing that storage space is an issue, students recommended reuse of non-recyclable plastic whenever possible. During a dumpster dive, the students were able to assess where and how much recyclable product (plastic bottles and aluminum cans) was being thrown into the landfill waste stream. In a building-wide survey, the students found that there were a limited number of recycling bins (4 comingled, 10 paper). They recommended increasing the number of recycling bins and signage about proper disposal of items around the building.

Paper waste represents a significant amount of the solid waste stream generated by the library. Students also surveyed library patrons and found that 19% do not recycle when in the library, while 8% recycle occasionally, indicating that some environmental education was needed in the library. Through the surveys they also found that the average student in the library prints 20 pages each week. Combined with faculty and administrative needs, the university consumed 435,000 sheets of high grade, bright white paper in the academic year of 2008-2009.

The transportation team based their assessment on a survey of all library staff transportation needs. They found that the staff releases 2,760 pounds of carbon dioxide each month during their commutes to work. Based on library staff home addresses, the students developed public transportation alternatives for each member and encouraged the administration to extend benefits to employees taking mass transit or carpooling.

Overall Impact

The project had numerous positive effects: students received practical experience in environmental research and in conducting an environmental audit, the Salve Regina community and library staff increased their awareness of the effects of the environmental impact of their actions, library workflows were changed to reduce environmental impact, a faculty/staff environmental group was created to effect change across campus, and numerous waste reduction policies were implemented to help library users reduce their environmental impact. Below we detail the effects within the library and on students.

Impact on Library Initiatives

As a result of the findings of the student-led carbon footprint assessment, sustainability issues were added to the library's strategic goals. The library established stated sustainability goals that reflected student findings and were posted to the library's sustainability page (Sustainability at McKillop Library, 2013).

To act on these goals, library staff formed a building-wide sustainability task force. As a result of student findings about the library's paper and electricity use, the building-wide task force developed an awareness-building campaign about patrons' use of resources through signage. Signs were posted near photocopiers, printers, and elevators with the aim of teaching patrons and staff about the effects of their actions on the environment.

Library staff also worked towards building awareness and incorporating environmental sustainability into its educational mission by inviting the student environmental group to develop a library display on water use. The student group created posters of facts about the worldwide water crisis, and library staff supplemented the display with library materials about water use and water policy. The group also sought to increase awareness about sustainability initiatives quietly operating all over campus. The Office of Mail Services was accepting packing materials to reuse and bring to local mail services businesses, and had successfully lobbied to allow only two printed event notices per office, rather than four hundred and twenty for each university staff member. The Office of Design Services offered environmentally sensitive printing options, and staff members in the University Athletic Center were repairing donated bikes to support a campus-wide shared bike initiative. As library staff members heard of these initiatives, they publicized them in the Office of Human Resources newsletter.

To improve the building's environmental quality, library staff members met with the director of cleaning services and learned about the company's commitment to green cleaners. Follow-up resulted in less toxic rug cleaners and improved coordination between library staff and the building's cleaning staff for recycling compliance. Library staff learned that cleaning staff needed cardboard boxes to be broken down and placed in one location to be properly recycled, and new workflows were instituted.

To act on the students' findings and decrease the library's rate of resource consumption, the University's Vice President for Mission Integration put the library on a short list to receive motion detecting lights installed in library bath-rooms and library staff members worked with the Office of Information Tech-nology to optimize public computer settings for increased energy savings. The Vice President also agreed to install a public filtered water fountain when the library staff volunteered to end their bottled water delivery service. This served a campus-wide goal to reduce the purchase of bottled water across campus.

As a result of the installation of a new print management system, library patrons made fewer unwanted printouts, and the library saw a reduction from 435,000 prints to 330,000 prints, a 25% reduction in paper use. Incrementally, over several years of purchase requests, McKillop Library was able to purchase enough bottle and paper recycling bins to strategically place four sets of bins and educational signage on each floor, resulting in large improvements in recycling rates. Each copier had a scrap paper tray placed next to it to encourage students to donate their unwanted prints for others to use.

Library staff members in the Department of Technical Services made a com-mitment to recycle all packing materials that passed through the office, as well as to recycle or donate all discards and unaccepted gift books. The Department of Technical Services also moved to a paperless ordering system, greatly reducing paper use by materials selectors and technical services staff. The cataloging spe-cialist made an agreement with the local public library to donate 500 DVD cases per year after the library moved to the Red Tag security system (which required Red Tag-compatible cases). This program continues, with the library donating all non-compatible DVD cases to the public library, significantly reducing their need to purchase replacements for damaged cases. Also, the archivist created a campus-wide recycling program for batteries and ink cartridges.

Impacts on Students' Learning Outcomes

The non-science majors in the BIO 140, "Humans and Their Environ-ment" course were the most successful section in achieving the learning goals, compared with the other twenty sections of the course between 2005 and 2010. The group had an equal proportion of honors students to the other sections and took the same content-based exams at three points through the semester; they performed as well or better than the other sections on the content exams (Figure 1A), exhibiting a high level of scientific and environmental literacy measured through the cumulative final exam (Figure 1B). The library project provided a successful learning opportunity for the students because (1) the problem was authentic, (2) library staff was supportive, encouraging, and responsive to the students, and (3) the library provided a real structure from which to base an environmental audit.

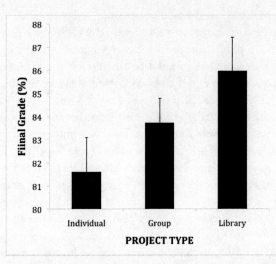

Figure 1A. Mean (se bars) of student scores on content-based exams in a non-majors environmental science course. Students in the course section that worked on the collaborative group library project (n = 23) and small group projects (n = 65) scored slightly higher than students working on individual projects (n = 68), Salve Regina University, 2007-2010.

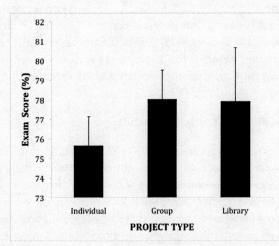

Figure 1B. Mean (se bars) of student final grades in general education science elective in environmental science. Students in the course section that worked on the collaborative group library project (n = 23) achieved slightly higher final course grade than sections of the course where students worked on small group projects (n = 65) or individual projects (n = 68), for their semester research project and paper, Salve Regina University, 2007-2010.

Grassroots Efforts

Building on local awareness of environmental issues, library staff members established a faculty/staff environmental group, GreenSalve. The group included faculty and staff from departments and offices across campus and created ties with administration and the student environmental group as it worked towards group goals. The group's mission is "[t]o move Salve Regina University towards environmental sustainability by altering our work processes, educating ourselves and students, or making changes in our lives to reduce our own environmental impact and to model sustainability."

GreenSalve mounted campaigns which have raised awareness about environmental issues and encouraged members of the Salve Regina community to green their work flow, commutes, and personal practices. GreenSalve members worked with the university president to institute the "Green Office" program, in which best practices for staff and faculty were printed on cards and hung outside offices whose occupants agreed to participate in the program. A "Green Miles" challenge encouraged faculty and staff to bike or walk to work instead of driving. A "Put Your Butts Here" program to eradicate cigarette litter was mounted one year, and the next, successfully taken over by the student environmental group. Each year, the group spearheads university and city participation in Earth Hour, a consciousness-raising exercise in which participants refrain from electricity use for one hour and instead join group activities around environmental education, and participates in the campus' Earth Day celebration. Building on ties developed during the library carbon audit, GreenSalve has also collaborated with the student environmental group and the administration's Environmental Advisory Board on consciousness raising events and actions to minimize the use of disposable water bottles on campus.

Broader Strategies for Advancing Environmental Sustainability

Since the early 1990s, awareness has been building of libraries' responsibility to be leaders in greening their missions and operations (Antonelli, 2008; Jankowska & Marcum, 2010). Library professional organizations in the United States and around the world have pushed to integrate environmental sustainability into the professional consciousness (Antonelli, 2008; Brodie, 2012; Jankowska & Marcum, 2010). Most authors writing about green libraries highlight green library buildings, greening staff workflows, or offering green programming. Fewer discuss collections and research instruction (Link, 2000). This gap is significant. Without leveraging their role as educators and providing high quality environmental content to build a community-wide awareness of the deeper issues surrounding environmental sustainability, librarians will find it difficult to convince funding agents to make large-scale changes. These changes, such as a commitment to green building and renovation, will result in financial savings over time but require an initial financial outlay. Libraries can help lay the groundwork for larger changes in the campus community not only by modeling green behavior, but by educating and building green collections and services. Supporting an environmental sustainability education program and acting on local issues can demonstrate staff and faculty commitment to environmental issues. This can move a library and its home institution onto a path that may result in more substantial institutional support for larger greening projects on campus.

The work presented here is an example of the library taking the initiative to actively engage with faculty and students to address university-wide concerns about sustainability, collect and analyze data from an environmental audit, and put the most salient recommendations into immediate action. In this case the university library has done far more than showcase sustainability, actively pursuing sustainability by modeling green behavior, altering workflows and public services, educating patrons in environmental science research, and collaborating to teach students research methods by providing information for an environmental audit. This has provided momentum for university action across campus.

Examples from universities nationwide show that grassroots efforts are most effective in concert with strong administrative support. Approaches that have proven effective for advancing an environmental sustainability agenda on other campuses include instituting an office of sustainability or a sustainability coordinator, creating a campus-wide sustainability plan, setting benchmarks, and creating a regular schedule for assessing progress. This demonstrates the three levels of environmental action: Personal, Policy, and Paradigm Shifts. Changing personal behavior is the most direct and immediate change, the easiest of the three to implement, but is by no means simple to carry out. Changing university policy is a top down approach to environmental change on campus, but far too often an administration signs a sustainability policy that fails to be implemented. Ultimately, a campus-wide Paradigm Shift is needed to achieve campus sustainability. In this scenario, sustainable options, choices, decisions and course themes are implemented as the status quo, instead of on a case-by-case basis when it can be justified on a short-term economic cost/benefit analysis.

Implementing Policy Change

Julian Keniry, Senior Director of the National Wildlife Federation's Campus Ecology Program, suggests (2003) that a successful campus-wide sustainability plan will fall directly in line with institutional mission and culture and be incorporated into strategic plans and budget statements. He also emphasizes the importance of creating a university action plan with timelines and benchmarks. An energy audit allows the institution to establish baseline levels of energy and resource consumption, which can be compared against later audits. These baselines provide the university with the opportunity to create clear goals and objectives with individualized timelines and benchmarks (Keniry, 2003). SRU completed an audit of the library, as reported here, meeting the learning goals for science and general education requirements while providing valuable benchmark information to the library and university. Later courses completed audits of other campus buildings and will soon return to the library to measure change since the 2009 audit.

SRU has a set of goals that address its commitment to environmental sustainability, but the university's published goals do not provide the types of hard benchmarks and timelines that Keniry (2003) suggests (see Appendix). The goals laid out in the university's sustainability policy help provide groups and individuals with a rationale for seeking to make changes that improve workflow or personal practices, changes that may inconvenience some but reduce resource consumption. They also provide groups and individuals with guidance and direction in developing new initiatives to educate students, faculty, and staff about environmental issues, and have supported many of the positive changes that the campus has seen in resource consumption and education.

Salve Regina's McKillop Library has taken the first steps in the university to set benchmarks for sustainability with measurable goals. While the sustainability page set goals in 2010, they have not been updated since (McKillop Library, 2013). When the BIO 240 class returns to the library to perform another assessment, the library will be on its way to being able to measure new data against the benchmarks, set timetables for goals and continue to work towards those time-specific goals. In the absence of a data collection system tailored to the needs of the specific institution and library and allotted staff or student resources to collect it, this is likely to be a problem in libraries and universities attempting to make meaningful policies to effect change in resource consumption and track the effectiveness of these policies.

Institutional structures supporting sustainability

As McKillop Library's experience shows, while grassroots work is an important part of any major campus initiative, a sustainability plan issued from campus leadership with clear goals, defined measurement mechanisms, and a timeline would help drive even more meaningful change. To be truly successful, institutions should enact their environmental management plans using a clear and permanent administrative structure to create policy, set objectives, monitor compliance, provide training and other awareness-building campaigns, coordinate communication, and maintain documentation (Eagan, Calhoun, Schott & Dayananda, 2008; Keniry, 2003)

The form the administrative structure should take depends on each school's organization, culture, and politics. Usually, the institution forms a permanent sustainability-focused committee or taskforce composed of student, faculty, and staff representatives (Eagan et al., 2008). The group can include representatives of major departmental stakeholders, such as student affairs, the university library, information technologies, dining services, student government, or other constituencies likely to be affected by the formation of new policies. This is to encourage collaboration and investment in the project by all parties (Eagan et al., 2008). At Salve Regina University, an Environmental Advisory Group meets regularly and is made up of administrative, staff, and faculty representatives. The group includes the university's strongest administrative proponent of environmental sustainability, the Vice President of Mission Integration. The advisory group has mounted certain successful initiatives. It has reduced the use of disposable water bottles on campus with alternatives such as free or reduced-price reusable bottles and filtered water stations in buildings across campus, and installed reduced-flow shower heads and toilets. It has also mandated the installation of motion detecting lights in select buildings across campus. In addition, the group has successfully advocated for the use of hybrid security vehicles when the older non-hybrids are retired, increased the number of recycling bins across campus, and supported initiatives that promote public transportation, bicycle use, and walking.

Libraries can play a pivotal role in promoting and achieving sustainability in several ways. Library staff may serve on the main sustainability steering committee or working group, or if seats are not available, support the committee's work by providing a strong, encapsulated operational model for environmental efficiency within the library building. At Salve Regina University, this is how the library has advanced the mission of environmental sustainability on campus.

Conclusion

Libraries as educational service organizations can shift their service model to create a balance for patrons between convenience and environmental sensitivity while educating the campus community about how lifestyle decisions affect the ecological balance of the planet. Campus sustainability practices and policies can, and logically should, start at the academic heart of the campus: the library.

Academic libraries can derive benefits from being active participants in a campus sustainability plan. The ability to forge or strengthen collaborative relationships with students, faculty and staff on campus, to improve the collection through targeted purchase of ecologically- and sustainability- focused materials across the disciplines, and to improve the visibility of library services are among the advantages to involvement. Libraries also have a responsibility to contribute, stemming from their contributions to a society that is on track for an unsustainable future. The potential for change is dramatic, however, and academic libraries can poise themselves to help catalyze this change by teaching, modeling, and offering a rich selection of challenging research materials to those who will take us through the next millennium.

References

American Association for the Advancement of Science. (2009). *Vision and change: a call to action. AAAS Vision and Change in Undergraduate Biology Education Initiative*. Retrieved from http://visionandchange.org/

Antonelli, M. (2008). The green library movement: An overview and beyond. *The Electronic Green Journal, 27*(1), 1-11.

Association of College and Research Libraries. (2013). *Information literacy competency standards for higher education*. Retrieved from http://www.ala.org/acrl/standards/informationliteracycompetency

Bordeau V.D. & Arnold, M.E. (2009). *The science process skills inventory. 4-H Youth Development Education*. Corvallis, OR: Oregon State University.

Brodie, M. (2012). Building the sustainable library at Macquarie University. *Australian Academic and Research Libraries, 43*(1) 4-16.

Eagan D., Calhoun T., Schoot, J., & Dayananda, P. (2008). *Guide to climate action planning*. Pathways to a Low Carbon Campus. Reston, VA: National Wildlife Federation.

Eccleston, C. H. (2011). *Environmental impact assessment: A guide to best professional practices*. Boca Raton, FL: CRC press.

Glasson, J., Therivel, R. & Chadwick, A. (2005). *Introduction to environmental impact assessment*, 3rd edition. New York: Routledge.

Jankowska, M. A., & Marcum, J. W. (2010). Sustainability challenge for academic libraries: Planning for the future. *College & Research Libraries, 71*(2), 160-170.

Keniry. (2003). Environmental management systems: A framework for planning green campuses. *Planning for Higher Education,* 31(3), 62-9.

Link, T. (2000). Transforming higher education through sustainability and environmental education. *Issues in Science and Technology Librarianship,* (Spring). Retrieved from: http://www.istl.org/00-spring/article4.html

McKillop Library. (2013). *Sustainability at McKillop Library.* Retrieved from http://salve.libguides.com/SustainabiltyMcKillopLibrary

Project 2061 (American Association for the Advancement of Science). (1989). Science for all Americans: A Project 2061 report on literacy goals in science, mathematics, and technology. Washington, D.C: American Association for the Advancement of Science.

Project 2061 (American Association for the Advancement of Science). (1993). Benchmarks for science literacy. New York: Oxford University Press.

Salve Regina University. (2013). *About sustainability at Salve.* Retrieved from http://www.salve.edu/about/green/about.aspx

Salve Regina University. (2013). *Salve Regina's mission.* Retrieved from http://www.salve.edu/about/catholicTradition/salveReginaMission.aspx

Appendix

Salve Regina University Sustainability Policy:

Create an environmentally literate and responsible community

- Integrate social and environmental responsibility into curricular development
- Foster student and faculty research of environmentally sustainable development
- Create and promote an informed network of people committed to the principles of environmental sustainability on campus

Practice Environmental Stewardship

- Promote water conservation, waste reduction, material reuse and recycling
- Encourage awareness of food consumption and strive towards promoting the ecological, sustainable and socially just production of food
- Engage in energy conservation by promoting the use of renewable energy resources, purchasing Energy Star appliances and practicing energy conservation behaviors
- Practice environmental stewardship of University property
- Promote sustainable modes of campus transportation
- Promote environmentally responsible building standards

(Salve Regina University, "About Sustainability at Salve" http://www.salve. edu/about/green)

Section Two

Building Collections Supporting Sustainability Curriculum

Building an Academic Library Collection to Support Sustainability

Amy Brunvand, Alison Regan, Joshua Lenart, Jessica Breiman, and Emily Bullough

Abstract

In their chapter, the authors make a case for collection development as it relates to sustainability. They identify two methods that a librarian should consider: 1) a "big ideas" collection to identify large-scale topics of sustainability and 2) smaller collections to cover areas of sustainability as they relate to specific topics. They cover formats and also provide an example of a case study performed.

Introduction

The study of sustainability encompasses many classic examples of what social scientists call "wicked problems," which is to say large, highly complex problems like climate change, food systems, or fossil fuel dependency, concerning multifaceted social planning and policy issues. Wicked problems are extremely difficult to solve because of interdependencies between a wide range of political, economic, and cultural constraints. Library collection development to support academic sustainability programs hints at a wicked problem, because it is a complex endeavor that requires interdisciplinary cooperation, tailoring of collections to local issues, and enough tact and diplomacy to avoid the pitfalls of academic turf wars.

Sustainability is still an emerging field, and a canon for sustainability studies and sustainability science is not yet well defined. Although a number of bibliometric articles have laid the groundwork to identify core subject areas and journals that define and support sustainability research, the conclusions of those studies are not in complete agreement.

Sustainability is an interdisciplinary and transdisciplinary area of study; one difficulty for librarians is that collection development requires working across organizational and bureaucratic boundaries that are often strongly institutionalized within various university departments as well as within library organization and funding structures. Librarians must work to identify texts and artifacts that constitute two strongly related but not identical aspects of the collection:

1) a "big ideas" collection that reflects the values and philosophy of sustainability and offers patrons a chance to reorient their thinking about what sustainability means in light of 21st century environmental constraints; and

2) a subject-based, interdisciplinary collection that relates existing academic disciplines to key themes and recent developments of the sustainability canon.

Librarians must understand that sustainability is not confined to any one particular curriculum or classroom; further, sustainability is a practical application of ideas such as green campus efforts that turn the university into a laboratory for practical sustainability. The academic library collection should support academic inquiry as well as enacted practices that include government policymaking, citizen activism, and a focus on the local culture and bioregion.

The Role of the Library Collection

University research libraries act as the primary storehouses for texts and artifacts on campus while also serving as a meeting place for faculty, students, and community members. University libraries host symposiums, working groups and conferences, and act as public spaces to engage in new conversations about our collective roles on this planet. Patrons may also use the library as a place to meet and exchange ideas about what it means to create a more sustainable future. Since academic programs—and funding—are often strongly divided between STEM research areas (science, technology, engineering, and mathematics) versus humanities and social sciences, the university library acts as perhaps the only interdisciplinary building on campus and contains research knowledge relevant to every field.

The library has the potential to lead innovation on campus, attracting, as it does, a cross-section of students, faculty, staff, and community users. Yet collection development remains mired in habitual, long-established processes for acquisitions. For example, Wilson and Edelman (1996) note that, "although the largest university component that promotes interdisciplinary research is the research university library, nowhere is the traditional discipline-based university structure more clearly evidenced than in collection development where the selection responsibilities of academic librarians are largely oriented toward academic departments" (p. 195). Since journal and database subscriptions are often paid annually and require higher-level administrative approval than monographs, supporting a new discipline with new subscriptions adds an additional layer of complexity and difficulty for librarians responsible for collection development.

The consequence of the way funds are distributed within the library (and the fact that the current economic crisis that has, in many cases, severely reduced funding) is that selectors may be protective of their limited budgets and resist purchasing items not squarely within the academic department for which they are responsible. Wilson and Edelman (1996) summarize the impacts and difficulties of interdisciplinary library collection development, writing that conventional collection development policy, "invites the undue perpetuation of collection gaps, particularly in nondisciplinary and inter-disciplinary areas" (p. 196). Their conclusion still holds true today: "Materials budget allocations based on existing departmental structures will not adequately address collection development issues, particularly in interdisciplinary fields" (p. 199). The library has a responsibility to support the curriculum and research needs of the entire university community; it is essential that libraries find a way to foster collection development for sustainability that reflects the interdisciplinary nature of the campus.

For librarians, it is important to take into account local needs and particular institutional areas of focus. Consider that the three universities in the Utah Academic Library Consortium with Carnegie Classifications of "very high" or "high" research activity each have different areas of focus regarding sustainability. In Utah, degree programs in natural resources and agricultural sciences are mainly taught at Utah State University (USU), the state's only land grant institution. Consequently, USU has a sustainability focus on agriculture, forestry, and fisheries, while the University of Utah offers programs that emphasize city planning, sustainable tourism, environmental humanities, and environmental law. At the University of Nevada, Las Vegas, the College of Hospitality Management's focus on Urban Sustainability necessarily drives the sustainability curriculum, and in turn, the sustainability collection.

The Role of Librarians

Librarians serve in various roles: departmental liaisons, subject specialists, reference consultants, sustainability instructors, and as green team members. As members of the university faculty, they may also guide campus policy. At the Marriott Library, collection development funds for monograph purchases are divided primarily between four teams—Science, Health, Engineering, and Mines (SHEM); Social Sciences, Education, Social Work, and Business (SEBS); Fine Arts, Architecture and Planning, and Humanities (FAAPH); and an International team rather than the more common system of distributing funds between individual departments and colleges. Members of these teams are subject specialists who are responsible for staying abreast with developments in their corresponding university departments, providing outreach and instructional support for these areas, and selecting new materials.

Since the university's interdisciplinary Environmental and Sustainability Studies major is housed in the College of Social and Behavioral Sciences, the librarian liaison for sustainability is a member of the SEBS team. Books selected by this liaison are charged to the SEBS budget; despite that many of the books in this field are closely tied to science or humanities. Liaisons from other teams are welcome to choose books related to sustainability as they see fit; teamwork is essential to ensure that gaps do not occur in the collection as cautioned by Wilson and Edelman (1996).

Each school's unique structure will affect decisions regarding librarian liaison assignment and fund distribution. What background should a sustainability librarian have? Burke (2011) makes a case for her sustainability assignment based on her background in anthropology; at the Marriott Library, the sustainability librarian has a professional background in government documents and a long history of environmental activism and journalism focused on Utah and Western issues. As for the interdisciplinary nature of sustainability, many subject specialties are appropriate, but a personal interest may be an even greater prerequisite for acting in this capacity.

Marriott Library Project

In the spring of 2012, the University of Utah J. Willard Marriott Library received funding from the Chevron Corporation to participate in the university's ongoing exploration of sustainability by conducting a curriculum audit to define the role of the library in providing research materials and information literacy support. This funding was used to form the Marriott Library Sustainability Working Group (MLSWG), which consisted of two librarians, two library employees enrolled in MLS programs, and a PhD candidate in the Department of English. The team produced the "University of Utah J. Willard Marriott Library Sustainability Collection Development Policy Report" (Brunvand, Breiman, Bullough, Lenart, & Regan, 2012), which led to the library making significant investments in new holdings.

The MLSWG began with a literature search in hopes of finding existing models for sustainability collection development. Many articles discuss green library facilities and operations, but only a few specifically address librarianship in support of academic sustainability curricula. A special issue of *Against the Grain* (December 2010/January 2011) focuses on environmental sustainability; one article by Burke (2011) discusses specific issues for academic librarians, including the challenge of interdisciplinary collection development, the obligation of libraries to support both curricula and green campus efforts, and the variety of approaches to sustainability in different disciplines. Charney (2011) surveyed 112 academic librarians in the United States instrumental in shaping sustainability on their campuses and describes sustainability librarianship in terms of research guide topics and campus connections as well as "touchy subjects" including academic "fiefdoms," territorialism between faculty members, and ambiguity concerning governance over librarian liaison areas. Charney, Smith, and Williams (2012) revisited this work with a four part webinar series on "Libraries for Sustainability" which resulted in a "Take Action" checklist for sustainability librarians.

In January 2013, the American Library Association approved a petition to start a new Sustainability Round Table with a mission to provide, "a professional forum for librarians to exchange ideas and concerns regarding sustainability in order to move toward a more equitable, healthy and economically viable society; and resources for the library community to support sustainability through curriculum development; collections; exhibits; events; advocacy, communication and library buildings and space design" (American Library Association Committee on Organization, 2013). As a consequence, the scholarship on sustainability librarianship is poised to expand in the near future.

Outside the field of librarianship the authors found that the emergence of interdisciplinary, interdepartmental environmental studies/science curriculums in the 1980s foreshadows the development of interdisciplinary sustainability curricula in the present time. Two particularly useful articles to contextualize the debate are Soulé and Press (1998), who criticize environmental studies programs as unfocused, and a response by Maniates and Whissel (2000) that identifies six valid programmatic responses as well as common failures of such programs. Currently, vigorous scholarly conversations are taking place regarding the emerging disciplines of sustainability studies and sustainability science, addressing such questions as: How to define the intellectual boundaries of sustainability as a discipline? How to maintain scientific objectivity versus an impulse toward public activism? How to structure interdisciplinary campus programs without losing academic focus? How to conceptualize an academic subject that is at least partly based on ethical values?

After conducting the literature review, the MLSWG began listing degree programs and campus organizations relating to sustainability. The University of Utah offers an interdepartmental undergraduate degree in Environmental and Sustainability Studies. The authors identified at least 10 other existing degree programs relevant to sustainability from nine different colleges as well as several programs under development. In Fall Semester 2012, the university began offering an undergraduate Integrated Certificate in Sustainability that includes courses across the curriculum. No single department manages the certificate program; instead, it is administered by the Office of Undergraduate Studies.

Besides degree programs, the university has an Office of Sustainability housed in Facilities Management to focus on greening the campus. In addition, the authors listed other campus involvement in sustainability such as research institutes, faculty and student groups, organizational memberships such as the Association for Advancement of Sustainability in Higher Education (AASHE), museums, community engagement opportunities, and special projects such as campus gardens and Green Teams (see Karren Nichols' chapter in section four).

The next step was to define how the library fits in with other sustainability offices and programs and how the collections support these efforts. Again, the authors found little guidance for sustainability collection development. Applin (2009) published a selected bibliography for building a sustainability collection; Visser (2009) issued *The top 50 sustainability books* skewed toward green business. The authors also found bibliographic essays on sustainability from a wide range of disciplines, and one member of the team developed a case study for ecopsychology to investigate how an interdisciplinary, subject-based sustainability collection might differ from a transdisciplinary collection reflecting the core precepts of sustainability. The authors conclude that there is still much work to be done to define a core of databases, reference sources, monographs, and journals.

Historical Sources and the Core Collection

The study of sustainability derives from an academic lineage that grew out of ecology, firmly rooted in the biological sciences. The pioneering ecologist Eugene Odum (1997) described ecology as the first truly interdisciplinary subject, and he subtitled the third revision of his influential textbook *Ecology: A bridge between science and society*. Hagen (2005) documents the pervasive influence of subsequent editions of Odum's ecology textbook and the debate over the intellectual boundaries of ecology as professional ecologists sought to define their role with regard to the emerging environmental activist movement. As ecological studies expanded its boundaries beyond just the hard sciences to include social sciences and humanities, colleges and universities began to develop interdisciplinary programs in environmental studies/science. Currently, sustainability studies/science seems to be undergoing a similar process of expansion to separate itself from environmental studies/science programs.

In an article about the evolution and structure of sustainability science, Bettencourt and Kaur (2011) plot the growing number of sustainability-related journal articles against a timeline of four key sustainability publications: "World Conservation Strategy" (International Union for Conservation of Nature and Natural Resources, 1980); "Our Common Future" (World Commission on Environment and Development, 1987), commonly referred to as the Brundtland Report; "Agenda 21" (United Nations Conference on Environment and Development , 1992); and "Our Common Journey" (National Research Council Board on Sustainable Development, 1999). The Brundtland Report in particular is typically considered the catalyst of the sustainability movement (Schubert & Lang, 2005). The report defined the current usage of the word sustainability; shifted usage of the word from a primary focus on agriculture/fisheries/forestry to include technology/industry/urbanization; influenced global, national, regional, and local environmental policies; and sowed the seeds for a new academic discipline. More recently, a new science-based discipline called "sustainability science" has split off from "sustainability studies," which is oriented toward social sciences and policy (Komiyama & Takeuchi, 2007). An editorial introducing a new sustainability section in *Proceedings of the National Academy of Sciences* (Clark, 2007) bemoans the "extreme dispersion" of interdisciplinary journals articles in a range of fields as, "limiting the opportunities for cross-fertilization and thus inhibiting development of the field" (p. 1738). A review committee found: "The most popular single journals carrying sustainability science articles capture no more than 5% of all of the important papers published and even then tend to focus on a single discipline or pair of disciplines (e.g., ecological economics) or a single issue area (e.g., agriculture or energy)" (p. 1738). This argues for the need to develop a core of high-impact journals in the field of sustainability.

An implication for library collections is that up until the publication of the Brundtland Report, sustainability was essentially an interdisciplinary research area grounded in existing disciplines such as ecology, environmental studies, economics, or international development; collecting in individual subject areas was generally sufficient to support early efforts at defining sustainability. After 1987, however, sustainability emerged as a nascent area of inquiry building upon its own research with its own set of classics, standard works, and core journals. As the number of sustainability-related articles increased throughout the 1990s, a variety of new journals were launched to meet academic and social demand and to help pull together dispersed research. As a consequence, existing library collections and collecting strategies are likely to leave collection gaps unless academic librarians deliberately focus efforts on sustainability collections. The authors discuss below specific considerations for sustainability collections in academic libraries.

Academic Journals

Librarians should be aware that there is an emerging new core of academic journals with a focus on sustainability and that many use open access publishing models. These new sustainability journals have not yet established high impact factors and are often not included with full-text databases or bundled subscriptions. As sustainability programs have gained a higher academic profile, researchers have tried to define the core disciplines and journals of sustainability. For example, Sherren (2007) surveyed attendees at two international sustainability events in order to describe a 10-subject core curriculum for undergraduates. Other studies used bibliometric analysis to identify the main academic fields that study sustainability issues and the core journals that publish sustainability articles. Schubert and Lang (2005) examined a set of articles that cite "Our Common Future"; Kajikawa, Ohno, Takeda, Matsushima, and Komiyama (2007) selected papers with a keyword search and then narrowed their corpus to just those papers that cited others within the set; Bettencourt and Kaur (2011) used the query "sustainability" and "sustainable development" in title, abstract, and keywords. Buter and Van Raan (2012) selected a seed set of journals with sustainability in the title, and also considered a set of articles that contain a word starting with "sustainab*" in the title. Quental and Lourenco (2012) identify the main references, authors, and journals for sustainable development. Each of these strategies produced slightly different results and identified a slightly different set of core academic disciplines.

Since regional magazines and alternative press publications are often not included in large bundled databases such as *Academic Search Premier*, it is difficult to search the full range of sustainability issues in a single research database. Subject specific databases are a useful resource for exploring disciplinary research; however, in utilizing these databases, researchers must consider a variety of pertinent questions, such as: Does the database include new sustainability journals and emerging forms of sustainability research? Do libraries need to expand their access to sustainability-focused databases instead of relying on sustainability continent within other databases? How can libraries promote regional materials and gray literature not present in commercial databases?

While there are a number of commercially produced article databases related to environmental studies/science, there is not yet a definitive database that pulls together a core of sustainability resources. Current available databases include the EBSCOhost products such as *GreenFILE*, *Environment Complete*, *Environment Index*, and *Left Index*, as well as Thomson Reuters' *Web of Science*. Exploratory research in sustainability related topics may be conducted in standard reference databases such as *CQ Researcher* and *Credo Reference*, as well as the interdisciplinary database *Academic Search Premier*. Another particularly valuable reference source is the annual "State of the World" report published by the Worldwatch Institute with the accompanying "Vital Signs" dataset.

Monographs

To evaluate the library's sustainability collection of monographs, the Marriott Library Sustainability Working Group needed to identify a core-reading list on sustainability. This task was not simple. No single Library of Congress classification contains the holistic field of sustainability. Although *Resources for College Libraries* offers core lists for ecology and environmental studies, it lacks a discrete subject heading for sustainability. While certain authors such as Wendell Berry, Edward Abbey, or Rachel Carson fall under the rubric of environmental studies, works by such authors do not necessarily address issues of sustainability. It is not hard to find bibliographic essays about sustainability in various academic disciplines, but only Applin (2009) and Visser (2009) make any attempt to define core sources of sustainability as its own area of study.

As part of an evaluation of Marriott Library collections, the MLSWG compiled a list of core monographs based on various bibliographies and bibliographic essays assembled during the course of the project. The committee added books that appeared on syllabi for courses approved to support the Integrated Certificate in Sustainability, as well as books specifically influential within our own political boundaries and bioregion. All of the core books the library lacked were purchased and added to the collection.

The MLSWG drafted a list with an explicit focus on the "big ideas" of sustainability based on Edwards (2005) summation: citizen engagement, concern for the environment, food systems, futures thinking, green economy, human dependence on natural systems, limits of the Earth's ecosystems, re-localization, and sustainability literacy. The keyword "sustainab*" is not definitive for monographs since only 8 percent of items on the list as of March 2013 contained any variation of that keyword. The University of Utah core list is a work in progress, but it is a starting point for a conversation between librarians and faculty. The list can assist faculty in integrating sustainability concepts into their courses and reading lists. Faculty, in turn, can offer suggestions that will add to the ongoing project of updating the list. It was also used as the basis of an Earth Day display to promote these new materials.

United Nations and Government Information

Many of the founding documents of sustainability came from United Nations and quasi-government sources and that government policy is a key aspect of sustainability. Depository collections representing all levels of government offer significant support to sustainability curricula. Sustainability librarians should be able to offer expertise in government information, including United Nations, international, federal, state, and local government publications and know how to follow the paper trail of environmental legislation and regulation. Many of these collections are available online and are therefore accessible to libraries without depository status. In depository libraries, government document specialists should develop an understanding of sustainability resources; at non-depository libraries, the sustainability librarian may be the logical person to take responsibility for knowing how to use and access this type of information.

Localization and Citizen Activism

A related consideration is public involvement and citizen activism. Any topic that has a strong policy component generates a response from lobbyists and citizen activism. In fact, part of the impetus to distinguish sustainability science as a discipline stems from the desire to distance the scientific and technical underpinnings of sustainable development from political agendas (Komiyama & Takeuchi, 2006). An essay launching the new journal *Sustainability Science* emphasized there is no one-size-fits-all solution to the problem of sustainability: "Any attempt to impose uniform solutions of global environmental problems will threaten the diversity of the earth's regions and cultures in the same way that economic globalization does now. Destroying this diversity will, in turn, prevent the realization of a society that is truly sustainable in the sense that it embraces human fulfillment, not merely survival" (Komiyama & Takeuch, 2006, p. 5). This pattern of localization translates into a distinctive publication pattern, since sustainability publications are regionally diverse and include many contributors from developing nations (Bettencourt & Kaur, 2001). As sustainability has such a strong regional component, relevant collections often include the types of materials within the domain of special collections that tend to be underrepresented in library collections. Keough and Schindler (2003-2004) outline a strategy to preserve the political history of the grassroots environmental movement. A similar strategy could be employed to document localized sustainability movements.

The diversity of sustainability publications also stems from a core value of sustainability sometimes called "localization," "relocalization," or "transition," which refer to grassroots efforts to build resilient communities based on local food and energy production (Quilley, 2009). Community engagement is also an important factor in academic programs. The STARS program of the Association for the Advancement of Sustainability in Higher Education (AASHE, 2012) ranks campus sustainability efforts and awards points for programs that encourage students to participate in community service and internships. Because of this, it is especially important for sustainability librarians to develop regional collections that reflect local concerns and efforts. Another implication is that not all important sustainability literature is in academic journals. Some key sustainability ideas come from popular/activist magazines such as *Orion*, *Yes!* or *Adbusters* (the Canadian magazine that triggered the Occupy Wall Street movement), as well as regional publications that are not bundled in any research databases. To collect the regional diversity of sustainability efforts, each academic library takes on a particular responsibility to reflect what sustainability means in the context of local conditions and local knowledge.

Conclusion

The effort detailed here provides useful background information for collecting institutions. All subject selectors should consider the interdisciplinary aspects of sustainability as related to their departmental area of responsibility. The transdisciplinary nature of sustainability studies/science requires an explicit effort to focus on sustainability across the curriculum. In order to bridge organization boundaries, librarians should work cooperatively with faculty, students, and library staff in both scholarly resources and collections library units to meet the needs of programs that do not fit within traditional departmental relationships or organizational purchasing plans.

The authors recommend a team approach to form a collection that supports sustainability-related sites across the entire campus community, including academics, facility management, community engagement, and student activism.

The authors also suggest conducting a scan of the university and community environment to help librarians tailor their core collection to reflect the unique aspects of their own bioregion and culture as well as their local needs and specific areas of emphasis within the university. It is also helpful to monitor what other universities are doing in this subject area in order to stay abreast of developments. Particular attention should be paid to areas of gray literature, such as government documents and publications generated by community activists. This is an emerging discipline for which the boundaries are not yet well defined. Librarians have an important role to play in identifying core sources, in particular new journals that have not yet established a reputation. Librarians could advise faculty and student researchers on how to conduct literature searches that cross-disciplinary boundaries or to incorporate the "big ideas" of sustainability into their projects. The authors hope the results of this work will prove useful to other libraries as they consider how they might best support sustainability across the curriculum and around colleges and universities.

References

American Library Association Committee on Organization, Report to Council Midwinter Meeting 2013—Seattle, Washington. (2013). 2012-2013 ALA CD#27.

Applin, M. B. (2009). Building a sustainability collection: A selected bibliography. *Reference Services Review, 37*(3), 313-325. doi:10.1108/00907320910982802

Association for the Advancement of Sustainability in Higher Education. (2012, February). *STARS: A program of AASHE: Version 1.2 technical manual.* Retrieved from http://www.aashe.org/files/documents/STARS/stars_1.2_technical_manual.pdf

Betterncourt, L. M. A., & Kauer, J. (2011). Evolution and structure of sustainability science. *PNAS, 108*(49), 19540-19545. doi:10.1073/pnas.1102712108

Brunvand, A., Breiman, J., Bullough, E., Lenart, J., & Regan, A. (2012). *University of Utah J. Willard Marriott Library sustainability collection development policy report.* Retrieved from http://content.lib.utah.edu/cdm/ref/collection/ir-eua/id/2620

Burke, M. (2011). Collection development and sustainability at the University of Florida. *Against the Grain, 22*(6), 18-20. Retrieved from http://www.against-the-grain.com/

Buter, R. K., & Van Raan, A. F. J. (2012). Identification and analysis of the highly cited knowledge base of sustainability science. *Sustainability Science, 8*(2), 253-267. doi:10.1007/s11625-012-0185-1

Charney, M. K. (2011, October). *Getting closer: The librarian, the curriculum and the Office of Sustainability.* Paper presented at the meeting of the Association for the Advancement of Sustainability in Higher Education, Pittsburgh, PA. Retrieved from http://www.aashe.org/resources/conference/getting-closer-librarian-curriculum-and-office-sustainability-0

Charney, M. K., Smith, B., & Williams, B. F. (2012). Libraries for sustainability [webinar series]. *pt.1 A call to action; pt. 2 Exploring sustainability practices in libraries; pt.3 Engagement in professional library organizations; pt.4 Exploring sustainability practices in libraries.*

Clark, W. C. (2007). Sustainability science: A room of its own [Editorial]. *Proceedings of the National Academy of Sciences, 104*(6), 1737-1738. doi:10.1073/pnas.0611291104

Edwards, A. R. (2005). *The sustainability revolution: Portrait of a paradigm shift.* Gabriola Island, BC: New Society Publishers.

Hagen, J. B. (2008). Teaching ecology during the environmental age, 1965-1980. *Environmental History, 13*(4), 704-723. Retrieved from http://environmentalhistory.net/

International Union for Conservation of Nature and Natural Resources. (1980). *World conservation strategy: Living resource conservation for sustainable development.* Retrieved from http://data.iucn.org/dbtw-wpd/edocs/WCS-004.pdf

Kajikawa, Y., Ohno, J., Takeda, Y., Matsushima, K., & Komiyama, H. (2007). Creating an academic landscape of sustainability science: An analysis of the citation network. *Sustainability Science, 2*(2), 221-231. doi:10.1007/s11625-007-0027-8

Keough, B., & Schindler, A. C. (2003-2004). Thinking globally, acting locally: Documenting environmental activism in New York State. *Archival Issues, 28*(2), 121-135. Retrieved from http://minds.wisconsin.edu/handle/1793/43546

Komiyama, H., & Takeuchi, K. (2006). Sustainability science: Building a new discipline. *Sustainability Science, 1*(1), 1-6. doi:10.1007/s11625-006-0007-4

Maniates, M. F., & Whissel, J. C. (2000). Environmental studies: The sky is not falling. *BioScience, 50*(6), 509-517 doi:10.1641/0006-3568(2000)050[0509:ESTSIN]2.0.CO;2

National Research Council Board on Sustainable Development. (1999). *Our common journey: A transition toward sustainability.* Washington, D.C.: National Academies Press.

Odum, E. P. (1997). *Ecology: A bridge between science and society.* Sunderland, MA: Siunauer Associates.

Quental, N., & Lourenco, J.M. (2012). References, authors, journals, and scientific disciplines underlying the sustainable development literature: a citation analysis. *Scientometrics. 90*, 361-381. doi:10:1007/s11192-011-0533-4

Quilley, Stephen. (2009). Transition Skills. In A. Stibbe & P. Villiers-Stuart (Eds.), Handbook of sustainability literacy: multimedia version. Brighton: University of Brighton. Retrieved from http://www.sustainability-literacy.org/.

Schubert, A., & Lang, I. (2005). The literature aftermath of the Brundtland Report "Our Common Future." A scientometric study based on citations in science and social science journals. *Environment, Development and Sustainability, 7*(1), 1-8. doi:10.1007/s10668-003-0177-5

Sherren, K. (2007). Is there a sustainability canon? An exploration and aggregation of expert opinions. *The Environmentalist, 27*(3), 341-347. doi:10.1007/s10669-007-9046-3

Soulé, M. E., & Press, D. (1998). What is environmental studies? *Bioscience, 48*(5), 397-405. doi:10.2307/1313379

United Nations Conference on Environment and Development. (1993). Agenda 21: *Programme of action for sustainable development; Rio Declaration on Environment and Development ; Statement of Forest Principles: The final text of agreements negotiated by governments at the United Nations Conference on Environment and Development (UNCED), 3-14 June 1992, Rio de Janeiro, Brazil.* New York, NY: United Nations Dept. of Public Information.

World Commission on Environment and Development. (1987). *Our common future.* Oxford: Oxford University Press.

Visser, W., & University of Cambridge. (2009). *The top 50 sustainability books.* Sheffield, U.K.: Greenleaf Publishing.

Wilson, M. C., & Edelman, H. (1996). Collection development in an interdisciplinary context. *Journal of Academic Librarianship, 22*(3), 195-200. doi:10.1016/S0099-1333(96)90058-0

Interdisciplinary Collaboration for Collection Development in Sustainability: Starting from Scratch

Kasia Leousis and Greg Schmidt

Abstract

While information resources relating to sustainability have long had a place in academic libraries, their collection has usually occurred through the efforts of individual subject specialists, each working toward the goal of building their discipline-specific collections rather than a cohesive and comprehensive sustainability collection. The development of specific sustainability programs at the university level presents academic libraries with the opportunity of changing the way these interdisciplinary collections are developed and managed. Auburn University Libraries' designation of a subject specialist for sustainability has opened the door for collaboration among librarians across multiple disciplines. Readers of this chapter will gain insight into how Auburn University Libraries created a subject specialist for sustainability studies, how the first year's budget was used to engage university scholars in helping to create a core sustainability collection, and how in subsequent years librarians across disciplines worked together to meet the needs of sustainability-related scholarship.

Introduction

Auburn University (AU) is a public institution located in Alabama with an enrollment of over 25,000 students. Designated a land-grant institution in

1872, Auburn has a long history of agricultural and engineering scholarship, including areas such as crop rotation and low-impact tillage that would now fall under the modern definition of sustainability. Auburn has also been active in research, teaching, and outreach in sustainable fisheries management, wildlife management, and energy efficient buildings and materials. Auburn's Office of Sustainability was founded in 2004 and in 2008 was organized into two divisions: Campus Sustainability Operations and Academic Sustainability Programs. The former division concerns itself with the institution's conduct as a sustainable organization, and contributes to decisions on construction, landscaping, energy and resource conservation, waste reduction, purchasing and other similar activities. The latter office focuses on training students in the concepts and application of sustainability, expanding incorporation of sustainability into the curriculum through faculty training workshops and fostering interdisciplinary sustainability research (Auburn University Office of Sustainability, 2013).

Auburn began offering a minor in Sustainability Studies in fall of 2008. The minor in sustainability exposes students to topics such as natural capitalism, the interdependence of economics environment and social equity, systems thinking, climate change and the future of energy, and biomimicry in human engineered systems. With the creation of the minor and the steady growth of the program, the libraries in 2010 assigned a librarian as liaison to the program and created a modest line in the materials budget for discretionary purchases related to sustainability. The newly appointed liaison to the sustainability program was quickly faced with the issue of both developing a core collection for undergraduate scholarship and supporting sustainability research across multiple disciplines.

Sustainability and Interdisciplinary Collection Development: A Literature Review

In 1987, sustainability emerged as a discipline separate from environmental studies when the World Commission on Environment and Development produced the Brundtland Report defining sustainable development (Riley, Grommes, & Thatcher, 2007, p. 184). In the United States, the President's Council on Sustainable Development, formed under President Bill Clinton in 1993, led to the development of collegiate and university curricula dedicated to promoting sustainability concepts in the classroom (Riley et al., 2007, p. 184). University libraries, by this time, had already begun to confront the challenge of interdisciplinary collection development in area, ethnic, and gender studies.

Collection development strategies for interdisciplinary or area studies programs is a recurring theme in library literature. Examining the interdisciplinary nature of research practices in the English Department at Oberlin College,

Carpenter (1990) concludes that the trend towards interdisciplinary research in the academy owes itself to three major factors: post-World War II growth of academic research; the emergence in the 1960s and 1970s of social movements focused on marginalized groups and the anti-authority (political and cultural) response to the Vietnam War; and the impact of advances in computer technology on academic research (p. 77). Interdisciplinary collecting ultimately requires monitoring current publishing in multiple subjects while separate funds divided by department or program inhibits the broad development of interdisciplinary areas (Carpenter, 1990, p. 82). Calculating the growth of interdisciplinary research, Wilson and Edelman (1996) searched *Dissertation Abstracts International* for the keywords "interdisciplinary research" appearing in the abstract or title and found 12 dissertations submitted from 1861-1981 versus 70 dissertations from 1982 to 1995 (p. 196). A similar cursory search of *ProQuest Dissertations & Theses A & I* for "interdisciplinary research" in the abstract or title reveals 331 dissertations from 1996 to 2012. If this keyword search is expanded to full text, 5070 dissertations appear in the results list. Dobson & Kushkowski (1996) evaluated collection strategies for interdisciplinary subjects based upon location of materials, access, and use by interdisciplinary scholars. They describe the difficulties involved with building a "consensus among scattered faculty as to what comprises an adequate local collection or adequate remote access" (Dobson & Kushkowski, 1996, p. 280). Gerhard (2000) addresses issues surrounding collection development of electronic resources as it pertains to interdisciplinary collections. Evaluation and selection guidance such as setting trial periods, consulting with faculty, defining selection criteria, and soliciting feedback from peer librarians is advised (Gerhard, 2000, p. 58).

Case studies address issues inherent with interdisciplinary collection development. At the University of Wisconsin-Madison, the Women's Studies Reading Area collection was developed (Jesudason, 1992) to acknowledge and further a growing academic interest in women's studies. Assessing and developing interdisciplinary library collections for the African American Studies department at Georgia State University "requires the targeted, careful use of limited funds, with disciplined, skilled choices based on whatever knowledge a bibliographer can gather" and, "understanding such factors as the history of a collection, the curriculum developed at an institution over time, and the needs of the students, faculty, and other library users" (Mosby, 1994, p. 198). Mosby (1994) argues that libraries are "where discipline boundaries blur" and this way of thinking benefits libraries and the university community as a whole (p. 211). Librarians from the George A. Smathers Library at the University of Florida addressed strategies for achieving effective interdisciplinary collection development while assessing the collections for American and British history (Hickey & Arlen,

2002). The authors recommend communication and collaboration strategies to address collection management for interdisciplinary areas. They advise setting regular meetings between bibliographers to discuss collections issues, sharing notification slips between approval plans, and allocating a portion of the collections budget for interdisciplinary purchases rather than strictly by department (Hickey & Arlen, 2002). Assessment of current collections for Black Studies through citation analysis of journal literature (Weissinger, 2002), developing a methodology for resource selection in Social Work (Jacoby, Murray, Alterman, & Welbourne, 2002), and analyzing the library approval plan for Geography (Bartolo, Wicks, & Ott, 2002) are three examples of collection development analysis for library resources pertaining to interdisciplinary areas. Taler (2011) presents a collection development strategy for Jewish Studies that advocates for building strong collections for this interdisciplinary program through selections based upon identified literary awards. Misco (2011), Slavic Studies Librarian at Miami University of Ohio, describes the challenges inherent to area studies collection development within the traditional subject specialist model and proposes communication and collaboration with other areas studies librarians as an effective method (p. 386) of dealing with collections issues. While evaluating and building the Asian American Studies collection at Pennsylvania State University, Masuchika (2012) proposes that librarians responsible for interdisciplinary collections development use a benchmarking process against comparable institutions with similar programs to address whether or not the library in question is able to currently support a new degree program (p. 6).

Canvassing the literature for publications specifically on environmental studies and sustainability collection management issues uncovers three key sources. A case study focusing on collection management strategies for environmental studies at Dartmouth College illustrates the issues inherent in coordinating collections for a broadly interdisciplinary area and proposes an alternative approach (DeFelice & Rinaldo, 1994). Four bibliographers from the Dartmouth College Library Collection Management and Development Committee with primary responsibility for environmental studies crafted a collection development policy that coordinated interdisciplinary materials housed in separate physical locations (DeFelice & Rinaldo, 1994). Reviewed every 3-5 years, this policy is "dynamic and updated frequently enough to reflect changes in the disciplines covered as well as the terminology" (DeFelice & Rinaldo, 1994, p. 340). Applin (2009), from the University of Southern Mississippi, conducted an extensive review of sustainability scholarship and published a selected annotated bibliography for collection development. Focused on academic libraries that support sustainability programs, this guide includes important reference works, subject databases, print and online journals, monographs, DVDs, and online sources and is the first published bibliography of its kind (Applin, 2009). Connell (2010) discusses three aspects of "green collection development" in academic libraries: selection of sustainability-related resources, the de-selection of materials and its impact on the environment, and an examination of the carbon footprints belonging to electronic and print materials (p. 2). The importance of curating a sustainability-related collection is emphasized as having a broad impact on the curriculum across campus as more academic programs address environmental issues (Connell, 2010, p. 3).

Canvassing the literature for collection development issues related to sustainability, we found three main categories of publications emerge over time: general collection development strategies for interdisciplinary and area studies, case studies that focused on particular institutions and interdisciplinary collections, and a few recently published sources that specifically address environmental studies and sustainability collection development. In the case of AU Libraries, the management of our collection development for sustainability has evolved over the years in response to increasing interest by academic programs and a campus-wide awareness of environmental issues. Our case study adds to the growing body of literature that relates to the challenges and opportunities of collecting for sustainability.

Year One

AU Libraries subject specialists assist students and faculty toward developing a library collection that meets the needs of the academic community. Sustainability is just one of 32 subject areas for which the libraries has created a materials purchase fund. Seventeen librarians at Auburn serve as the departmental liaisons and subject specialists charged with collection development. With interdisciplinary subjects such as sustainability, there can be significant overlap with established disciplines such as agriculture, business, and sociology among others.

Auburn's first yearly allotment to the sustainability materials fund was $3000 and occurred midway through the fiscal year. This initial allocation was intended to allow for the creation of a core collection in coordination with the Sustainability Studies students and faculty. The librarian was told that in following years the allocated funding would be in the range of $1000 to $1500. Building a useful interdisciplinary core collection from the ground up with limited financial resources requires careful selection with consideration given to both relevance and cost. At the initial stages of collection management, even conceptualizing and expressing what material constitutes a "core collection" for an interdisciplinary topic such as sustainability is a challenge. While an academic library is certain to contain a large number of sustainability-related information sources, without a specific collecting agenda, there are likely to be areas overlooked and underrepresented in the library holdings. The librarian's goal for the first year of collection development was to gain an understanding of the sustainability titles already in the collection, consult with academic faculty from the Sustainability Program regarding their perception of what a core collection should consist of and how Auburn's current collections met their expectations, and then use the first year's funding to build a strong core collection of sustainability works.

Understanding the Collection

As sustainability-related publications are numerous and range from titles oriented toward a general audience to those written for discipline-specific research, the fundamental endeavor undertaken by the new sustainability liaison was to survey the library collection and compile a bibliography of current holdings. This was a critical step that would inform both the faculty consultation and the subsequent collecting effort. This survey of holdings was accomplished through an open-ended exploration of the library catalog and the subject headings assigned to sustainability titles as they were found. Keyword searching the catalog using general search terms such as "green"; "sustainable"; and "ecological" proved useful as a starting effort. These buzzwords of the sustainability movement are frequently used in both titles and subject headings. As catalog classifications for sustainability titles were identified, a picture of Auburn's collections began to emerge. General "sustainable living" and "green living" titles tended to be concentrated in the social science ranges including economics, commerce, and business. Discipline-specific sustainability titles were concentrated largely in agriculture, engineering, architecture, and building science classifications. From the catalog searching effort, the library liaison recorded for each major topical area several of the most current and relevant titles that appeared to be written at an undergraduate and general audience level. This list would be used as part of the faculty consultation process.

Defining the Core Collection

The faculty assigned to the Academic Sustainability Programs, particularly those who had helped create the minor, were grateful to have a library liaison and enthusiastic about a collaborative effort to build a useful core collection. The librarian arranged for a 2-hour consultation held at the library with program leaders. This consultation was intended to incorporate elements of a reference interview and an informal focus group. The first meeting with Sustainability faculty showcased the interdisciplinary holdings of sustainability materials and solicited advice from teaching faculty on identifying gaps in the library's current holdings. The librarian pulled the volumes from the initial list of potential core collection titles and this physical collection served as an ice-breaker to the meeting and an example of the library commitment to supporting sustainability teaching at Auburn. Faculty identified several authors important enough to merit collecting their complete works. Faculty also offered suggestions for important works not represented in the cross section, suggested sustainability-related terms for future searching efforts, gave lists of required reading for their classes, and advised on discipline-specific titles important to their own areas of expertise.

The consultation ended with a discussion of the teaching faculty's recommendation for an interdisciplinary sustainability core collection oriented toward undergraduates. Consulting with sustainability teaching faculty is critical to crafting a collecting strategy for a core undergraduate collection. Since Auburn's approval plan for purchases only covers titles published by university presses, the librarian felt that general-audience titles may be underrepresented in the collection. Given the academic sustainability program's emphasis on undergraduate studies and the academic minor in Sustainability, the librarian's initial perception was that a "core" undergraduate collection needed to be weighted toward sustainability literacy and general, popular titles on "green" living. Sustainability faculty agreed with this assessment, but suggested that there were undergraduate-level overviews and introductions to discipline-specific sustainability studies that would also be important to collect. From their teaching experience, they found that general titles may be useful for class discussions and readings, but for research projects undergraduates still needed "entry level" works on specific sustainability topics for engineering, agriculture, biological sciences, wildlife sciences, and building sciences. The need for a strong basic collection on green business practices was the most commonly expressed opinion.

Building the Core Collection

Following the faculty consultation, the sustainability liaison crafted a strategy to spend approximately $1500 of the initial $3000 toward a core collection, with the remaining funds held for discretionary purchases and meeting purchase requests. The first collecting priority was to meet the specific core materials requests made by sustainability faculty, regardless of costs. Where their selections were for discipline-specific, graduate level material, the request was forwarded to the relevant subject librarian. Given the limited budget, the second consideration was that of cost. For materials not requested by sustainability faculty, the librarian decided to give priority to materials that cost below $100. While this was an arbitrary number, it helped to both increase the amount of materials purchased and to orient purchases toward general and undergraduate materials.

The process of reviewing materials for selection involved three main tools: "Choice Reviews Online," Amazon, and YBP's Global Online Bibliographic Information (GOBI[3]) purchasing platform. "Choice Reviews Online" serves well to inform a book selector of the perceived quality of the work and its readership level. For the core collection building process, the librarian chose to limit the "Choice Reviews Online" results to essential and highly recommended works relating to sustainability written for general and undergraduate readers. This effort gave the librarian a pool of several hundred titles from which to select potential core titles. Amazon, though less useful for filtering results by readership level and perceived quality, was useful in gauging the sales numbers, and hence popularity, of sustainability-related works. It was useful for finding popular titles and those that had not been reviewed by *Choice*. For the final analysis and selection of materials identified through *Choice* and Amazon, the librarian used the GOBI[3] tool offered through YBP, the academic division of Baker & Taylor. This tool enabled the librarian to review purchasing statistics for identified titles that were considered worthwhile by other academic library selectors.

The summary for the abbreviated seven month fiscal period of sustainability collection development reveals that during 2010-2011, 59 volumes were purchased using sustainability funds. The average cost for the volumes was $44. Of the titles purchased, 31 were written at the popular and general academic level and 24 at the advanced academic and professional level. Four DVDs were purchased at the request of teaching faculty for use in the classroom. Of the materials purchased, 14 were direct requests from faculty and students in the Sustainability Program.

Year Two

In 2011, a new liaison to AU's College of Architecture, Design and Construction joined the library's faculty. Sustainability and "green building" is an important aspect of teaching and research in design disciplines. In 1998, the U.S. Green Building Council established the Leadership in Energy and Environmental Design (LEED™) rating system and students at Auburn have the opportunity to attend class in one of Alabama's LEED™ Gold certified structures, the M. Miller Gorrie Center, where the McWhorter School of Building Science is located. In the current architectural education landscape, sustainability is largely integrated across collegiate schools of architecture. Borden (2008) argues that "most, if not all architectural schools, are acutely aware of the relevance of sustainability, and even the most cursory of glances at the various summer degree shows held around the world demonstrate an incredible variety of approaches" (p. 46). At Auburn, design students learn about sustainability through courses in architectural materials and methods, community planning, environmental design, landscape and interior architecture, and building science.

Although the study of sustainable materials and green building concepts are incorporated into almost every program at AU's College of Architecture, Design and Construction, there are no library funds specifically allocated to sustainability-related materials in the design disciplines. Dealing with a lack of dedicated funds has proven an opportunity for collaboration between the liaison for these design programs and the library liaison for sustainability. Sustainability in architecture, design, and building sciences, "involves many issues, including building for posterity; maintaining, preserving, and adapting, rather than replacing, the existing building stock; and environmental, social, and cultural responsibility and awareness" (Brady, 1996, p. 41) and therefore the liaisons' first step towards collaboration was to share approval plan slips and identify areas of overlap between the two profiles. Sharing approval slips allowed both liaisons to track monograph selections and consult on joint purchases. The liaisons also coordinated funds on larger purchases, such as the online database *BuildingGreen Suite* from *BuildingGreen.com*. Recognizing interest from faculty in both areas, the liaisons arranged for a trial and solicited faculty input before deciding to add the resource. After receiving positive feedback from design and sustainability faculty, funds were split according to the size of the department, with design paying about ¾ of the annual cost. The new library liaison for design disciplines arrived with financial support from the library and college for new subscriptions which allowed for interdisciplinary purchases related to sustainability such as the *Journal of Green Building*. The additional funds served as an opportunity to support Brady's (1996) argument that sustainability taught through architectural education "must be a philosophy that informs the education of an architect at every level" (p. 42) by increasing library resources for this interdisciplinary subject. The liaisons found that selecting and adding online resources jointly, using funds from both budgets, is considerably more straightforward than joint purchases for print items. Because the architecture, design, and construction collections are primarily housed in the branch library rather than the main library, decisions about where to locate print titles are always made in consultation with the library liaison for sustainability.

AU conducts an annual workshop for faculty to build sustainability objectives into course plans. The sustainability liaison has been invited to speak at these workshops and has used the opportunity to build awareness of the sustainability fund and solicit input from faculty across campus. During the second fiscal year 2011-2012, library funding for collection development of sustainability was dropped from $3000 to $1500. The collaborative purchase of *Building-Green Suite* required the use of $300 from the fund. With the remaining $1200, 25 volumes were purchased. The average cost for the volumes purchased during the second year of the sustainability fund was $48. Of the 25 titles purchased, 8 were written at the popular and general academic level and 17 at the advanced academic and professional level. Of the materials purchased, 8 were direct requests from faculty and students in the Sustainability Program.

Conclusion

The library liaison for sustainability continues to contact subject specialists when selecting discipline-specific titles over $100 and asks them to purchase the volume or at least contribute a majority of the cost. The sustainability materials fund has not risen over time. Ongoing collaborative purchases include sustainable farming practices media in cooperation with the agriculture specialist, renewal of the *BuildingGreen Suite* with a combination of sustainability and design funds, and the purchase of sustainability pedagogy works by the education library liaison. Recently, design and sustainability library liaisons both received emails from their respective faculty members about purchasing an expensive DVD set for each physical library. Because of the high cost, the liaisons decided to coordinate the purchase by splitting payment based upon where the videos would be housed.

The materials budget will always be an important factor in a collection strategy for sustainability. A designated funding line under the direction of a sustainability liaison is the optimal arrangement, but one that may not be economically feasible for some libraries. The appointment of a sustainability liaison for collection development, even if the budget for sustainability discipline is negligible, still enables the academic library to begin meeting the communication challenges of interdisciplinary collecting. Serving as the information clearinghouse between the library and faculty engaged in sustainability at the university, a dedicated liaison can aid both groups' effectiveness. A sustainability liaison can field requests from faculty and students, identify important works for the collection, review the collection for weaknesses, and then approach fund managers for specific disciplines with recommendations. Comprehensive oversight of sustainability-related purchases remains a primary challenge for Auburn's sustainability liaison to address. Purchases relating to sustainability may occur at the request of many different subject librarians. Coordinating with acquisitions and the ordering unit may be necessary to develop a reporting mechanism to track sustainability-related purchases.

The sustainability liaison is ideally situated to communicate to teaching faculty across disciplines regarding the acquisition of important information resources for sustainability research. Library subject specialists can also benefit from the creation of a sustainability liaison, learning about faculty research and the development of new courses in sustainability across disciplines. Referring to the influence of Vitruvius and his *Ten Books of Architecture* written circa 27 B.C.-A.D. 14, on the fundamental objectives of architecture programs, Brady (1996) concludes that "the concept of sustainability, as the ability to endure, has been a fundamental issue of architecture as holistic design since its earliest practice" (p. 32). This precept can easily be applied to sustainability as a fundamental part of interdisciplinary collection development across many disciplines. As such, the sustainability liaison is not the gatekeeper of the sustainability-related materials at the library. If not for the efforts of subject librarians across multiple disciplines, our sustainability collection would not be as strong.

References

Applin, M. B. (2009). Building a sustainability collection: A selected bibliography. *Reference Services Review, 37*(3), 313–325.

Auburn University Office of Sustainability. (2013.) *Who we are.* Retrieved from http://www.auburn.edu/projects/sustainability/sustain-web/

Bartolo, L. M., Wicks, D. A., & Ott, V. A. (2002). Border crossing in a research university: An exploratory analysis of a library approval plan profile of Geography. *Collection Management, 27*(3/4), 29-44.

Borden, I. (2008). Sustainability and architectural design. *Space,* (492), 46–47.

Brady, D. A. (1996). The education of an architect: Continuity and change. *Journal of architectural education, 50*(1), 32–49.

Carpenter, E. (1990). Toward interdisciplinarity in literary research: Some implications for collection development. *Collection Management, 13*(1/2), 75–86.

Connell, V. (2010). Greening the library: Collection development decisions. *Endnotes: The Journal of the New Members Round Table, 1*(1), 1–15.

DeFelice, B., & Rinaldo, C. (1994). Crossing subject boundaries: Collection management of environmental studies in a multi-library system. *Library Resources & Technical Services, 38*(4), 333–341.

Dobson, C., & Kushkowski, J. D. (1996). Collection evaluation for interdisciplinary fields: A comprehensive approach. *Journal of Academic Librarianship, 22*(4), 279-284.

Gerhard, K. H. (2000). Challenges in electronic collection building in interdisciplinary studies. *Collection Management, 25*(1/2), 51-65.

Hickey, D., & Arlen, S. (2002). Falling through the cracks: Just how much "history" is history? *Library Collections, Acquisitions, & Technical Services, 26*(2), 97-106.

Jacoby, B. E., Murray, J., Alterman, I., & Welbourne, P. (2002). Resource selection for an interdisciplinary field: A methodology. *Journal of the Medical Library Association, 90*(4), 393–398.

Jesudason, M. (1992). Building a Women's Studies reading area collection: University of Wisconsin-Madison, College Library experience. *Reference Services Review, 20*(1), 81–93.

Masuchika, G. (2012). Building by benchmarking: A method of creating and evaluating an Asian American Studies collection. *Library Collections, Acquisitions, & Technical Services, 36*(1/2), 1–7.

Misco, M. (2011). Disciplinary points of departure: How area studies librarians fit within the subject paradigm. *College & Undergraduate Libraries*, *18*(4), 385–390.

Mosby, A. P. (1994). Coalition building to build collections. *Reference Librarian*, (45/46), 197–212.

Riley, D. R., Grommes, A. V., & Thatcher, C. (2007). Teaching sustainability in building design and engineering. *Journal of Green Building*, *2*(1), 175–195.

Taler, I. (2011). The Jewish Studies book awards: A collection development strategy for non-sectarian academic libraries. *Collection Building*, *30*(1), 11–38.

Weissinger, T. (2002). Black Studies scholarly communication: A citation analysis of periodical literature. *Collection Management*, *27*(3/4), 45-56.

Wilson, M. C., & Edelman, H. (1996). Collection development in an interdisciplinary context. *Journal of Academic Librarianship*, *22*(3), 195-200.

Section Three

Sustainable Scholarship

Connecting Journal Articles with Their Underlying Data: Encouraging Sustainable Scholarship through the Public Knowledge Project and Dataverse Network Integration Project

Eleni Castro

Abstract

Collaboration between academic institutions and publishers is needed for scholarly output to be shared and preserved in a sustainable manner. An example of this type of cooperation, through interoperability, is currently taking place with the Public Knowledge Project (PKP)-Dataverse Network integration project. This collaboration will focus on connecting journal publications with their underlying data through the integration of two well-established open source systems: PKP's Open Journal Systems (OJS) developed by Stanford and Simon Fraser University; and Harvard's Dataverse Network web application developed by the Institute for Quantitative Social Science (IQSS). This paper will provide an overview of the project, its technology, expected outcomes, benefits and challenges.

Introduction

As the Information Age progresses, it is imperative that academic institutions work closely with publishers so that research data can be shared, reused and preserved in a sustainable manner. Supported by a two year, $1M grant from the Alfred P. Sloan Foundation, the Public Knowledge Project (PKP) and

Dataverse Network integration project, will collaborate through interoperability to connect journal publications with their underlying research data. The end result being to help increase the replication and reuse of research outputs by improving the infrastructure for, practice of, and incentives related to data publication and citation. This will be achieved by integrating two well-established open source systems: Open Journal Systems (OJS) (Willinsky, 2005) developed by PKP, an organization dedicated to improving the scholarly and public quality of research, which includes Stanford and Simon Fraser University; and Harvard's Dataverse Network web application (Crosas, 2011, 2013; King, 2007) developed by the Institute for Quantitative Social Science (IQSS). The technical aim in integrating these two systems is for an article's underlying research data to be seamlessly deposited into the Harvard Dataverse Network during the OJS journal article submission process. This paper will provide a brief discussion on the importance of collaborating and sharing research data, an overview of the project as it currently stands, and some of its expected benefits and challenges.

Why Collaborate and Share Research Data?

Before going into the details of the PKP-Dataverse Network Integration Project here is some background behind the reasoning for this particular undertaking. Borgman provides "four rationales" for sharing research data: reproduce or to verify research, make results of publicly funded research available to the public, enable others to ask new questions of extant data, advance the state of research and innovation (2012, p. 26).

Additionally, in Hodson and Jones' most recent blog post (July 16, 2013) for The Guardian they mention the Royal Society's landmark report, Science as an Open Enterprise, which "stresses the potential for data reuse and a need for rapid data sharing so that we can respond to global challenges, such as flu epidemics or disaster risks." If research data is made openly available it not only helps the scholarly community to advance scientific research, but can also have a positive impact on the wider population as well.

Indicatively, various members of the research data community have recently asserted that the cooperation of journals is necessary (Ghergina & Katsanidou, 2013) for research data to be "made available alongside its published work in order to validate and advance scientific research" (JISC, 2012). More specifically, Vlaeminck (2013) proposes collaboration among key stakeholders such as journals, research libraries, and data centers "for building up the necessary e-infrastructure...to ensure effective sharing and reuse [of research data]".

Open Journal Systems (OJS)

One of the open source systems that will be used for this integration project is PKP's OJS, which was started in 2001 and provides the technical infrastructure for the management and publishing of peer-reviewed journals. This system facilitates every stage of the refereed publishing process, from submissions through to online publication and indexing. Through OJS, PKP seeks to encourage open access publishing and "improve both the scholarly and public quality of refereed research" (PKP, n.d.). As of December 2012, OJS has over 5000 journals publishing on a regular basis (defined as over 10 articles per year, see Figure 1).

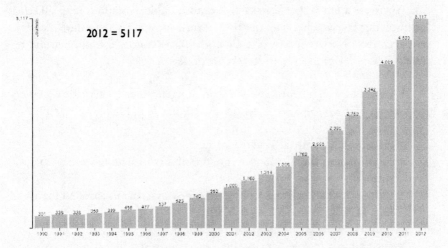

Figure 1. Number of new OJS Journals with at least 10 articles published per year.
Credits: Juan Alperin, PKP.

Some of OJS's current features include:

- technical infrastructure for an entire editorial management workflow (submission, peer review, indexing);
- 'plugin' architecture (a la WordPress, Drupal, etc) to easily add new features without the need to change the entire core code base;
- universal metadata standards (e.g. expandable Dublin Core);
- interoperability with other systems through standard protocols (e.g. OAI-PMH, and APIs);
- support for generating DOIs for permanent linking of articles; and

- the option for backups and replication of journals in different locations (e.g. LOCKSS) so access is never lost.

Dataverse Network

The other open source system that will be used for this project is the Dataverse Network web application, which started in 2006 at IQSS. The Dataverse Network allows researchers to publish, share, cite, extract and analyze research data. It takes care of long-term preservation and good archival practices, while the researchers and data producers are recognized for and keep control of their data. There are a handful of Dataverse Network implementations (e.g. ODUM Institute) but Harvard hosts an instance of this web application called the Harvard Dataverse Network, which is a worldwide repository for all scientific research data. Some of its current features include:

- support for all file formats, with additional features for statistical formats (e.g. STATA, SPSS, R), astronomy format (e.g. FITS), and graph formats (e.g. GraphML);
- extracting file and variable metadata;
- re-formatting files for long term accessibility so data never become obsolete;
- support for backups and replication of research data in different locations (e.g. LOCKSS) so data is never lost;
- universal metadata standards (e.g. DDI, Dublin Core);
- generating a formal data citation and permanent link to datasets using the Handle and DOI systems; and
- interoperability with other applications through standard protocols (e.g. OAI-PMH and APIs).

Integration Between the Two Systems

The described project will integrate OJS and Dataverse Network to allow for the underlying research data deposit to occur during the article submission process. More specifically, this project will work with publishers to enable journals to seamlessly manage the submission, review, and publication of data associated with published articles. As a result of this cooperation, it is anticipated that the project will help increase awareness among journal editors and publishers regarding the importance of data sharing and preservation to support published research results.

On a more technical level, this project will lead to the development of an OJS plugin and Dataverse Deposit API (SWORDv2-compliant[1]); allowing authors to efficiently submit their article and datasets at the same time through OJS, while the underlying data are automatically deposited into the Harvard Dataverse Network. At the time of writing this paper, both the OJS and Dataverse Network development teams are in the process of implementing support for the SWORDv2-compliant API. The plugin that is currently being developed will complement OJS' current mechanism for handling a given article's supplementary files option (i.e., those which are not provided inline in the published HTML or PDF document -- often, underlying research data), and will also provide access through a permanent identifier and link to Dataverse Network data analysis tools at the journal/article level.

Beta versions of the plugin in OJS and the Dataverse Network Deposit API-were made available late Fall 2013 for a pre-selected group of OJS Journals to provide feedback on its functionality and usability. This test group will consist of approximately 50 journals spanning multiple disciplines and publishers (e.g. Social Science, Medical, Public Health, Science and Technology). Based on this initial round of feedback, both the OJS and Dataverse Network developers will work on revising the plugin and API. The end goal is to prominently include the data deposit functionality in an upcoming release (Spring 2014) of both OJS and Dataverse Network applications. Concurrent with the release, the project documentation, best practices (data management, review and citation), code and API will be made openly available for anyone who: has an instance of OJS or Dataverse Network; would like to add this functionality to their own repository or journal management system.

Data Publication Workflows

Prior to working on the development of the plugin and API, the PKP-Dataverse Integration Project team drafted possible data publication use cases and workflows for the integration between the two systems. This documentation

---

1. According to the official SWORD website (http://swordapp.org/), "SWORD is a lightweight protocol for depositing principally content (any content!) into repositories from one location to another. It stands for Simple Web-service Offering Repository Deposit and is a profile of the Atom Publishing Protocol (known as APP or ATOMPUB)." This project will be using the most recent version of the protocol, which is SWORDv2.

was sent out to several publishers for review to ensure that all relevant use cases or steps in the publication workflow had been considered. Given the publishers feedback, the team drafted the following data publication workflows that will be considered for this implementation:

- Workflow A is for authors that deposit their research data *at the same time* as they submit their article to the OJS journal;
- Workflow B is for authors that submit their article to the OJS journal but already have their research data in a repository, and therefore only need to include a data citation with a persistent link pointing to their data; and
- Workflow C is for authors that would deposit their research data *after* they submit their article to an OJS journal.

For example, Workflow A would have the following data publication steps:

1) author submits their article, and underlying research data with metadata to the journal's OJS article submission system;
2) editors and/or peer reviewers review the article and its underlying research data,
3) if the article is approved for publication the underlying research data (datasets, documentation, code/scripts, and other file types) and its corresponding metadata are automatically deposited from OJS into the Harvard Dataverse Network through the Data Deposit API;
4) a permanent identifier (i.e. Data Citation) will be automatically generated from the Dataverse Network that will allow the data to be linked, cited and tracked;
5) a data citation with permanent URL will be included with the journal article in OJS enabling users to easily access the underlying research data; and
6) a bibliographic citation of the journal article with permanent URL will be included in the Dataverse Network for users to access the corresponding article in OJS.

Expected Outcomes

Since the development of the technology for the PKP-Dataverse Network Integration Project is still at a nascent stage, it is difficult to predict accurately the outcomes. Nevertheless, outlined in the following paragraphs are some of the project's foreseeable benefits and challenges.

Challenges to Integration

The lack of precedents is one of the main challenges with this project since this is the first attempt at automating the integration between a journal publishing system and a research data repository using the SWORDv2 API. Since it is under documented it is expected that the project will encounter some unforeseen obstacles, which would require more development time to ensure the release of a fully functional plugin and API. However, concurrent with this project's efforts EDaWaX is working on a similar research data publication project (http://www. edawax.de/about/). The project coordinator has been communicating with the EDaWaX Project Manager, Sven Vlaeminck, and it is hoped that by sharing development and implementation experiences with this team it will help with building a more robust plugin and API.

Another issue is that, even though "[t]he notion of reproducibility as a scientific standard began with Robert Boyle and discussions within the Invisible College in the 1660s," there are still barriers within the scientific community regarding the sharing of research data (Leveque, Mitchell, & Stodden, 2012, p.13). Not only is reproducibility, if not properly documented, difficult to accomplish, in some instances researchers do not want to share research data for reasons such as being "scooped" on new data prior to publication or fear of misinterpretation (Donovan and Baker, 2010, p.29). In this sense, there are technological, as well as social barriers to data sharing. However, recognizing the social obstacles to data publication, international and governmental agencies such as OSTP's Memorandum of February 22, 2013, and G8's Science Ministers Statement are making top down policies and statements to publicly share research data. This zeitgeist shift in data sharing indicates that it is only a matter of time before the wider academic community will be interested (forcefully or willingly) in utilizing the type of technology that is being developed by this project.

Benefits to Integration

One of the advantages to this integration is that currently emerging data journals, also known as "data sharing as publication" (Alexandria Publishing Institute, 2012), exclusively publish data, rather than traditional research articles. One example is Ubiquity Press' *Journal of Open Psychology Data*, who will also be pilot testing integration between OJS and the Dataverse Network. With these recent changes in publishing and research funding policies, an increasing number of researchers will need a place to deposit their data to meet publisher and granting agency requirements, and this project will facilitate all stakeholders in that process.

An additional benefit is that by facilitating the research data sharing process, an increase in the visibility, reuse and sustainable preservation of research data is expected. Since the underlying research data can be preserved for the long-term in the Harvard Dataverse Network, or other Dataverse Network instances, authors will be able to deposit varied data types in robust reusable preservation-friendly formats (i.e. CSV). Furthermore, with an increase in research dataset visibility, it is expected that there will be an increase in data citation, replication and reuse essential to scholarly work. More specifically, this will be due in part to:

- permanent two-way linking of the published article in OJS with its underlying research data in the Dataverse Network;
- data files in the Dataverse Network will be discoverable, indexed, and exposed to both commercial search engines and academic indexing services.

Finally, interoperability will allow for streamlining the authors' article and data submission processes between the two systems and others. Authors will no longer need to go to different places to deposit different components of their research. Additionally, since the code and API will be open source - built using universal metadata standards and standard protocols, the application of this technology can therefore expand beyond OJS and Dataverse Network to other publishing management systems and repositories. This broader usage, in turn, can help to improve the code and API for the benefit of the wider research data sharing community.

Conclusion

The PKP-Dataverse Network Integration Project hopes to open up new avenues for improving the access, reuse, management and sharing of research data with the active participation of academic journals. Furthermore, the release of the open source plugin and API will be accompanied by detailed documentation and best practices that will guide stakeholders in the successful implementation of the technology, along with suggestions and templates for data management, review, and citation policies. By focusing on collaboration and interoperability through open access systems this project has the potential to expand ideas and technology to other repositories and journal management systems. Doing so can lead to the development of a truly collaborative, sustainable research data infrastructure. Ultimately, this integration will help increase the replication and reuse of research data by improving the infrastructure for, practice of, and incentives related to sharing data publication and citation.

References

Alexandria Archive Institute. (2012). Data Journals. Retrieved from http:// alexandriaarchive.org/projects/data-journals/

Borgman, C. L. (2012). The conundrum of sharing research data. *Journal of the American Society for Information Science and Technology*, 63(6), 1059-1078. doi: 10.1002/asi.22634

Crosas, M. (2011). The Dataverse Network™: An Open-Source application for sharing, discovering and preserving data. *D-lib Magazine* 17(1/2).

Crosas M. (2013). A data sharing story. *Journal of eScience Librarianship*, 1(3), 173-179.

Donovan, Joan M; & Baker, Karen S. (2011). The shape of information management: fostering collaboration across data, science, and technology in a design studio. UC San Diego: Scripps Institution of Oceanography. Retrieved from http://escholarship.org/uc/item/42s1q6mt

Gherghina, S., & Katsanidou, A. (2013). Data availability in political science journals. *European Political Science* 12, 333-349. doi:10.1057/eps.2013.8

JISC (2012, August 9). Innovative Research Data Publication. Retrieved from http://www.jisc.ac.uk/

King, G. (2007). An introduction to the Dataverse Network as an infrastructure for data sharing. *Sociological Methods and Research*, 32(2), 173–199.

LeVeque, R. J., Mitchell, I. M., & Stodden, V. (2012). Reproducible research for scientific computing: Tools and strategies for changing the culture. *Computing in Science and Engineering*, 14(4), 13-17.

Public Knowledge Project. (2012). Open Journal Systems. Retrieved from http://pkp.sfu.ca/ojs/

Hodson, S., & Jones, S. (2013, July 16). Higher Education Network. Seven rules of successful research data management in universities. *Guardian Professional*. Retrieved from http://www.theguardian.com/higher-education-network/blog/2013/jul/16/research-data-management-top-tips

Vlaeminck, S. (2013). Data management in scholarly journals and possible roles for libraries – Some insights from EDaWaX. *LIBER Quarterly, 23*(1), 48-79. Retrieved from http://liber.library.uu.nl/index.php/lq/article/view/URN%3ANBN%3ANL%3AUI%3A10-1-114595/8827

Willinsky, J. (2005). Open Jsournal Systems: An example of open source software for journal management and publishing. *Library Hi-Tech*, 23 (4), 504-519.

Library Publishing Services for Sustainability

Barbara DeFelice

Abstract

In this chapter, the author makes a case for library liaisons to be involved in providing new publishing opportunities for faculty and students interested in sustainability. The author believes this is a good way to spread the word about sustainability not only within the faculty but also to students and the general public. Academic research concerning sustainability should be available openly, so it is accessible to broad audiences. The author presents various projects completed by the Dartmouth College Library to spur "open access" to work on sustainability held by the library in both paper and digital formats, and to new scholarship.

Introduction

The dissemination of research in sustainabilty is a key goal of two recent projects involving the Dartmouth College Library (DCL) in partnership with local and national organizations. The DCL is exploring a sustainable publishing model through the development of the open access journal *Elementa: Science of the Anthropocene*, and promoting broader access to a seminal book in sustainability, Donella Meadows' et al., 1972 "*The Limits to Growth: A Report for the*

Club of Rome's Project on the Predicament of Mankind", through digitizing it. These projects have a common goal: providing open access to important material for research and teaching in areas relating to a sustainability. In this chapter, the author uses the term "sustainability" in reference to the content of the scholarship and "sustainable" to describe a model of journal publishing.

Dartmouth has several sustainability initiatives, including a Sustainability Minor, the Kapuscinski Sustainability Science Collaboratory, and the Sustainability Project, which engages the institution in sustainability practices. The Dartmouth College Library's work in digital publishing supports the goal stated on the web page of the Sustainability Project Learning and Culture Vision, Goals and Metrics: "Adapt and transform our teaching, research, creative expression and campus culture to push the edges of sustainability" (Dartmouth College 2013).

Identifying Needs for Scholarly Communication in Sustainability

The two digital publishing projects described in this chapter address needs for scholarly communication that supports sustainability sciences, studies and practice. They include:

- publishing outlets for multidisciplinary work that may include disparate approaches to knowledge and understanding, such as scientific research and artistic expression;
- publishing services for topics which have recently emerged but are not fully defined or recognized;
- the imperative to produce work that is accessible to legislators and the general public, so that it can influence government policy and legislation;
- the need to have research results be open access to be effective in supporting a transition to sustainability policies and practices;
- the need to share information resources with collaborators from outside the academic institution;
- the need to reach the unintended reader to influence social norms.

These needs were identified through outreach to faculty in the Environmental Studies Department, and became more focused through discussions with the faculty member holding Dartmouth's first Sherman Fairchild Distinguished Professor of Sustainability Science and participation in Dartmouth's Sustainability Project events. Among the best practices of Dartmouth College Library's strong library liaison program is "advocating with authors and editors for sustainable models of scholarly and educational publishing" (Dartmouth College Library, 2013). In the author's role as the outreach librarian for Environmental Studies, she finds that this practice provides an important means of understanding the shifts in scholarly publishing norms and expectations. The Dartmouth Sustainability Project (2013) is broadly inclusive, so librarians can stay current by attending events, providing input when invited, and participating in campus sustainability programs. Over the past few years, Dartmouth's Sustainability Project and the Sustainability Collaboratory offered opportunities such as participation in the Culture and Learning Working Group for the Sustainability Steering Committee, a "Sustainability Minor Meet and Greet", and the current "Sustainability Salons". Based on the author's experience the key components of outreach to discover publishing needs in sustainability include:

- being present at key programs, offering to present library resources and services as part of cross campus sustainability events, and accepting invitations to offer input on program development and direction;
- knowing where faculty publish, such as the journals in which they publish, or for which they serve as editors or reviewers
- discovering unmet needs in publishing; for emerging fields, there may be few satisfactory choices, and current commercial publishing models may not meet the imperative of broader reach and impact;
- discussing the career paths of their students; when these paths lead to work with organizations involved with environmental and sustainability issues, the students are likely to cease having access to library digital resources such as journals which they need for thorough research for their work;
- asking faculty about their recent or current publishing projects; asking what would be the ideal journal or other kind of publishing outlet for their field;
- suggesting that faculty try to retain their copyright; authors in sustainability areas often want to provide broader uses of their material and to share materials with collaborators worldwide with no barriers of cost;
- sharing information about the pay walls around materials needed for research and teaching, including the license or terms of use restrictions that often are attached to these materials.

Identifying Next Steps and New Roles

As a result of conversations with faculty, a team of librarians built the Sustainability Studies Library Research Guide (2013), which includes a list of journals in the field, openly available resources, and a section on collections of the papers of environmentalists included in the Dartmouth College Library Rauner Special Collections (2013). Due to these contacts and conversations, when opportunities arose to collaborate on publishing projects, librarians knew there was a strong match between the projects and the needs that had been identified for disseminating sustainable scholarship.

Libraries are becoming more involved in campus based publishing initiatives. Some of these initiatives involve partnerships with a university press (Crow, 2009), which is a potential solution to the crisis in scholarly publishing of monographs. Other paths involve the library hosting journals and conference papers through open source, commercial, or locally developed publishing platforms (Mullins et al., 2012). The Dartmouth College Library's Digital Program has been successful with several of these approaches, due to strong digital production and mark-up units, a close working relationship with the University Press of New England, and the use of open source and locally developed publishing services and infrastructure.

Each of the publishing projects presented here has a different genesis and result, but both contribute to learning and research in sustainability through complex collaborations involving the Dartmouth College Library's Digital Publishing Program, which is part of Dartmouth's Digital Library Program. Following are details on the goals and genesis of each of these projects.

The First Project

Figure 1. *Elementa: Science of the Anthropocene* logo

When the not-for-profit publisher BioOne approached the Dartmouth College Library about being a partner in a new open access journal publishing program, the Library had a journal publishing program, experience with developing digital scholarly editions of works from Special Collections, and an e-book partnership with the University Press of New England. BioOne's proposal to collaborate on an infrastructure for a new, open access journal with a sustainable business model was well received. As librarians spoke with faculty around campus about the opportunity, it became clear that sustainability teaching and research programs on campus would benefit from new modes of publishing. Two faculty members, who were deeply engaged in discussions of this new journal, were also committed to the idea that research must be applied and communicated effectively to forward a transition to sustainability. After accepting invitations to become Co-Editors-in-Chief, they further developed the scope of their domain in Elementa "Sustainability Transitions" noting that, "[o]ur current state of knowledge is insufficient to say how or whether humans can guide transitions to sustainability." (BioOne, 2013) This new open access journal is *Elementa: Science of the Anthropocene* (see Figure 1), and it currently has six domains: Atmospheric Science, Ecology, Earth and Environmental Science, Ocean Science, Sustainable Engineering, Sustainability Transitions.

The Dartmouth College Library is providing the staffing infrastructure for the manuscript peer review system and the publishing platform, technical expertise on XML, and administrative support. BioOne is providing the capital, marketing, communications, and key leadership for the project. This innovative project will provide a hub of scholarship through the six domains that are part of *Elementa* in the first year. These domains are critical to understand the impacts humans have on the environment and to develop ways to mitigate the negative impacts. As Anne Kapuscinski and David Peart wrote in their abstract for a talk at the 2013 Annual Meeting of the American Association for the Advancement of Science (AAAS): "We need to develop and promote highly respected journals that encourage interdisciplinary, innovative, and rigorous contributions to the new knowledge that can drive sustainability transitions in the "real world" of economic realities, human motivation, cultural context, power, and politics" (Kapuscinski & Peart, 2013).

The *Limits to Growth* Story

Donella Meadows was a Dartmouth faculty member, and her papers were housed at the Sustainability Institute in Hartland, Vermont. The Dartmouth College Library's Rauner Special Collections was asked to take these papers by request of a faculty member and the Sustainability Institute. The papers fit well into the Special Collections Library Manuscript Selection Policy guidelines. Through conversations about uses of the collection in teaching and research, the library staff realized that digitization of some of the collection would be valuable but required funding. As a starting place, the Sustainability Institute provided funding for the Dartmouth College Library to digitize the first edition of "Limits to Growth: a Report to the Club of Rome's Project on the Predicament of Mankind" and make it openly accessible. For this project, the Library provided the XML mark-up work, created the HTML and PDF versions, and presented the work on a digital collections web page, in close collaboration with staff from the Donella Meadows Institute (DMI), a private non-profit organization based in Norwich, Vermont. The book is highly cited and used in classes and having this edition widely available and open access is a benefit to a broad audience.

Conclusion

The Dartmouth College Library is supporting the dissemination of scholarship and research in sustainability through collaborative projects with faculty and with off campus partners. The library identified the following essential tools for library publishing services for sustainability:

- liaison or outreach program including the sustainability curriculum, faculty teaching and research, the campus sustainability program, aspirations of students, and regional programs;
- conversation with faculty about their experiences with current publishing opportunities and their aspirations for different options in the future;
- awareness of materials locally available, such as in Special Collections, that support teaching and learning in sustainability;
- support in terms of expertise, technologies, and an administrative infrastructure for digital library publishing services;
- reports and links on campus based publishing and publishing collaborations from the Scholarly Publishing and Academic Research Coalition (SPARC) and other sources;
- collaborators and partners; librarians can seek these and be open to them when opportunities arise.

The two disparate projects described in this chapter illustrate ways librarians can make unique contributions to sustainability teaching and research in their institutions through supporting open access publishing. Based on the author's experience with both projects, important key tools to help librarians make contributions include outreach to those involved in sustainability curricula and research, knowledge of the scholarly communication needs of faculty and students in an emerging interdisciplinary field, willingness to work with partners outside the immediate campus community, and an infrastructure that supports campus based publishing.

Libraries have always played a role in the scholarly communication ecosystem. In the networked digital information environment, that role is transitioning into support for dissemination of scholarship through new paths. Sustainability is emerging as an important way of thinking and acting for the long term health of the planet and people. Librarians can assume key roles in addressing these issues by providing publishing support for faculty and students who are working on the challenges of sustainability.

References

BioOne. (2013). *Elementa: Science of the anthropocene. Scope of sustainability transitions.* Retrieved from http://elementascience.org/about/aims-and-scope/#sustainability-sciences

Crow, R. (2009). *Campus-based publishing partnerships: A guide to critical issues.* SPARC. Retrieved from http://www.arl.org/sparc/partnering/guide/

Dartmouth College (2013). *Sustainability Project Learning and Culture: Vision, Goals and Metrics.* Retrieved from http://sustainability.dartmouth.edu/people/culture-and-learning-workgroup/learning-and-culture-vision-goals-and-metrics

Dartmouth College Library (2013). *Dartmouth College Library liaisons: Engaging with our community.* Retrieved from http://www.dartmouth.edu/~library/home/staffweb/liaison.html

Dartmouth College Library Digital Program (2013). Retreived from http://www.dartmouth.edu/~library/digital/

Dartmouth College Library Publishing. (2013). *Limits to growth: A report for the Club of Rome's project on the predicament of mankind.* Retrived from http://www.dartmouth.edu/~library/digital/publishing/meadows/ltg/

Dartmouth College Library Rauner Special Collections. (2013). *Manuscript selection policy.*

Retrived from http://www.dartmouth.edu/~library/rauner/donating/mssel.html

Dartmouth Sustainability Project. (2013). Retreived from http://sustainability.dartmouth.edu/

Elementa: Science of the Anthropocene. (2013). Retreived from http://elementa-science.org/

Kapuscinski, A., & Peart, D. (2013). Shared learning systems for sustainability. [Abstract] Paper presented at the session "What are the Roles of Knowledge Institutions in Sustainability?" at the Annual Meeting of the American Association for the Advancement of Science, Boston, MA.

Mullins, J. L., Murray-Rust, C., Ogburn, J. L., Crow, R., Ivins, O., Mower, A., Watkinson, C. (2012). *Library publishing services: Strategies for success. Final Research Report.*
SPARC. Retrieved from http://wp.sparc.arl.org/lps/

Dartmouth College Library. (2013). *Sustainability Studies Library Research Guide.* Retreived from http://researchguides.dartmouth.edu/sustainability

Community Archiving and Sustainability: Denison University's Homestead

Joshua Finnell

Abstract

This chapter provides an overview of one of the oldest sustainable communities among liberal arts colleges, the Denison University Homestead. Through the financial assistance of an Andrew W. Mellon Foundation Grant, Denison Libraries and both past and current Homesteaders created a digital archive documenting the cultural impact of this pioneering experiment on campus culture. As a community archiving initiative, this project presented unique challenges and opportunities in negotiating copyright and permissions with past and present Homesteaders, creating controlled, but community-specific metadata and communicating the importance of this resource to both the campus and wider community.

Introduction

In 2007, Denison University established an Environmental Taskforce to explore issues related to environmental sustainability on campus. Though the university established a recycling program in 1984 and developed the curriculum for an Environmental Studies program in 1994, no long-term strategic plan committed to the research, funding, and implementation of continually emerging sustainability practices existed. In a two-year period, the taskforce installed solar panels on the William Howard Doane Library, completed a campus environmental audit and, among other initiatives, successfully created a permanent committee within the university council governance system: The Campus Sustainability Committee. The hiring of the university's first Campus Sustainability Coordinator signified an institutional commitment to sustainability in all areas of campus life, from building construction to curriculum development.

The hiring of the university's first Campus Sustainability Coordinator was significant both as a financial commitment to sustainability practices on campus and as a symbolic gesture. Jeremy King is not only an alumnus ('97) of the university, but also a former resident of the Homestead. A student-run intentional community within the university residency system, the Homestead is a living-learning experiment focused on ecologically sustainable living. Created in 1977, this environmental community marked the beginning of sustainability efforts at Denison University (DU). The hiring of a former Homesteader as the first Campus Sustainability Coordinator in 2009 affirmed the sustainability efforts this community has contributed to the university for the last three decades.

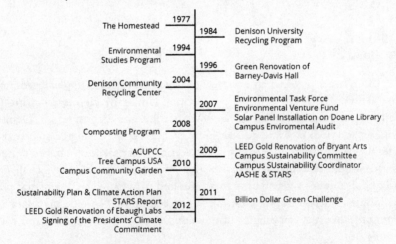

Figure 1. Timeline of sustainability at Denison University. Source: Denson University http://www.denison.edu/sustainability/history_of_sustainability.html

However, the history of Denison University's effort at promoting sustainability was not readily accessible to interested students, faculty, or researchers. While the William Howard Doane Library housed archival papers related to the financing and administrative aspects of creating this living-learning community, the Homestead itself had amassed a stockpile of papers, photographs, and documents within the attic of a cabin. Together, these two separate collections held the history of sustainability efforts at DU.

This chapter provides an overview of how, through an Andrew W. Mellon Foundation Grant, the digital archive of DU's Homestead was created. As a community archiving initiative, this project presented unique challenges and opportunities in negotiating copyright and permissions with past and present Homesteaders, creating controlled, but community-specific metadata and communicating the importance of this resource to both the campus and wider community. To contextualize the genesis of the Andrew W. Mellon Foundation Grant, it is first important to understand the Homestead's history and structure.

History of the Homestead

"In this world of growth and mobility, the emphasis placed on individual development is far from the level desired by most. What is needed is an experience that will affect a way of thinking. This way of thought would make the individual more aware of himself and the world around him. The concept of the Homestead is just such an experience" (Alrutz, 1977a).

On April 23, 1977, biology professor Dr. Robert W. Alrutz established the alternative living experiment at Denison University known as the Homestead. Almost every sustainable practice at DU leads back to Dr. Alrutz. He was instrumental in the university's acquisition and development of the 350-acre Biological Reserve, assisted in the creation of the university Recycling Program, and developed the Environmental Studies Program. The Homestead represented both a natural extension of Dr. Alrutz's interest in environmental sustainability as well as a response to the energy crises dominating the headlines in the 1970s.

After several meetings with the university president, board of trustees, campus affairs council, the campus community, and the surrounding community, three 24'x24' sustainable cabins were finally constructed, complete with a well for potable water and a garden to produce food, on a ten-acre plot of land approximately 1 mile north of the university. The twelve original members of the Homestead, along with Dr. Alrutz, were responsible for the construction and maintenance of this residential dwelling. As a learning experiment in sustainable construction, the expectation was that cabins would be deconstructed and repurposed into new forms of housing every three to five years.

Students interested in living at the Homestead would need to fill out an application indicating their interest in this alternative living experiment, and agree to the shared work responsibilities as outlined in the Homestead constitution. Students could stay as little as a semester or their entire four years at DU. Coupled with the expectations associated with living at the Homestead, inhabitants were also required to enroll in a Homestead Seminar focused on consensus-building in an intentional community, sustainable agricultural practices, and a student-driven topic series (Alrutz, 1977b). Speakers in the topic series were chosen from among current faculty as well as community members. This topic series would become a cornerstone of community involvement and create continuity with the current curricular interests of faculty members across disciplines. Some of the first topic speakers presented on pre-19th century human community, population problems and solutions, and alternative energy (Alrutz, 1977c). These seminars were intended to inspire students to execute a sustainable project during each semester they lived at the Homestead. Projects focused on researching and implementing evolving sustainable living practices.

Functioning as a liaison between the Homestead, the university, and the community, the Homestead Advisory Board (HAB) was established to review curricular elements of the Homestead, oversee construction of and physical modifications of buildings and land, and audit fiscal transactions (Alrutz, 1977d). Consisting of members of the Homestead, faculty, staff, and community, HAB now also serves an advocacy function for the Homestead. As Dr. Alrutz's original plan to rebuild cabins every three to five years proved both financially and practically infeasible, HAB has served a major role in the modification and rehabilitation of the original cabins.

For the last 35 years, in varying forms, the Homestead has maintained this focus and structure: seminar speakers have been identified each term; students research, document, and execute sustainability practices; the HAB has overseen new construction; and roughly 12 students each term inhabit the Homestead. To strengthen continuity within this transient community, a reunion is held every five years bringing generations of inhabitants back to the Homestead during the summer months to share stories, photographs, and memories. Naturally, the documentation on these activities was loosely stored in shoeboxes, bags, and photo albums at the Homestead. Over several decades, however, the archive was slowly eroding away due to environmental deterioration.

Interested in organizing and preserving this history, two students chose to digitize the archive as their Homestead Seminar project in the fall of 2011. Attempts at creating a digital archive of the Homestead had previously been attempted by former Homesteaders, but none of these projects involved working with a librarian. Agreeing to oversee the project, the author created workspace in the library's digitization lab for the students to begin sorting and organizing the various piles of items accumulated at the Homestead. As a clearer picture of the breadth of the community archive emerged, it became evident that this project exceeded the parameters of a semester-long seminar project. The archive presented a challenge not only in size, totaling 2,600 items, but also in description; many of the items lacked recognizable identifiers. The students were willing to work on this project beyond the spring semester, but the success of this project would require a significant commitment of time, input from both past and current members, and financial support. With these considerations in mind, members of the Homestead Advisory Board collaborated on submitting an application to the Andrew W. Mellon Foundation Next Generation Libraries Grant.

Andrew W. Mellon Grant

In 2009, the Five Colleges of Ohio Libraries (The College of Wooster, University, Kenyon College, Oberlin College, and Ohio Wesleyan University) received an Andrew W. Mellon Foundation *Next Steps in the Next Generation Library Grant*. The focus of this grant centered on both the construction of the Five Colleges of Ohio Digital Collections Portal and the dissemination of collaborative development grants between faculty and librarians. The Five Colleges of Ohio Digital Collections Portal was constructed within the OhioLINK Digital Resource Commons on the open-source, digital repository software DuraSpace (DSpace). Each institution established their own oversight committee, consisting of librarians, technologists, and faculty members, to approve project proposals.

After several discussions among HAB members and current Homesteaders, Linda Krumholz, associate professor of English and chair of the HAB, in conjunction with the author successfully submitted a proposal to digitize the Homestead archive. As the grant articulated, this project focused on a local collection of curricular interest to DU and the Ohio Five Colleges and primarily involved students in the selection, creation, and description of materials. In addition, the 35-year reunion of the Homestead was scheduled for summer 2012, presenting a perfect opportunity to record oral histories, collect donated items, and obtain crowdsourced metadata from a cross-section of former inhabitants of the Homestead.

Since the upcoming reunion was central to the success of the project, four current Homesteaders were hired in late spring to learn how to use digital recorders, conduct oral histories, use digital cameras, and prepare for the event. In addition, the project required the procurement of copyright permissions for many of the items in the archive, as well as informed consent from reunion attendees contributing their oral histories. Practically, this involved researching and drafting both a copyright statement and informed consent form to be presented to the Denison University Internal Review Board for Human Participants Research.

Copyright and Permissions

The understanding and application of intellectual property law is both difficult and confusing, especially within the academic environment. June Besek, Executive Director of the Kernochan Center for Law, Media and the Arts at Columbia Law School, succinctly summarizes the complications of copyright and archives in *Copyright Issues Relevant to the Creation of a Digital Archive: a Preliminary Assessment* (Besek, 2003). Moreover, obtaining permissions, whether they are informed consent or copyright, is a challenge. As was discovered in the creation of the Jon Cohen AIDS Research Collection at the University of Michigan, the biggest obstacle to getting permission is non-response (Akmon, 2010). The reunion provided a rare opportunity to contact every past Homesteader, the invitation was used to not only secure an RSVP, but also to collect copyright permissions from copyright owners, but also from individuals who appeared in the collection of photographs. Without attribution on any of the items in the archive, identifying and focusing on individual photographers, artists, and writers was futile. Permission from everyone who had ever lived at the Homestead was needed.

Also, it was important to respect the rights of this community and its archive. The custody and collection of the Homestead archive was a community-driven, grassroots effort. Since the beginning, this community was developed within the larger, institutional community of DU. However, geographically distanced from the university and focused on individual sustainability; the Homestead has always maintained a separate identity. The paucity of archival materials related to the Homestead in the university archives pointed to this distinction. As a non-Homesteader, and a representative of the university library, the author was aware of the symbolic nature of attempting to administratively control the archive through the collection of copyright. Andrew Flinn warns of this bravado when partnering with community archives when he writes:

> "This approach ...remains wedded to a very top-down custodial view of professional activity. It does not focus on the creators and custodians of these community archives, who often distrust or are at least wary of the intentions of heritage professionals."(Flinn, 2007, p. 163)

Therefore, current Homesteaders conducted the collection of copyright and permissions. Much like the Jon Cohen AIDS Research project at the University of Michigan, non-response proved to be the biggest obstacle. Though Homesteaders indicated interest in attending the reunion, very few copyright forms were returned with signatures. As a solution, current Homesteaders were provided with permission forms to distribute at the reunion, allowing for a more personal, community-oriented approach. After the reunion, these permission forms were sent to the library and kept on file. Not all former Homesteaders wish to have their image or name associated with the digital archive. Those members who wished to remain anonymous had their names recorded in a notebook during the reunion. Any photographs they appeared in, or documents containing their names, were not digitized. However, before excluding individuals from the archive, it was still necessary to identify the majority of individuals represented in the 2,600 photographs and letters in the archive.

Metadata

In *Management of Metadata for Digital Heritage Collections*, Laursen, Christiansen, and Olsen (2012) outline a general flow structure for creating metadata for digital heritage collections:

- Identification of metadata sources
- Analysis of metadata sources
- Selection of metadata sources
- Designing a metadata model
- Implementing the metadata model
- Documentation

In the identification phase, the students hired to work on the digitization project compiled names, and years of residency, for former Homesteaders from the handwritten rosters in the archive. This list of residents consisted of both human and non-human inhabitants, including pets throughout the years. An initial identification of metadata resulted in only 10% of items in the archive being easily identified. Knowing that a majority of former Homesteaders would be attending, it was hoped that reunion participants would fill in the missing 90%.

However, appropriately harnessing the knowledge of the reunion participants without disrupting the joyous nature of the reunion proved difficult. The initial plan was based on the success of the Library of Congress Flickr Pilot Project (2008), wherein users tagging photographs uploaded to Flickr-aggregated metadata. This approach would prove impossible to implement, as there is no Internet and limited electricity at the Homestead. As an alternative, several photograph posters were created using Picasa. The posters were printed and placed in each one of the cabins during the reunion as seen on Figure 2. In this way, attendees could write names, dates, and other relevant information on the posters at any point during the reunion without formalized instruction.

Figure 2. Photo posters in the basement. Credit: Ryan Culligan, 2012

Figure 3. Working in the Digitization Lab. Credit: Joshua Finnell, 2012

At the end of the reunion, the posters were returned to the library and hung on the walls of the digitization room. In the selection and designing of a metadata schema, a hybrid model of Library of Congress Subject Headings and community language was adopted. An excellent example of community language would be the number of references to the yard in front of the cabins as the *lower beach*. The metadata collected from the photo posters were matched against official Homestead rosters found in the archive. Throughout the designing process, an emphasis was placed on the necessity of a controlled vocabulary to ensure precision in retrieval. The agreed upon model was a negotiation between community language and the foundational elements of cataloging and classification. The final product was implemented into a modified Dublin Core schema and uploaded to the Denison Resource Commons.

Over a four-month period, students manually digitized, cataloged, and uploaded items into the Denison Resource Commons Portal as seen on Figure 3. During this process, Homesteaders who attended the reunion continued to send their own personal photographs and documents to be added to the archive. By the end of the summer, the archive was robust enough to begin announcing its completion to the university community, and students felt confident enough to present on the process of its creations.

Communication and Marketing of the Archive

In 1932, Shiyali Ramamrita Ranganathan wrote:

"It's no wonder that, when the library has been extending its scope, changing its outlook and altering its very character and functions, there should be adequate understanding among the public as to what has been going on" (Ranganathan, 1931, p. 315).

Not only was it important for us to communicate the completion of the project to the Homestead community, but also the larger Denison community. Additionally, as stipulated by the terms of the Mellon grant, there was a responsibility to communicate the results of the project to the Five Colleges of Ohio. On a broader scale, there was a deliberate effort to document and communicate the archiving process to similar intentional communities, both within and outside of a university setting.

Since the archiving process was deeply embedded into the reunion, the completion of the project was communicated clearly to the broader Homestead community. Working with the Office of University Communications at DU, the Homesteaders produced a story on the reunion and the archiving project for the university website (Denison University, 2012b). In addition, an article on the archiving process appeared in the fall 2012 issue of Denison Magazine, distributed to alumni across the globe (Denison University, 2012a, p. 3). Both articles served to remind the Denison community of the long history of the Homestead, as well as its uniqueness among American Liberal Arts Colleges.

The focus of this project was collaboration between faculty and librarians, Linda Krumholz, in collaboration with the Homesteaders who worked on the project and the author, presented on the archiving process at DU's Faculty Lunch Series (Finnell, Krumholz & Culligan, 2012). This opportunity not only allowed marketing the archive to faculty for curricular use, but also to discuss the intellectual process of designing and executing a project of this scope. Consequently, the project underscored the importance of documenting sustainability practices at Denison.

Marketing the Homestead archive as a resource to the Five Colleges of Ohio, the Homesteaders presented at the Next Generation Libraries Institute at The College of Wooster in the summer of 2012 (Plummer, Culligan & Jochem, 2012). The students gained valuable experience in presenting at a professional conference and were able to connect with similar intentional communities across the Five Colleges. Whereas previous marketing focused on the end product, this conference allowed students to discuss the library-centric aspects of the process in terms of choosing a metadata scheme and obtaining copyright and informed consent.

Outside of the Five Colleges of Ohio, it was important to market the archive to the general public as well. In 2013, an article detailing the Homestead archive appeared in *Communities Magazine*, the primary resource for information about intentional communities in North America. Also, DU's Dean of Students and a Homestead student will present on the project at the 2013 Association of College and University Housing Officers – International Conference. From professional conference to magazine publications, this project has, in the words of Ranganathan, provided an *"adequate understanding among the public as to what has been going on."*

The Future of the Homestead Archive

As every archivist knows, the documentation of history is an ongoing process. The Homestead is a dynamic, thriving community with new ideas and approaches to sustainability manifesting from a constant influx of new members. This presents obvious challenges to the maintenance and scope of the archive. What items from the community need to be preserved? Who is responsible for the collection and preservation of those items? Will current homesteaders always want to be associated with the Homestead by inclusion in the archive? As Dean Seeman points out in *Naming Names: The Ethics of Identification in Digital Library Metadata* will someone who gave consent to appear in the archive still feel that way twenty years later (Seeman, 2012, p. 328)? What privilege does one accord the historical accuracy of the archive against the individual right over personal identity? These are conversations that will continue between current and future members of the Homestead and HAB (for more information on the ethics and construction of community archives, see appendix A).

Coupled with these challenges was the opportunity for current and future Homesteaders to negotiate the evolving identity of the Homestead through the collective memory of the archive. The absence of a historical record at the Homestead had a significant impact on current Homesteaders' ability to articulate the history of commonality shared between inhabitants in 1977 and 2013. As a repository of not only sustainability projects but also diary entries written while living at the Homestead, current and future members have the ability to gain a historical insight that is broader in scope than their temporary residency. This perspective becomes operationally important as the core mission and focus of the Homestead is constantly negotiated against advances in sustainable technology.

The importance of the project in archiving sustainability efforts at DU cannot be understated. In *Teaching Sustainability, Teaching Sustainably*, Bartels and Parker remind us that sustainability is both a regulatory concept and a guiding ideal. Whereas the regulatory concept allows one to compare the relative destructiveness of various practices, the guiding ideal allows for the definition of target outcomes (Bartels & Parker, 2012). The Homestead provides DU with a living-learning experiment wherein emerging sustainability approaches are researched and applied to housing, food production, and energy consumption. These practices, in turn, serve as a guiding ideal in establishing long-term sustainability goals for the broader community. The digitally preserved and accessible Homestead archive now serves as a rich, historical record of sustainability practices, and the people involved with them, at DU.

References

Akmon, D. (2010). Only with your permission: how rights holders respond (or don't respond) to requests to display archival materials online. *Archival Science, 10*(1), 45–64.

Alrutz, B. (1977a). Homestead Justificaton. Retrieved from http://drc.denison.edu/bitstream/handle/2374.DEN/3910/Formation%20Documents%20_0027.pdf?sequence=1

Alrutz, B. (1977b). Format for Homestead Seminar Courses. Retrieved from http://drc.denison.edu/handle/2374.DEN/3912

Alrutz, B. (1977c). 1977 Seminar Schedule. Retrieved from http://drc.denison.edu/handle/2374.DEN/3777

Alrutz, B. (1977d). Description of HAB. Retrieved from http://drc.denison.edu/handle/2374.DEN/3911

Bartels, A.B., & Parker, K.A. (2012). *Teaching sustainability/teaching sustainably*. Sterling, Va.: Stylus Pub.

Besek, J. M. (2003). *Copyright issues relevant to the creation of a digital archive: a preliminary assessment*. Washington, D.C.: Council on Library and Information Resources : Library of Congress.

Denison University. (2012a). Alumni society: the homies come home. *Denison Magazine Online, Fall*. Retrieved from http://denisonmagazine.com/2012/articles/alumni-society-3/3/

Denison University. (2012b, June 18). Home again « TheDEN [Denison University]. *The DEN*. Retrieved March 21, 2013, from http://www.denison.edu/theden/2012/06/home-again/

Finnell, J., Krumholz, L., & Culligan, R. (2012). The Homestead at 35: archives and the future. *Faculty Lunch Series*. Lecture conducted from Denison University, Granville, Oh.

Flinn, A. (2007). Community histories, community archives: some opportunities and challenges. *Journal of the Society of Archivists, 28*(2), 151–176.

Laursen, D., Christiansen, K. F., & Olsen, L. L. (2012). Management of metadata for digital heritage collections. *Microform & Digitization Review, 41*(3/4), 151–158.

Library of Congress. Prints and Photographs Division, Springer, M., Dulabahn, B., Michel, P., Natanson, B., Reser, D. W., Library of Congress. Office of Strategic Initiatives. (2008). *For the common good the Library of Congress Flickr pilot project*. Washington, D.C: Library of Congress, Prints and Photographs Division. Retrieved from http://purl.access.gpo.gov/GPO/LPS108390

Plummer, K., Culligan, R., & Jochem, H. (2012). Homestead archive project lightning talks presentation. *Denison Resource Commons*. Retrieved March 21, 2013, from http://drc.denison.edu/handle/2374.DEN/2579

Ranganathan, S. R. (1931). *The five laws of library science*. London: Madras Library Association.

Seeman, D. (2012). Naming names: the ethics of identification in digital library metadata. *Knowledge Organization, 39*(5), 325–331.

Appendix A

Books and Articles Related to Community Archiving

Bicknese, D. (2003). Institutional repositories and the institution's repository: what is the role of university archives with an institution's on-line digital repository? *Archival Issues: Journal of the Midwest Archives Conference, 28*(2), 81–93.

Cannon, B. (2009). *Preserving communities a guide to archiving for community organizations*. Halifax, N.S.: B. Cannon.

Bastian, J.A. & Alexander, B. (2009) *Community archives: the shaping of memory*. London: Facet.

Flinn, A. (2007). Community histories, community archives: some opportunities and challenges. *Journal of the Society of Archivists, 28*(2), 151–176.

Flinn, A. (2011). Archival activism: independent and community-led archives, radical public history and the heritage professions. *InterActions: UCLA Journal of Education and Information Studies, 7*(2).

Flinn, A., Stevens, M., & Shepherd, E. (2009). Whose memories, whose archives? Independent community archives, autonomy and the mainstream. *Archival Science, 9*(1/2), 71–86.

Keough, B., & Schindler, A. C. (2003). Thinking globally, acting locally: documenting environmental activism in New York state. *Archival Issues: Journal of the Midwest Archives Conference, 28*(2), 121–135.

Millar, L. (2010). *Archives: principles and practice*. New York: Neal-Schuman Publishers.

Newman, J. (2012). Sustaining community archives. *APLIS, 25*(1), 37–45.

Ritchie, D. A. (2003). *Doing oral history : A practical guide*. Oxford: Oxford University Press.

Ronchi, A. M. (2009). *eCulture: cultural content in the digital age.* London: Springer.

Stielow, F. J. (2003). *Building digital archives, descriptions, and displays: a how-to-do-it manual for archivists and librarians.* New York: Neal-Schuman Publishers.

Theimer, K. (2010). *Web 2.0 tools and strategies for archives and local history collections.* New York: Neal-Schuman Publishers.

Section Four

The Landscape for Changes

The Triple Bottom Line: Portable Applications and Best Practices for Sustainability in Academic Libraries

Anne Marie Casey, Jon E. Cawthorne, Kathleen DeLong, Irene M.H. Herold, and Adriene Lim

Abstract

Triple Bottom Line Accounting (TBLA) refers to a method of measuring the economic, environmental, and community service impacts of an organization rather than the traditional practice of measuring just the financial bottom line. This chapter explores TBLA from a historical point-of-view; offers examples in higher education and discusses the implications for academic libraries. It concludes with ideas for the implementation of TBLA in libraries.

Introduction

In 1994, John Elkington coined 'triple bottom line' (TBL) as a new term to advance his sustainability agenda. He wrote: "Sustainable development involves the simultaneous pursuit of economic prosperity, environmental quality, and social equity. Companies aiming for sustainability need to perform not against a single, financial bottom line but against the triple bottom line" (Elkington, 1998, p. 397).

Elkington's definition intended to go beyond previous constructions of sustainable development (SD) and corporate social responsibility (CSR) to encompass an approach that emphasizes economic prosperity, social development and environmental quality as an integrated method of doing business. This definition implies a shift away from the emphasis of organizations on short-term financial goals to long-term social, environmental, and economic impacts. The approach is intended to be holistic, from the development of the vision, mission, and values of a company, to its management practices, including accounting and reporting.

Triple Bottom Line Accounting (TBLA) or sustainability accounting focuses on the value to society that is created or destroyed by an organization's activities or business. Richardson (2004) identifies two high level components of the TBLA framework. First is the restatement of traditional accounts to highlight financial flows that are sustainability related; second is additional accounting undertaken to show the financial value of economic, environmental, and social performance upon external stakeholders. Richardson highlights the danger inherent in accounting for only those items that can be reduced to monetary value and the difficulties of converting environmental practices and performance into financial values, much less the extension to the sphere of social performance and impact. She also stresses that financial valuation of economic, environmental, and social bottom lines places these factors into silos that allows them to be traded-off against one another. Richardson argues for moving beyond this thinking to a systemic approach that focuses upon qualitative processes such as diversity, learning, adaptation, and self-organization rather than defining and setting of financial, environmental, and social performance targets to be achieved and perhaps traded-off against one another.

In terms of implementing TBL, Adams, Frost, and Webber (2004) determined that there are no generally or widely accepted accounting standards or metrics to measure environmental or social performance. Mintz (2011) acknowledges that while managers' attention to the social and environmental impacts of their organizations has increased, it is difficult to develop standard accounting measures similar to those in financial accounting. He recommends that organizations develop Key Performance Indicators (KPI) or quantifiable measures linked to their own missions, goals, and stakeholder expectations. Rogers and Hudson (2011) caution that while businesses need to internalize their social and environmental impacts; they also need to instill the realities of the economic environment into their environmental and social policies.

Critics of TBL include Norman and MacDonald (2004) who question whether the paradigm of TBL is anything but a marketing ploy. They argue that, prior to the TBL model, the belief in attaining CSR had already led to a broader movement sometimes referred to as Social and Ethical Accounting, Auditing, and Reporting (SEAAR), producing "a variety of competing standards and standard-setting bodies, including the Global Reporting Initiative, the SA

8000 from Social Accountability International, the AA 1000 from Accountability, as well as parts of various ISO standards" (p. 247).

Despite criticisms of TBL and Elkington's original definition, the TBL concept continues to be important in thinking about sustainability and its application to management in both for-profit and public spheres. In this chapter, the focus is upon TBL and sustainability applications, and their importance in higher education and to academic libraries.

Sustainability in Higher Education

Kelly (2008) writes that sustainability in higher education has usually focused on energy, but it is not a single issue. Sustainability, he argues, should not be confused with incremental technology approaches to managing the environment or making the existing campus or consumer culture greener but rather should be viewed as a question of culture: what gives meaning and purpose to human beings. He concludes that universities should become sustainable learning communities, where everyone is an educator and a learner (Kelly, 2008).

Sherman (2008) suggests that sustainability should be viewed as a way to think critically about individual and collective roles in ecological, economic, and social systems and move away from prescriptive lists of what we should do. He advocates for inclusion of sustainability in the curricula of all disciplines, fully integrating it into every aspect of a student's education. To do this, he promotes sustainability as a *big idea*, which he defines as a concept, theme, debate, paradox, question, theory, or principle central to a course of study. For all three areas: social, economic, and environmental, his definition of sustainability coalesces around the concept of limits and future need. The *biggest idea* according to Sherman (2008) is that sustainability reveals interconnectedness across space and time, involving a study of what matters for the future.

Sustainability and its inclusion in all aspects of higher education has been increasing in prominence since 2000. Organizations, such as the Sustainable Endowments Institute, track and measure sustainability initiatives in colleges and universities. The organization's *College Sustainability Report Card* (Sustainable Endowments Institute, 2012), issued from 2007 to 2012, profiles the sustainability efforts of 300 colleges and universities in the United States and Canada. Other organizations like the International Sustainable Campus Network (ISCN) have established sustainability goals to which many institutions of higher education aspire. Founded in 2007, the ISCN provides, "a global forum to support leading colleges, universities, and corporate campuses in the exchange of information, ideas, and best practices for achieving sustainable campus operations and integrating sustainability in research and teaching" (ISCN, 2013).

In 2010, the ISCN, in partnership with the Global University Leaders Forum (GULF), developed the ISCN-GULF Sustainable Campus Charter. Signatories to this document, of which nearly half are U.S. universities, set three principle goals:

- Buildings and their sustainability impacts
- Campus-wide planning and target setting
- Integration of research, teaching, facilities, and outreach (ISCN, 2013).

Other institutions, such as Holme Lacy College (HLC), have conducted audits that measure their TBL impacts. Using the Royal Institution of Chartered Surveyors (RICS) project appraisal tool for sustainability (RICS, 2001), HLC measured environmental, social, and economic impacts of the college to interrelate the three and encourage systems thinking (Dawe, Vetter, & Martin, 2004). Through this method they looked at the institution's ecological footprint, calculating transportation, building energy use and waste; surveyed internal and external stakeholders for the social issues section; and gathered economic data on the impact of the institution locally and regionally based upon income and expenditures. This review formed the basis for the creation of ecological footprint targets for the institution but met with mixed success as the acknowledgement of intuitive versus data-driven judgments conflicted at times with economic needs (Dawe, Vetter, & Martin).

Other colleges and universities are establishing units that focus on implementing sustainability initiatives. The Center for Regional Sustainability (CRS) at San Diego State University fosters research and establishes collaborations across the university and with partners from business, government, and education to generate solutions that will enhance the natural environment, economic vitality, and social equity in the San Diego County, Imperial County, and northern Baja California region (SDSU, n.d.). It draws on scholars, students, community members, businesses, and NGO›s to identify key challenges that need attention, set goals for achieving progress toward a sustainable region, establish benchmarks for meeting those goals, and report on progress. The model provided by SDSU is an example of a number of plans being developed by higher education institutions. Whether incorporated in a sustainability audit, as a scoping review of positive and negative impacts of the social, economic, and environmental status quo, or as a question of culture or curriculum, sustainability is a topic of discussion in academia today.

TBL or Sustainability in Academic Libraries

The literature of Library and Information Science (LIS) contains relatively little on TBL or sustainability. Much of what is available focuses on the planning of new libraries as green buildings and efforts to conserve energy and recycle resources (e.g., Barnes, 2008; Cunningham, 2012; Krige & Kriazis, 2010). In 2011, *Library Journal* launched a series acknowledging new library buildings that demonstrate environmental, social, and economic impacts. The 2012 organizations to receive the designation of New Landmark Libraries (NLL) are all academic. At the top of this list is the Goucher [College] Athenaeum, which is Gold LEED-certified, offers services and space for the campus community as well as members of the general public, and operates a 24-hour restaurant (Schaper, 2012) combining environmental, social, and economic impacts from its opening day.

Among other LIS works which look beyond library buildings, Link (2000) asks librarians to understand the ecology of knowledge and review the issues related to social, economic, and environmental sustainability. The author provides some of the early concepts of TBL, highlights examples of sustainability at the Michigan State University Libraries, and encourages librarians to participate actively in institutional initiatives. Link states that assessment is a critical component for long-term sustainability success.

Jankowska and Marcum (2010) discuss the challenges to sustainability planning faced by academic libraries which they attribute to the development of blended models of maintaining traditional print materials, increasing electronic resources, and providing new Library 2.0 services. The authors question whether this hybrid can be socially, economically, or environmentally sustainable. They point out that academic libraries do not appear to be establishing sustainability indicators to the degree found elsewhere in higher education and advocate for libraries to establish a framework of indicators to help assess their impacts and progress.

Jankowska and Marcum (2010) refer to the maintenance of the print and electronic collections simultaneously as one that poses challenges in terms of the environment (printing, electricity, etc.), the social (duplicate workflows that may be problematic to staff), and economic (the cost of maintaining print and electronic collections). Other authors have addressed this issue and present it as a major challenge to the sustainability of academic libraries. Since the 1980s, serials expenditures and commitments in academic libraries have steadily grown to become the major part of the materials budget, and in many cases, have overtaken the funding for other types of materials, such as books and media. Walters (2008) describes this trend as one that poses a serious long-term problem in that "it reduces the economic sustainability of the library as a whole" (p.578). He suggests that academic libraries refocus on the priority of book collections in undergraduate libraries to move away from the unsustainable model of ever-increasing journal cost commitments. Marcum (2008), addressing this issue, advocates for a renewed emphasis on collection development to ensure the on-going sustainability of library collections.

Whether employing the framework proposed by Jankowska and Marcum (2010) or another method, it is vital that academic libraries develop new models of sustainability and community-impact accounting in general and for collection management in particular. Currently libraries appear to graft new methods of service and information resource provision onto traditional approaches without monitoring their effects on the environment or the priorities of their users. To remain viable and engage in leadership in academia, libraries need to measure their economic, environmental and community impacts and develop new models that enable them to support the three areas effectively.

Examples of TBL-based Applications and Best Practices for Academic Libraries

Academic institutions already employ a wide variety of best practices which when pulled together could contribute to TBL-based applications. Many of these have risen from the prestige of having LEED certified buildings, recycling programs, inclusive planning processes, and budget and resource councils.[1] When attempting to integrate the best TBL applications and practices related to social, environmental, and economic impacts into their operations academic libraries could:

- Perform a comparative analysis, benchmarking against comparator libraries, the levels of employees' skills, salaries, wages, and workloads, to determine if labor practices are fair and sustainable within the library to set targets for compensation equity (social and economic impacts).
- Gather and report on quantitative data about the use of library resources by outside groups (e.g. local businesses or the general public) and obtain

---

1. Keene State College (KSC) in New Hampshire is a case study in all of these practices. Although KSC has not implemented an overt TBL practice, it has LEED-certified buildings, an inclusive annual planning process tied to strategic planning and goals, a budget and resource council for economic efficiencies, and a recycling program that placed 97th out of 293 schools in the per capita classic competition category of Recyclemania and third in New Hampshire, with 13.93 cumulative recyclable pounds per person

qualitative data about how the library has affected community members' lives, information needs, and research projects (social impact).

- Begin an incentive program for all students, faculty, and staff to implement ideas related to environmentally sustainable practices (e.g. waste reduction or energy conservation). Recognition in campus media outlets and on a plaque in the library would serve as a reminder that environmentally sustainable practices are not only implemented but also valued in the academic library (environmental impact).

- Determine KPIs through strategic planning for social, environmental, and economic impacts by using a tool such as the RICS for the library as a whole. Base library evaluation at all levels on these key indicators in regard to resource efficiency and effectiveness (environmental, social, and economic impacts).

- Conduct an audit of the areas library staff frequent within the building. Underutilized spaces may be identified which could then be re-purposed for innovative new uses, saving the cost of a physical renovation. For example, an underused staff lounge might function better and turn into a profit-generating space by repurposing it as a student café (social, environmental, and economic impacts).

- Create an inviting environment by displaying works of art created from recycled materials on library walls. This will increase traffic into the building as people come to view the art, and create an aesthetically pleasing space. Once an environment for displays is established, the library could leverage it to solicit donations of more artwork or funding for maintenance and preservation (social, environmental, and economic impacts).

- Implement print management to contain printing costs and hold individuals financially-accountable for waste. This would reduce the carbon footprint for paper and toner delivery, reduce recycling, and encourage usage of what is needed, not what is possible (environmental and economic impacts).

- Convert print holdings to electronic to save paper and library space that can be repurposed. This allows access to library information anytime from anywhere (social and environmental impacts).

- Install timer lights in all rooms to reduce electricity usage and increase savings (environmental and economic impacts).

- Implement power saving measures for all computers by purchasing thin clients for online public access computers in the library to reduce energy consumption and save money (environmental and economic impacts).

- Conduct business with «green» and «fair trade» vendors for purchasing transactions whenever possible (social and environmental impacts).

- Encourage telecommuting and videoconferencing to reduce travel to work and to meetings (social and environmental impacts).
- Install low flow stools in all restrooms to reduce the amount of water used per flush and sensor-activated faucets that automatically switch on and off based on the proximity of a person to the faucet (environmental and economic impacts).
- Perform annual maintenance on HVAC building systems, making sure that full advantage of balanced air flow is achieved, filters are clean, valves are functional, and humidity is controlled. This will reduce reliance on air conditioning and strain on heating and cooling systems, not only maximizing the functionality of the systems but also avoiding costly repairs that routine maintenance could prevent (environmental and economic impacts).
- Report upon the social and financial returns achieved through library-based jobs and job training for employees, measuring the economic impact of these jobs on the community (social and economic impacts).

Strategic Planning Models

Much of the literature on strategically incorporating TBL into an organization concentrates on for-profit institutions; however, many of the general principles might translate well to an academic library. Rigby and Taber (2008) suggest four steps to increase an organization's sustainability advantage. The first is to determine the vision for the organization. They urge leaders to ask what TBL means to their particular enterprise. This is an important place to begin because environmental issues vary according to geographic location and type of organization while social issues evolve and change over time (Papmehl, 2002).

The second step that Rigby and Taber (2008) suggest is to assess where the organization is at the starting point. Many organizations may have begun to incorporate environmental and social concerns into their *modus operandi* but have not formally acknowledged or assessed them. Step three urges organizations to implement new strategies that evolve from environmental and socially-conscious values while the fourth step encourages constant assessment of outcomes.

Wirtenberg (2008), who studied the qualities of nine sustainable companies, has developed the *Sustainability Pyramid* comprised of "seven core qualities associated with implementing sustainability strategies and achieving triple bottom line... results" (p.16). The foundation level consists of corporate values consistent with sustainability, management's visible support of sustainability efforts, and the placement of those efforts as central to the strategic plan. The middle level, which Wirtenberg calls *traction*, includes developing sustainability metrics and aligning formal and informal organizational systems around sustainability goals and values. The top of the pyramid or the *collaborative integration* level is comprised of the core qualities of systems integration and stakeholder engagement.

Siegal and Longworth (2009) echo and extend these steps and core qualities in their advice to CEOs on incorporating corporate social responsibility into organizations. They recommend that leaders develop green initiatives before claiming them publicly. They cite examples of corporations that have claimed to have gone green while only having made surface changes which had no long-term effect and which hurt those organizations' credibility when revealed to be an unsubstantiated claim. The authors urge leaders to achieve stakeholder engagement in taking steps towards sustainability as well as to identify and focus on those efforts that maximize the organization and have the greatest impact. Finally, they suggest that assigning someone in the organization the role of chief sustainability officer might assist the process of implementing and maintaining corporate social responsibility in organizations.

Metrics

Much of the literature on developing TBL metrics discusses the difficulties of creating meaningful measures. Financial accounting standards are common, but measuring the impact of sustainability and corporate responsibility are not as simple. Papmehl writes, "While generally accepted accounting principles (GAAP) guide financial reporting, no standardized metrics exist for measuring an organization's environmental and social costs and benefits" (p. 22). Not only is there no universal standard for calculating TBL, there is no accepted standard for the measures of the social and environmental categories (Slaper, 2011). However, several approaches to measurement have been suggested. One is the incorporation of sustainability and social responsibility efforts into the balanced scorecard approach (Hubbard, 2009; León-Soriano, Muñoz-Torres, Chalmeta-Rosaleñ, 2010). Another is to develop types of measures for each category that reflect particular impacts relevant to a given institution (Marsh, 2010; Slaper, 2011). Searcy (2009) provides guidance to managers setting metrics this way by proposing a series of questions that might assist them in developing a sustainability performance measurement system. Pourdehnad and Smith (2012) advance the idea of organizations developing a means to track and learn from TBL-related management decisions, much as commercial aviation tracks and learns from crashes, to develop benchmarks for measuring social and environmental impacts.

As a library begins the process of making the strategic changes to support sustainability and social responsibility efforts, a simpler approach to developing TBL metrics might be to benchmark efforts in these areas at the start of the planning process and set outcomes for each of the goals. An example of such a metric might be to reduce the amount of printing done in a library in a year by a specified amount and to measure the outcome based on the boxes of paper and number of print cartridges purchased. Other metrics that tie directly into the previously suggested best practices would be reduction of water, heat, and electricity usage, which are all metered services, so not only would lower costs be captured, but usage of these resources would also be reduced. As with the strategic planning process discussed above, TBL metrics for academic libraries will also need to be locally defined, because of the unique geographic, cultural, environmental, and social concerns faced by every organization.

Conclusion

To effect innovation and implement TBL in academic libraries, library leaders need to engage in two different but integrated processes: change management and change leadership. The former refers to project management aspects of the proposed innovation. Change management involves the study and direction of the practical aspects of embarking on a new venture, such as changes in finances and accounting, personnel distribution, and new ways of doing business (Griffith-Cooper & King, 2007). Most organizational leaders handle this part of the process well. In fact, it is common for a leader to expect change to occur successfully through the communication of the project design and implementation (Brenner, 2008).

Change leadership refers to a set of techniques and principles related to influencing acceptance while reducing resistance among the people in the organization (Griffith-Cooper & King, 2007). This part of the process is often overlooked by those in leadership positions due to their overemphasis on the rational and cognitive aspects of an innovative venture. This oversight may be the principle reason why change initiatives fail (Brenner, 2008). Brenner suggests that it is important to build and launch a change campaign from an organization's strategic platform. By doing this, a leader signals to employees that a change like TBL is related to the already-agreed-upon values of the organization.

Leaders too often rely on top-down communication and do not factor in the need to answer questions and incorporate the input of all members of the organization. Communication about sustainability initiatives is no exception and must straddle the line between telling people what to do and urging them to do the right thing. If communication is not straightforward and honest, the message could be heard as "green washing" or doing something just to look environmentally savvy (Bolch, 2008, p.59). Wirtenberg (2008) suggests that leaders engage in authentic conversations with their employees to build a sustainability culture. She also emphasizes two fundamental elements to moving to a culture of sustainability in business and other enterprises. The first is to integrate sustainable values, strategies, principles, metrics, and practices into the core business plans of the company and the second is to develop leaders throughout the enterprise that wholeheartedly support the sustainability initiatives.

Quinn and Dalton (2009) offer recommendations for leadership behavior based on their study of leaders in organizations with a history of sustainability practices. The first of these focuses on the importance of the way the leader sets the direction and suggests that a positive, enthusiastic introduction elicits stronger buy-in from stakeholders. Quinn and Dalton also report that leaders successful in establishing sustainability initiatives tend to use the language of the particular organizational environment (e.g., an academic library) when communicating about new initiatives.

Initiating and implementing TBL in academic libraries will require leadership throughout the organization as well as a strong and grounded belief that TBL, which integrates economic, environmental, and social performance, is integral to the sustainable future of libraries. Making the environmental impacts in the construction of new academic library buildings a high priority is a vital step in this process. However, it is equally important for academic library leaders to consider their overall social, environmental, and economic impacts on their communities, from planning to assessment, as a way to demonstrate their value. Incorporating TBL practices is likely to be a unique experience for each library, but with the models from other industries, it should be possible to adopt TBL as a priority of the organization.

References

Adams, C., Frost, G., & Webber, W. (2004). Triple bottom line: A review of the literature. In A. Henriques & J. Richardson (Eds.). *The triple bottom line: Does it all add up?* (pp. 17-25). London: Earthscan.

Barnes, L.L. (2008, October). Libraries can go green. *ILA Reporter, 47*.

Bolch, M. (2008). Speaking green. *HRMagazine, 53(6)*, 58-61.

Brenner, M. (2008). It's all about people: Change management's greatest lever. *Business Strategy Series, 9*(3), 132-137.

Cunningham, H. (2012). Partnering for paper reduction. *Feliciter, 58*(1), 18.

Dawe, G.F.M., Vetter, A., & Martin. S. (2004). An overview of ecological footprinting and other tools and their application to the development of sustainability process: Audit and methodology at Holme Lacy College, UK. *International Journal of Sustainability in Higher Education, 5*(4), 340-371.

Elkington, J. (1998). *Cannibals with forks: The triple bottom line of 21ˢᵗ century business.* Gabriola Island, BC: New Society Publishers.

Griffith-Cooper, B., & King, K. (2007). The partnership between project management and organizational change: Integrating change management with change leadership. *Performance Improvement 46*(1), 14-20.

Hubbard, G. (2009). Measuring organizational performance: Beyond the triple bottom line. *Business Strategy and the Environment, 19*, 171-191.

International Sustainable Campus Network (ISCN). (2013). *The ISCN mission and approach.* Retrieved from http://www.international-sustainable-campus-network.org/about/introduction-and-analysis.html

Jankowska, M. A., & Marcum, J. W. (2010). Sustainability challenge for academic libraries: Planning for the future. *College & Research Libraries, 71*(2), 160-170.

Kelly, T. (2008). Higher education and sustainability: Universities can have no greater mission than this – Earth Day and every day. Retrieved from http://www.sustainableunh.unh.edu/highereducation

Krige, B., & Kriazis, J. (2010). Sustainability key to Macquarie University's new library. *inCite, 31*(9), 18.

León-Soriano, R., Muñoz-Torres, M. J., & Chalmeta-Rosaleñ, R. (2010). Methodology for sustainability strategic planning and management. *Industrial Management + Data Systems, 110*(2), 249-268. doi: 10.1108/02635571011020331

Link, T. (2000). Transforming higher education through sustainability and environmental education. *Issues in Science and Technology Librarianship.* Retrieved from http://www.istl.org/00-spring/article4.html

Marcum, J.W. (2008). Collection building barter: a proposal. *The Bottom Line: Managing Library Finances, 21*(2), 49-51.

Marsh, C. M. H. (2010). Sustainability and financial management. *Finance, 124*(1), 54-56.

Mintz, S. M. (2011). Triple bottom line reporting for CPAs. *The CPA Journal, 81*(12), 26-33.

Norman, W., & MacDonald, C. (2004). Getting to the bottom of "Triple Bottom Line." *Business Ethics Quarterly, 14*(2), 243-262.

Papmehl, A. (2002). Beyond the GAAP. *CMA Management, 76*(5), 20-25.

Pourdehnad, J., & Peter A.C. Smith. (2012). Sustainability, organizational learning, and lessons learned from aviation. *The Learning Organization, 19*(1), 77-86. doi: 10.1108/09696471211190374

Quinn, L., & Dalton, M. (2009). Leading for sustainability: Implementing the tasks of leadership. *Corporate Governance, 9*(1), 21-38. doi: 10.1108/14720700910936038

Richardson, J. (2004). Accounting for sustainability: Measuring quantities or enhancing qualities? In A. Henriques & J. Richardson (Eds.). *The triple bottom line: Does it all add up?* (pp. 34-44). London: Earthscan.

RICS. (2001). *Comprehensive project appraisal: Towards sustainability.* Policy Unit Paper, Royal Institution of Chartered Surveyors, London.

Rigby, D., & Tager, S. (2008). Learning the advantages of sustainable growth. *Strategy & Leadership, 36*(4), 24-28.

Rogers, K., & Hudson, B. (2011). The triple bottom line: The synergies of transformative perceptions and practices for sustainability. *OD Practitioner, 43*(4), 3-9.

San Diego State University. (n.d.). *Center for Regional Sustainability.* Retrieved from http://crs.sdsu.edu/dus/regionalsustainability/

Schaper, L. (2012, July 1). Standing tall on campus. *Library Journal, 137*(12), 20-23.

Searcy, C. (2009). Setting a course in corporate sustainability performance measurement. *Measuring Business Excellence, 13*(3), 49-57. doi: 10.1108/13683040910984329

Sherman, D.J. (2008). Sustainability: What's the big idea? A strategy for transforming the higher education curriculum. *Mary Ann Liebert, Inc., 1*(3), 188-195. doi: 10.1089/SUS.2008.9960.

Siegal, Y., & Longworth, A. (2009, January/February). Sustainability for CEOs. *Chief Executive, 238*, 45-48.

Slaper, T. F., & Hall, T. J. (2011). The triple bottom line: What is it and how does it work? *Indiana Business Review, 86*(1), 4-8.

Sustainable Endowments Institute. (2012). *The College Sustainability Report Card.* Retrieved from http://www.greenreportcard.org/

Walters, W.H. (2008). Journal prices, book acquisitions, and sustainable college library collections. *College & Research Libraries, 69*(6), 576-86.

Wirtenberg, J. (2008). Leaving a legacy: Do it by building a sustainable enterprise. *Leadership Excellence, 25*(11), 16.

Becoming Sustainability Leaders: A Professional Development Experience for Librarians

Madeleine Charney

Abstract

In this chapter, the author describes her work instructing other library and information professionals during a two-week course on sustainability. The author details the interactions amongst librarians, who are sincerely invested in sustainability-related issues.

Introduction

In January 2013, the Sustainability Studies Librarian at the University of Massachusetts Amherst was invited to teach a two-week online course through Library Juice Academy, which offers professional development workshops for librarians and other library staff. The course, *The Sustainability Movement on Campus: Forming a Library Action Plan for Engagement* was intended to expand the network of library professionals interested in deepening their role and finding allies in the sustainability movement, particularly in higher education. Others who were eager to jump start their engagement were equally welcome-- for we all learn from one another. To better understand the elusive term "sustainability," the author considers this definition from *The Sustainability Revolution*, a book by Andres R. Edward (2005) in which he frames sustainability as, "…

an alternative that supports economic viability and healthy ecosystems by modifying consumption patterns and implementing a more equitable social framework" (p.3).

Forming a Library Action Plan for Engagement

The main goal of the course was to empower librarians to explore ways to engage in sustainability activities at their libraries and institutions as well within the library profession. Such activities include areas of teaching, outreach, and collaboration, as well as facilities design and management as seen in Appendix 1.

The course content was not to be received passively but rather, it was offered as a spur for participants to reflect on their roles within the grid of sustainability education. Girding this new cohort with confidence in their leadership potential, this quote from Vaclav Havel was placed at the top of the syllabus: "We must not be afraid of dreaming the seemingly impossible if we want the seemingly impossible to become a reality" (Quotd.org , n.d.).

The course welcomed 12 participants into a guided experience, including seven academic librarians and a paraprofessional, one school librarian, and three library school students. The course commenced with introductions on the forum for Moodle (the course management system). Participants' subject specialties, mirroring the multi-disciplinary nature of sustainability, spanned a number of disciplines, from poetry, government documents, and life sciences to urban planning, special collections, and mathematics. Four others self-identified as reference or instruction librarians. Many were already involved with library and campus sustainability committees. Beyond sharing their professional backgrounds, participants wrote of their passion for community gardening, raising chickens, biking, volunteering for environmental organizations, making art (as sustainably as possible) and other creative, health-minded, community-related activities. Within the very first day, participants were finding common ground. For instance, one participant mentioned a campus garden project she oversees and another participant responded, saying she had been a leader at the same site years before. Their delight in this connection and continuity was clear. A library school student responded to a string of the posts, "I had no idea Sustainability in libraries was so big on the North/Eastern front, or that it could reach out in so many different areas, and this really inspires me to keep at it, and to keep looking into research, and formulating my own while I work on my MLIS!" (Anonymous, personal communication, January 8, 2013).

In the introduction, participants were asked: "What motivated you to take this course?" Repeatedly, participants wrote of the intersection of their personal

and professional lives. One participant responded: "My investment in sustainability comes into play in my personal life. Like [another participant] and others
in the course, I am interested in permaculture. Because I live in the desert, I am
especially interested in water harvesting and solar power" (Anonymous, personal
communication, January 8, 2013). Another participant reflected: "Having seen
how campus and community sustainability programs have made a difference
in my life, I'd like to help to contribute so that others can benefit. ... My other
motivation is the desire to have my personal interest in sustainability and permaculture not be completely separate from my work life as a special collections librarian, as it is now" (Anonymous, personal communication, January 9, 2013).
After hearing the previous response, another participant stated: "I am motivated
daily by my student staff workers, who, despite their majors and career goals,
hold a social and environmental consciousness that amazes me, and gives me
hope for the future" (Anonymous, January 9, 2013). The websites, related readings, and Facebook page recommendations flew back and forth, flavoring the
forum with the communitarian spirit characteristic of sustainability activism.

The course got underway with a leadership assessment exercise, in which
participants reflected on their individual styles and considered their individual
potential for capacity building. Readings (see Appendix 2) were drawn from
book chapters, professional and scholarly publications, and reports, all written
by and for librarians. Participants also viewed short videos of students' campus
sustainability projects. Along the way, participants were invited to consider their
relationships within their libraries and campus networks with their sights on
making connections to specific groups (e.g. sustainability-related committees)
and people (e.g. sustainability managers).

An early reading assignment, the text of the American College and University Presidents Climate Commitment (ACUPCC), framed the course within the
context of climate change and higher education. The 650 campus administrators
who signed the ACUPCC acknowledge they are, "deeply concerned about the
unprecedented scale and speed of global warming and its potential for large-
scale, adverse health, social, economic and ecological effects" (ACUPCC, 2006,
para. 1). More than an exercise in ethics, administrators are bound to carry out
certain actions within two years of signing. This includes developing an institutional action plan for becoming climate neutral, which includes, "Actions to
make climate neutrality and sustainability a part of the curriculum and other
educational experience for all students" (ACUPCC, para 5). Being familiar with
this text helps participants justify their engagement with sustainability issues in
the workplace. Since three Canadians were enrolled, the course also touched on
the Talloires Declaration, an official statement signed by over 360 university
administrators in over 40 countries, including Canada (Talloires, 2001, para. 1).

Both of these administrative statements offer a "green light" for activities once fueled mostly by grassroots efforts.

Day-by-day, participants identified an area to explore for an intended action: Campus, Library Building, Library Outreach, Faculty, Students, and Library Colleagues. The intention included a timeframe for completion: right away, during the next semester, within the year, or an alternative timeframe. Participants were given the option to share their intended actions in the Moodle forum and many took advantage of the opportunity. Reading others' actions cultivated cross-pollination and inspiration to move forward; "You may have given me another action item! I haven't seen any cisterns on campus, but I could talk to someone in our sustainability office and see if they have plans to install any" (Anonymous, personal communication, January 10, 2013). Postings were also peppered with comments such as "I've been meaning to ..." and "I should be..." and "We haven't started that yet but intend to..." Participants longed to engage sustainability issues but were constrained by time and institutional barriers. At times there were expressions of frustration. For example, "While I found it relatively easy to make changes and get 'buy in' in my previous positions, I find it much more difficult to make changes in an academic environment -- there's a lot of bureaucracy and it is often so difficult to figure out just who (if anyone) is responsible for what on an academic campus" (Anonymous, personal communication, January 11, 2013).

The final part of the course looked at the library profession and potential for advancing sustainability engagement. All were encouraged to join the Sustainability Librarians LinkedIn group, which was launched by Beth Filar Williams, University of North Carolina Greensboro in 2011 and now boasts 270 members. Some mentioned their efforts to *persuade* ALA to approve the Resolution on Divestment of Holdings in Fossil Fuel Companies and Libraries' Role in a Peaceful Transition to a Fossil-Free Economy (ALA 2013). The timing of this conversation was perfect as the author was concurrently working with a small group of librarians to initiate a Sustainability Round Table under ALA. The approval process for the Round Table provided more fodder for our course discussion. Some participants stepped up to help promote signing the e-petition (with one continuing to play an active role in planning future activities). Less than two weeks after the culmination of the course, ALA's Council passed a motion brought by the Committee on Organization to create a Sustainability Round Table (SustainRT), described as, "a forum for ALA members to exchange ideas and concerns regarding sustainability in order to move toward a more equitable, healthy, and economically viable society"(Borman, 2013, para. 3). SustainRT was born!

The course culminated with the submission of a seven-part Action Plan that matched the needs of each participant's library and institution and suited their comfort levels for professional involvement. In solidarity, the instructor wrote and shared her own Action Plan along with the class as well as offering individual feedback as the course progressed. Intended to be a fluid document, updated and revised over time, the instructor recommended posting the plan prominently in work areas. The course wrapped up with well wishes and obvious connections amongst the cohort such as "Hope to meet you all one day in person...This will be a lifelong passion of mine, so I'm sure we will." "It is so inspirational to see the wonderful ideas and plans everyone is creating. I am looking forward to the creation of a Sustainability Roundtable where I hope we can meet face to face. Keep up the good work everyone. You are the change." "It is nice to be enrolled in a class with like-minded folks." One participant closely echoed the author's own vision for the future when she wrote, "I hope one day, it [sustainability] will become just as common as eating and exercising, without requiring the word "conscious" anywhere, as it will become a necessary part of daily life!...I guess for now we serve as ambassadors of knowledge and can send these messages out to many in the various other ways that they might understand."

Conclusions

Besides coming away with a tailored Action Plan, participants had tapped into a group of like-minded library staff and learned about professional forums for support around sustainability projects and ideas. They became aware of opportunities for collaboration within their libraries and institutions as well as acknowledging gaps in funding, communication, and willingness to engage with an eye toward solving these problems.

As for the instructor's motivation for engaging in the sustainability movement on campus, an anecdote comes to mind. A student group on her campus recently presented a request to the Faculty Senate -- the campus divests from fossil fuel investments. Stating the irony of teaching sustainability while promoting a main culprit of climate change, the students were articulate and clearly impassioned about the topic. However, when questioned about the factual basis of their argument, their response did not instill confidence in their audience. Their citations were randomly selected web sites with little or no evidence-based sources. Librarians are a vital part of the force working to train the next generation of leaders in a globally challenged society. Helping shape students critical thinking skills and guiding them toward reliable resources will go a long way toward their efforts on campus, in their professions, and as citizens advocating for a healthier, more equitable society. Had these students sought the assistance of a librarian, their presentation would likely have been more potent and productive.

The time is running out in May 2013, the planet's CO2 levels climbed higher than they have been in at least 800,000 years. Perhaps crossing the 400 ppm mark will play a role in awakening the public to the dangers of runaway climate change (Montaigne, 2013, para. 3). There is an urgency underlying the work of librarians to be part of this awakening. Librarians need to be gadflies, support one another as professionals, foster communities of learning, empower the next generation of leaders and envision together so that the seemingly impossible becomes a reality.

References

American College & University Presidents' Climate Commitment (ACUPCC) (2006). Text of the American College & University Presidents' Climate Commitment. Retrieved from http://www.presidentsclimatecommitment. org/about/commitment

American Library Association (2013, July 1). 2012-2013 ALA CD#42. Resolution on Divestment of Holdings in Fossil Fuel Companies and Libraries' Role in a Peaceful Transition to a Fossil Free Economy. Retrieved from http://www.ala.org/aboutala/sites/ala.org.aboutala/files/content/governance/council/council_documents/2013_annual_council_docs/cd_42_ fossil fuel Chicago-7-1-2013 (f).pdf

Borman, L. (2013, January 29). Inside scoop: News and views from inside AL. Council II session. Blog posted to http://americanlibrariesmagazine.org/ inside-scoop/council-iisession

Edwards, A.R. (2005). *The Sustainability revolution: Portrait of a paradigm shift*. Gabriol Island, Canada: New Society Publishers.

Montaigne, F. (2013, May 14). Record 400ppm CO2 milestone 'feels like we're moving into another era.' *Guardian UK*. Retrieved from http:// www.guardian.co.uk/environment/2013/may/14/record-400ppm-co2- carbonemissions

Quotd.org. Václav Havel, 1936 – 2011. Retrieved from http://www.qotd.org/ search/search.html?aid=6820&page=3

Talloires Declaration (2001). Retrieved from http://www.ulsf.org/programs_ talloires.html

Appendix 1:

Example of a Seven-part Action Plan

Part One - My Campus

Action(s) I plan to take:

A. Check on current status of Sustainability Committee

By when: <u>right away</u> / spring 2013 / within the year/ other:

B. Arrange for a joint announcement of our Sustainability Research Guide from the Library and the Office of Sustainability in the University's weekly email newsletter.

By when: <u>right away</u>/spring 2013/within the year/other:

Part Two - My Library - Building

Action(s) I plan to take:

A. Share ideas from *Greening Libraries* book with Facilities Department

By when: right away / <u>spring 2013</u> / within the year/ other:

B.Discuss forming a library green team

By when: <u>right away</u> / spring 2013 / within the year/ other:

C. Add "Turn me off" stickers to lights and computers throughout our buildings. Deploy members of our Green Team to attach the stickers in both public and staff areas.

By when: right away / spring 2013 <u>/ within the year</u>/ other:

Part Three - My Library - Outreach

Action(s) I plan to take:

A. Continue development of Sustainability Libguide and promote it to faculty

By when: <u>right away</u> / spring 2013 / within the year/ other:

B. Propose an exhibition for Earth Day 2013 highlighting books, DVDs, databases, and the Sustainability Research Guide.

By when: <u>right away</u> / spring 2013 / within the year/ other:

Part Four - My Colleagues (librarians and other staff at our library)

Action(s) I plan to take:

A. Raise green issues at each staff meeting

By when: <u>right away</u> / spring 2013 / within the year/ other:

B. Our collection development with regard to sustainability collections is a bit all over the place right now...In addition to the Environmental and Agricultural Studies librarians, I will invite other librarians to the table: Architecture, Civil Engineering, Transportation Engineering, Physical Geography, Sociology, Philosophy, and Anthropology.

By when: right away / spring 2013 / <u>within the year</u>/ other:

Part Five- My Faculty

Action(s) I plan to take:

A. Inquire whether faculty training is planned and offer support in the form of library services.

By when: right away / spring 2013 / within the year/ other: summer 2013

B. Find out if my campus has developed Learning Outcomes for sustainability curricula.

By when: right away / spring 2013 / within the year/ other: summer 2013

Part Six - My Students

Action(s) I plan to take:

A. Suggest service learning opportunities in the Library, in collaboration with the Office of Sustainability. Ideally these opportunities would align with curriculum, be interdisciplinary, and bring faculty onboard as well. For instance, a design competition tied to sustainability and library space or perhaps a waste audit.

By when: right away / spring 2013 / within the year/ <u>other: within the next couple of years</u>

Part Seven - My Library Associations and Professional Networks

Action(s) I plan to take:

A. Campaign for ALA to disinvest from fossil fuel stocks

By when: <u>right away</u> / spring 2013 / within the year/ other:

B. Be a more active member of the Sustainability Librarians LinkedIn Group

By when: right away / <u>spring 2013</u> / within the year/ other:

Appendix 2

Selected course readings

Andresen, C., Gustavson, A., Hisle, D. & Reynolds, M. (2012). Tending the garden: Growing your own green library committee. In Antonelli, M. & McCullough, M. (Eds.). *Greening libraries* (pp. 93-103). Los Angeles: Library Juice Press.

Association for the Advancement of Sustainability in Higher Education. (2010). *Sustainability curriculum in higher education: A call to action.* Retrieved from http://www.aashe.org/files/A_Call_to_Action_final%282%29.pdf

Breiman, J., Brunvand, A., Bullough, E., Lenart, J., & Regan, A. (2012). University of Utah J.

Willard Marriott Library: Sustainability collection development policy report. Retrieved from http://content.lib.utah.edu/utils/getfile/collection/ireua/id/2620/filename/2621.pdf

Charney, M., & Connare, C. (2012, Fall). Sustainability fund fuels activities at the University of Massachusetts Amherst Libraries. *College Libraries Section of the Association of College and Research Libraries* 28 (2): 4-5. Retrieved from http://www.ala.org/acrl/sites/ala.org.acrl/files/content/aboutacrl/directoryofleadership/sections/cls/clswebsite/newsletters/cls_fall2012.pdf

Crowe, K. (2010). Student affairs connection: Promoting the library through co-curricular activities. *Collaborative Librarianship* 2 (3): 154-158. Retrieved from http://collaborativelibrarianship.org/index.php/jocl/article/view/77

Duke University. (2010). AASHE list of faculty professional development groups. Duke University, Trillium Project Web site. Retrieved from http://sites.duke.edu/trillium/

Forrest, C., Munro, K. & Kate Zoellner. (2012). Toward sustainable conferences: Going green at the 2009 ACRL national conference in Seattle. In Antonelli, M. & McCullough, M. (Eds.). *Greening libraries* (pp. 141-155). Los Angeles: Library Juice Press.

Academic Libraries as Sustainability Leaders

Karren E. Nichols

Abstract

Academic libraries are living laboratories where students, faculty, and staff can easily connect to find the space and resources to explore environmental sustainability and enhance the learning experience. The J. Willard Marriott Library recognized this in 2008 when it made a formal commitment to becoming a sustainability leader at the University of Utah. Throughout this chapter the readers will find a case study for the Marriott Library Waste Pod Solution and several examples of projects that incorporate sustainability related projects, student/staff collaboration, and provide examples of the library as a living laboratory. All the projects have influenced patron and staff behavior and brought greater awareness of sustainability issues to campus.

Introduction

As the central hub for information on campus, the academic library has a responsibility to support not only teaching and its patrons' research needs but also to provide an environment filled with learning opportunities. The J. Willard Marriott Library recognized this in 2008 when the University of Utah signed the American College & University Presidents' Climate Commitment and made the decision to become a sustainability leader on campus. The library demonstrated its commitment by devoting staff resources to sustainability efforts and recruiting volunteers to spearhead a wide-variety of sustainability programs.

The library provides the perfect arena to test out new ideas, gauge attitudes, and educate for sustainability. Since 2008, the Marriott Library has implemented a large number of green initiatives and become the model for green teams across the University of Utah campus. These initiatives have ranged from participating in the creation of the University's climate action plan and piloting a campus green team expansion program, to providing student internships and implementing an expanded recycling and waste reduction program within the library.

Funding for these efforts have come from a variety of sources including one corporate and one anonymous individual donor, the Sustainable Campus Initiative Fund that is paid for by a student fee of $2.50/ semester (http://sustainability.utah.edu/get-involved/students/sustainable-campus-fund.php), Associated Students of the University of Utah (ASUU), the Rocky Mountain Blue Sky Utility Match, library funds, and funds from the Office of the University President. The education piece has been crucial to the success of the sustainability initiatives. The library has, for example, created a number of highly persuasive displays that demonstrate the outcomes of changing individual behaviors in such arenas as printing, recycling, and non-sustainable consumption behaviors. The installation of water bottle filling stations that count the number of plastic water bottles saved allows for a series of non-confrontational "teaching moments." The library has had many testimonials from employees, for example, that such efforts have led to behavioral changes and a greater awareness of the kind of proactive choices people can make in order to have a smaller carbon foot-print.

Figure 1. Recycling Station in Knowledge Commons, Marriott Library.

What makes sustainability projects unique in an academic library is that there are unlimited opportunities for student, staff, and faculty collaboration. For example, we have worked to connect sustainability initiatives with student internships or class projects. These kinds of collaborations enhance the learning experience and can offer real life work experience and opportunities to learn from each other while gaining new perspective. This chapter offers a case study of the Marriott Library Waste Pod Solution, a description of the campus Green Team Expansion, a description of projects paid for by the Sustainable Campus Initiative Fund (SCIF) and student internships.

Case Study: Marriott Library Waste Pod Solution

The Marriott Library, at any time, employs approximately 190 full-time staff and 160 part-time staff. The building is 517,000 net square feet, with a gate count exceeding 1.5 million annually. The library does not employ custodial staff. Custodial staff are managed and employed by Campus Facilities Management. The library's facilities manager liaises with campus facilities to ensure library needs are met.

The Marriott Library Green Committee (MLGC) is a group of staff, faculty, and students, charged with identifying and implementing sustainability solutions in the library. In December 2009, the MLGC was asked to consider the possibility of all library staff assisting with the Library's recycling efforts. Specifically, the request was to remove paper recycling from individual work spaces to a centralized location. The desired outcome of this effort was to free up custodial staff time so that more attention could be paid to public areas, thus improving the public face of our building. The catalyst for this was a recession-driven, campus-wide reduction in custodial staff and a lower custodial service level being assigned to the Library.

Marriott Library Waste Pod Solution

In 2008, Director Joyce Ogburn of the J. Willard Marriott Library convened a staff task force to develop recommendations for enhancing sustainable practices in the library. The report led to the formation of a standing Green Committee and many positive changes. In the spring of 2010, the library expanded its recycling program by implementing centralized waste stations in its staff areas. These waste pods make it convenient for staff and faculty to deposit and sort all waste from workspaces into separate containers for aluminum, cardboard, papers, and plastics. Additional drop-off points were also designated for battery recycling in both public and staff areas. Waste pods and additional drop-off points make recycling easy and encourage staff to throw away less and recycle more. The library continues to recycle, re-purpose, and re-use items such as furniture, Styrofoam, packing materials, and telephone books.

Figure 2. Marriott Library highlight from the University of Utah, Energy and Environmental Stewardship Initiative: 2010 Climate Action Plan (Office Sustainability, 2010.)

It was the position of the MLGC that discontinuing removal of only mixed paper and office pack from office/cubicle/work spaces would have a negative impact on recycling efforts, resulting in paper ending up in trash cans. The committee believed that requiring staff to remove all waste from office/cubicle/work spaces and sort into conveniently located waste pods that contained receptacles for plastics, aluminum, mixed paper, office pack, cardboard, and trash, would not only reduce the amount of time custodial staff spent collecting waste but also increase amount of recycling being collected and reduce the amount of waste being produced as individuals became more aware of and active in the process. These waste pods would be located in non-public areas library-wide.

A waste pod is a centralized location designated for staff to deposit all waste from their workspaces. Waste is defined as trash and all recyclables designated by campus to be collected by custodial staff. Each pod has clearly identified containers for the deposit of mixed paper, office pack, plastic, cardboard, aluminum, and trash. The bin labels were designed to reflect the same color and similar image as purchased recycling quads used in public space as seen in Figure 1. No new bins were purchased for this project. The containers were created by repurposing existing trash bins into recycling bins as seen on Figure 3.

Waste pods also reduced the frequency custodial staff needed to visit each office/cubicle/work area. At that time, custodians would visit each office/cubicle/work area several times per week: three times per week to pick up trash, three times per week to pick up recycling, and once to vacuum. Each of these tasks was often performed by a different staff member. Implementation of centralized waste pods resulted in custodial staff needing to visit office/cubicle/work areas only once per week to vacuum and once or twice per week to collect items at the designated waste pod locations.

This recommendation was presented to and accepted by the library's executive council in January 2010. It was further agreed that to maintain individual accountability for compliance with waste removal procedures, language supporting library and university commitments to sustainability was added to the Marriott Library organization-wide competencies.

Figure 3. Staff Waste Pod, Marriott Library.

Implementation

The time line for implementation of this project was six months. Roll out of this project began in February of 2010 and the project was completed in August, 2010.

PHASE 1: The first phase of this project included meeting with the custodial team leader and library facilities manager to determine locations for each waste pod and identify individual and group responsibilities. Pods were placed in visible locations so they could be easily found and accessible to staff.

The custodial team leader was responsible for the designation and training of staff that would be responsible for collecting waste at each pod. The custodial team leader was also responsible for determining the frequency each pod would be checked, making any necessary adjustments to this schedule and reporting any problems to the library facilities manager.

The MLGC was responsible for project planning, oversight of project implementation, and developing training and reference material for each department to ease the staff's transition to this new workflow. The committee was also responsible for coordinating with the library facilities manager and campus recycling to design the new labels and signage for the waste pods.

The library facilities manager was responsible for overseeing the efforts of campus custodians and the MLGC to ensure that the overall needs of the library were being met. Final approval of location of waste pods, signage placement, and any space use changes fell to the library facilities manager. Library facilities staff would assist with the gathering, setup and labeling of bins for each waste pod once the roll out schedule was set. A recycling liaison was established in each department to assist with training and be the point of contact for staff questions in their area. A peer-to-peer training model was used to educate members in each area on how to properly sort and dispose of waste.

PHASE 2: Meetings were scheduled with each department to answer questions and address any unique needs. Departments such as acquisitions and library computing required additional bins due to the high volume of cardboard and to collect packing materials for reuse and Styrofoam for recycling. Intra Library Loan and areas of Special Collections required additional 90 gallon bins for mixed paper and office pack. Areas that included copy machines and printers were staged with additional office pack bins that custodians were responsible for emptying.

Since the fifth floor of the library contained the greatest concentration of staff work areas, it was decided that roll out of waste pods would begin on that floor and work its way down to level one. Department meetings and area pod setups were done in the same week. Smaller departments shared a single waste pod but had their own training session and recycling liaison. A total of 20 waste pods were setup building wide.

Outcomes

The desired outcomes for this project were met. All staff members were actively involved in the library recycling program and custodial time was reallocated to allow more time to clean in public spaces. Initially, the library anticipated that weekly or bi-weekly pickup of waste and recyclables at pods would be sufficient. It was determined that a daily check of waste pods was necessary to eliminate odors and keep materials from piling up. Ongoing reminders about what and how to recycle items are provided to staff via email, at staff meetings, and through a variety of rotating posters and exhibits.

Campus Green Team Expansion Pilot

In 2011, the Marriot Library participated in a campus pilot program that focused on the expansion of green teams and the development of tools to provide teams with project resources and a uniform approach. This pilot included funding from the Office of the University President to purchase five hours per week, for a period of one year of Marriott Library staff's time to dedicate to this project. During this project, campus green teams increased from 8 to 18. The project committee consisted of five members from different University of Utah departments: two from the Office of Sustainability, one from the Energy Management Office, one from the Marriott Library, and one from Recycling and Waste Management. The library was chosen to participate in this pilot based on its already demonstrated successes with its own green team.

A Green Teams eToolkit. It was created by the library as a resource for campus green teams using LibGuides, a SpringShare product (http://campus-guides.lib.utah.edu/content.php?pid=225954&sid=1871399). This resource includes an explanation for having a green team, information on how to connect with advisors and resources on campus, including other green teams, and documents and media to help teams get started.

The library regularly hosts a mix of sustainability related events, organized by students, staff, and faculty, such as Green Team Workshops, Social Soups, the Annual Green Teams Summit, the Innovative Sustainability Summit, and the Presidents Sustainability Advisory Board. Offering meeting space for these groups and co-hosting or sponsoring events is one of the many ways the library remains visible on campus. At the end of this pilot, the library hosted the first annual Green Teams Summit, organized by the University of Utah's Office of Sustainability.

Rooftop Garden Projects. A rooftop garden was installed above the library's three-and-a-half story Automated Retrieval Center (ARC) to protect the structure and to increase the energy efficiency of the building. This garden can be seen from the third floor study space. Currently, two student sustainability research projects are being conducted in this garden space. Both of these projects are funded by SCIF. The University of Utah Beekeepers Association has space on the rooftop garden designated to house multiple hives. These hives provide students hands on experience with beekeeping, while learning about the importance of bees in our environment. It also provides great benefit to our garden blooms, which are all drought resistant plants and native to Utah.

University of Utah Apiary Project: Beehives on Campus. The U of U Apiary project was funded through SCIF. The project teaches beekeeping, assigns students to care for individual hives, produces local honey for the University Farmers Market, and is used for research purposes. The research component of this project will participate in a longitudinal study looking at the effects of global warming on the timing of flowering plants and nectar flows. The data collected from this project will be synthesized by a NASA scientist, the results then sent back to the University. Future research projects will include purchasing pollen traps to identify the types of plants bees use to collect pollen.

Green Roof Lysimeters. The Green Roof Lysimeter project is a Civil and Environmental Engineering research project. Two to three small green roof lysimeters will be placed on the library's rooftop garden. The project will explore green roof choices and identify what works best in the local climate and the specific environmental benefits. The project will result in recommendations to campus on how green roofs could impact storm water runoff and/or impact building energy consumption.

Water Bottle Filling Station Project: Just Fill It! Just Fill It! is an exhibit designed and created by students to increase awareness of the negative impact of plastic bottles on our environment and to encourage people to use refillable water bottles. The exhibit, as seen in Figure 4, was installed in conjunction with the installation of the water bottle filling stations seen in Figure 5 and was funded through the same SCIF grant. Within 18 months of installation of two water bottle filling stations, the equivalent of 254,054 plastic water bottles had been

Figure 4. Just Fill It! Exhibit, Marriott Library.

diverted from the landfill. The creation of an
exhibit to accompany the new filling stations
expanded the student learning opportunity
and added a patron education component to
the project. By working directly with the library facilities manager, students learned how
to plan and implement a project that required
working with multiple departments on campus to get the water bottle filling stations
installed. Students then employed research
skills to find credible data sources to use in
the exhibit and walked through the creative
process for design. Water bottles used in the
exhibit were collected from the library's waste
stream for reuse. This exhibit is now part of the library's rotating exhibit collection and runs annually.

Figure 5. Water Bottle Filling
Stations, Marriott Library.

The Life Cycle of Paper. *The Life Cycle of Paper* exhibit seen in Figure 6
was one of two exhibits created as part of a larger project, *The Paper Project*,
which was designed to educate and create awareness about paper consumption,
print alternatives, environ-
mental impacts, and indi-
vidual choice. This project
was funded through SCIF.
The exhibit focused on increasing awareness of the
impact of small behavior
changes on paper con-
sumption. An exhibit was
created that told the story
of paper, showing the
reduction of paper con-
sumed per person in the
United States by simply
changing margins, using a
smaller font, duplex print-

Figure 6. The Paper Project :
The Life Cycle of Paper Exhibit,
Marriott Library.

ing, etc. This exhibit was a collaborative effort of the MLGC and the University
of Utah's Enviro Club, an ASUU student group. During this project students
held think-tanks to identify what components to include in the exhibit's design
that would catch the attention of students. The result was an exhibit that told

a story, identified both global and local impacts, and was multi-dimensional in design. This exhibit is now part of the library's rotating exhibit collection.

Print Smart & Print Alternatives. The *Print Smart & Print* Alternatives exhibit was one of two exhibits created and funded as part of a larger SCIF project, *The Paper Project.* This exhibit focused primarily on library resources as seen in Figure 7, as well as our archival responsibilities as a research institution. It informed patrons as to why the Marriott Library chose not to move to 100% post-consumer recycled paper in all staff spaces, what print alternative resources are available in the library, and emphasized the reduction and recycling of paper if you must print. As a result of this project, grant funds were used to purchase the initial

Figure 7. Print Alternatives Exhibit, Window 2, Marriott Library.

quantities of paper required to switch to 30% post-consumer recycled paper in all public space and fourteen new recycling quads in student study spaces throughout the library. The library chose not to move to recycled content paper in staff spaces at this time but is looking at how to incorporate it without compromising institutional archival requirements. During the creation of this exhibit, students learned about preservation and archiving requirements. Staff and faculty learned that the quality of post-consumer content paper has greatly improved over the past several years and that there is a cost savings associated with its use. This exhibit is now part of the library's rotating exhibit collection.

Energy Reduction Projects (Lighting and Solar). A lighting improvement project was funded by an anonymous individual donor in the amount of $10,000. This project reduced energy usage by reprogramming existing lighting zones and installing motion sensors. In addition, exhibit spaces were placed on manual switches so wall wash lighting could be turned off when an exhibit space is not in use. Additional energy reduction and alternative energy projects are in progress. These projects include: installing solar panels on the library roof, funded through Associated Students at the University of Utah, Rocky Mountain Blue Sky Grant Program, and SCIF; replacing lighting from the 1960s installed in concrete that we were unable to address until now due to lack of funding, which is now being funded through campus facilities; a proposal for an energy dashboard to display library energy usage and direct students to related research information and tools, potentially being funded by a corporate grant combined with campus grant.

My U Signature Experience (MUSE) Intern. My U Signature Experience (http://muse.utah.edu/) is an internship program at the University of Utah designed to enhance internship experiences and provide students with opportunities for professional development they can take out into the world with them when they graduate (University of Utah, 2013). The MUSE program matches funding to provide paid internships for students. The intern worked with the library's sustainability coordinator and MLGC to develop content for web pages, compile project information, organize lecture series and discussion panels for the academic year 2011-2012, and assist in the development of data collection processes to track outcomes of committee initiatives. The intern was paid $10.00 per hour ($5.00 from MUSE/ $5.00 library funded), and worked 10-12 hours per week for twelve weeks. This internship provided the opportunity for the student to improve project planning and implementation skills, provide the committee with a student perspective on projects, and expand his/her knowledge of the sustainability efforts of the Marriott Library and campus.

Sustainability Interns, Curriculum Review. Three interns were hired who worked with two librarians to conduct a thorough review of sustainability curricula and library holdings in sustainability studies and sustainability science. This project was funded through a corporate grant. (See chapter by Brunvand et. al. in this book).

Collaboration with faculty and students to enhance the learning experience. The library provides space for students to fulfill course requirements while providing the library with valuable information. Teaching faculty to collaborate with librarians on projects related to sustainability. This project required no funding. MLGC and a group of communication students worked together to design a survey geared towards gauging student attitudes about recycling. This survey was a class assignment. Students collected 199 survey responses and provided the MLGC with a summary report and recommendation to improve our program.

Outreach/Increasing Visibility

Tabling at Earth Fest each year is another way the library maintains visibility. The library gives away free books while taking the opportunity to talk to students about the sustainability projects and resources available at the library. This is also a good time to gather feedback from students to find out what they would like to see happening at the library and gauge awareness of existing services.

Conclusion

During the run of exhibits, custodial staff members have noticed a significant reduction in recycling contamination. This leads the library to believe that visually interesting reminders have a strong impact on behavior change. Without being preachy, the Marriot Library has changed patron and staff behavior and brought greater awareness of sustainability issues to the campus. From academic year 2010-11 to 2011-12, the library saw an increase in plastics collected for recycling of 28% and an increase of 47% in aluminum.

Marriot Library —like most libraries—is the heart of the campus community. As a focal point for events, exhibits, and educational materials, it serves as a logical place to foreground campus efforts to be greener by making our ecological footprint smaller.

References

Just Fill It! Exhibit, J. Willard Marriott Library. Personal photograph by Karren Nichols. August 2011.

Marriott Library Green Task Force. (2008). *Recommendations for Greening the J. Willard Marriott Library.* Retrieved from http://www.lib.utah.edu/pdf/GTF_Final_Report.pdf

Office of Sustainability, University of Utah. (2010). *Energy and Environmental Stewardship Initiative: 2010 Climate Action Plan.* Retrieved from http://sustainability.utah.edu/static-content/pdf/EESI_2010_web2.pdf

Office of Sustainability, University of Utah. (2013). *Sustainable Campus Initiative Fund.* Retrieved from http://sustainability.utah.edu/get-involved/students/sustainable-campus-fund.php

Print Alternatives Exhibit, Window 2, J. Willard Marriott Library. Personal photograph by Karren Nichols. April 2012.

Recycling Station in Knowledge Commons, J. Willard Marriott Library. Personal photograph by Karren Nichols. April 2012.

Staff Waste Pod, J. Willard Marriott Library. Personal photograph by Karren Nichols. June 2013.

The Paper Project: The Life Cycle of Paper Exhibit, J. Willard Marriott Library. Personal photograph by Karren Nichols. April 2012.

University of Utah. (2013). *My U Signature Experience.* Retrieved from http://muse.utah.edu/

Water Bottle Filling Stations, J. Willard Marriott Library. Personal photograph by Karren Nichols. August 2011.

Greening the Mothership: Growing the Environmental Sustainability Group at the University of California, San Diego Library

Kim Kane and Annelise Sklar

Abstract

Using the University of California (UC) San Diego Library's Environmental Sustainability Group as a case study, this chapter walks readers through establishing a need for sustainability efforts within an academic library, communicating that need to the library's administration and other stakeholders, and launching an official library group to work on those issues. It also describes sustainability activities an academic library can undertake, and the resources needed—or not—to accomplish them and measure their success. This chapter is aimed at libraries just starting to plan environmental sustainability activities, or those who want to formalize their current endeavors into their library organization.

Introduction

It takes commitment from the organization, along with people and time, to accomplish a library's green initiatives. In this chapter, the authors profile the UC San Diego Library's Environmental Sustainability Group (ESG) and discuss the creation of an official group within a library to carry out the actual work associated with a library's sustainability efforts.

Sustainability in Universities

Green initiatives in the academic setting are certainly nothing new, dating back at least as far as the 1960s, when Middlebury College launched the United States' first Environmental Studies major. Today, green activities and sustainable initiatives are an integral part of many college campus cultures. The Princeton Review notes that among the 12,000 college applicants surveyed for the 2010 College Hopes & Worries Survey, 64 percent of respondents said they would value having information about a college's commitment to the environment and 23 percent said such information would "very much" impact their decision to apply to or attend the school (2011). In fact, there are now at least five separate green and sustainability ratings of universities and colleges (Galbraith, 2009).

As of early 2013, 665 colleges and universities have signed onto the American College & University Presidents' Climate Commitment (ACUPCC). It is:

"…a high-visibility effort to address global climate disruption undertaken by a network of colleges and universities that have made institutional commitments to eliminate net greenhouse gas emissions from specified campus operations, and to promote the research and educational efforts of higher education to equip society to re-stabilize the earth's climate." (Presidents' Climate Commitment, 2013a)

The commitment was started at the Association for the Advancement of Sustainability in Higher Education (AASHE) conference in October 2006. This commitment encourages campuses who sign on to find ways to achieve climate neutrality at their campus and asks universities and colleges who sign to create a Campus Action Plan (CAP) for their campus. So far, 516 colleges and universities have submitted their Climate Action Plans (Presidents' Climate Commitment, 2013b).

Sustainability in Academic Libraries

Libraries, on the other hand, began talking about green initiatives in earnest in the 1990s. Antonelli (2008) traces the earliest articles on green libraries to the early 1990s and then a second wave of green library scholarship to 2003. Common green themes in the library literature include building green (generally meaning LEED-certified) library buildings and making already existing buildings more sustainable, offering green library programs to library users, and greening library associations. Jankowska and Marcum (2010) identify four major categories of sustainability and green library issues commonly discussed in the literature since the 1990s: (1) sustainability of scholarship and collections,

(2) green library operations and practices, (3) green library buildings, and (4) measuring and improving sustainability. They also note that even in providing paperless, born-digital information to users, libraries continue to consume large amounts of nonrenewable resources such as energy, water, computer paper, and electronic equipment. Nationally, library environmental sustainability issues such as these are addressed by the American Library Association's Social Responsibilities Round Table (SRRT)'s Task Force on the Environment (TFOE), which was founded in 1989 (2013) and newly formed Sustainability Round Table (2013). However, a quick Google search for the terms like "green libraries" also returns hundreds of results for individual library- and librarian-run blogs, Libguides, etc., with titles like "Going Green at Your Library," "The Green Library," and "Green Libraries" that promote green activities on a local library level.

Sustainability on the UC San Diego Campus

Even with the current trends toward being green, UC San Diego is perhaps more committed to sustainability than many other institutions because of its history. Back in 1957, UC San Diego's founder and Scripps Institute of Oceanography Director Roger Revelle warned that greenhouse gases from industrialization could endanger the planet (UC San Diego Sustainability, 2013). The following year, UC San Diego geochemist Charles Keeling began his precise measurement of atmospheric carbon dioxide, and by 1961, he had proved that atmospheric CO_2 was rising dramatically (Our Heritage of Sustainability, 2013). In 1967, the university named its second (of now six) colleges after environmentalist and Sierra Club founder John Muir.

The University of California system was also an early signatory on the ACUPCC, President Robert C. Dynes having signed in March 2007. In December 2008, UC San Diego launched its campus wide Climate Action Plan, which outlines the various sustainable activities and initiatives the university, will undertake to achieve climate neutrality and provides campus departments with guidance for achieving those goals. UC San Diego strives to be climate neutral by 2025. The university is also a member of the AASHE, which administers the Sustainability Tracking Assessment and Rating System (STARS) survey that evaluates institutions in a variety of areas related to sustainability. In 2011, UC San Diego was one of the first ten colleges and universities to receive a "gold" rating in STARS (Graham, 2011).

The campus currently claims initiatives and research on clean energy, climate, green education, fuel alternatives, green building, alternative transportation, waste diversion, and water. It also has its own natural gas cogeneration plant and has installed photovoltaic panels on some of the rooftops on campus; between them the university generates about 85% of its electrical needs (Clean Energy, 2013). Approximately 59% of campus commuters use some sort of alternative transportation including walking and bicycling to campus (Alternative Transportation, 2013). According to the STARS report submitted in 2011, UC San Diego has 257 sustainability related courses, out of 6,319 courses offered (Sustainability Tracking, Assessment & Rating System, 2011). The campus also has approximately 20 student organizations with sustainability in their mission statements and a Sustainability Resource Center (SRC) that "serves as a hub for materials and initiatives related to local, national and global sustainability. The SRC is a partnership between the Sustainability Program Office and the Student Sustainability Collective dedicated to balancing environmental, social and economic stewardship" (UC San Diego Sustainability Resource Center, 2013).

The UC San Diego Library

The UC San Diego Library considers itself the "intellectual foundation for the dynamic and innovative UC San Diego campus" (A Message from the University Librarian, 2010). The Library is a member of the Association of Research Libraries, among other consortia, and highly dedicated to innovation and digital initiatives, providing "access to more than 7 million digital and print volumes, journals, and multimedia materials to meet the knowledge demands of scholars, students, and members of the public" (About the UC San Diego Library, 2010).

The Library at UC San Diego currently consists of two buildings, Geisel Library and the Biomedical Library building, and has approximately 250 staff and librarians. The campus has an enrollment of approximately 29,000 students (Campus Profile, 2011), and the libraries, both of which have prime central locations on campus, are vibrant places that overflow with library users throughout the day and evening. With an annual gate count of over two million (A Message from the University Librarian, 2010), the library buildings are so busy, in fact, that one section of the Geisel Library building has recently been designated as a 24/5-hour study area for students.

The Environmental Sustainability Group (ESG) at the Library

Given the library locale, it is not surprising that several individual UC San Diego Library staff members have long been interested in sustainability. Local library legend has it that many years before the formation of the current Environmental Sustainability Group, the Library actually had another green team that, among other things, encouraged staff to recycle and to conserve water and electricity in the building, but no current staff remember why or how it ceased to exist.

It should be noted that, even on a campus as green as UC San Diego, the creation of the current Environmental Sustainability Group was staff-initiated. One of the authors of this chapter, Kim Kane, approached the Director of Library Administrative Services with the idea of creating an internal sustainability group. The Library Administration approved the request to form the group and appointed a group chair. They provided the following official charge, which shows the work the group was encouraged to do, including development of best practices.

The ESG is charged with developing and recommending comprehensive strategies and institutional practices that promote sustainability, including measures to make more efficient use of resources as well as decrease production of waste (see Appendix I with advice on creating sustainability group at your library).

Functions of the ESG

- Detail our sustainability practices and evaluate their effectiveness.
- Draft policies intended to maximize the Libraries' activities in the following areas:
  - Products/equipment made from sustainable items;
  - Recycling and otherwise decreasing waste;
  - Water conservation;
  - Energy efficiency;
- Share sustainability information and best practices with Library employees.

The original members were volunteers plus one designated representative from the Library's Facilities Management Department. However, the Library has since begun a lengthy organizational restructuring process that will move people and units around. In the meantime, members who leave the group have been replaced by volunteers from anywhere within the Library. The group meets monthly, and, as an official Library committee, posts agendas and takes minutes to document action items. The group has a folder on the Library's shared drive to store working documents and communicates via email in between meetings. While the group has no allotted budget, it can submit requests to the Library Administration for consideration. However, most projects the ESG undertakes require very little to no funding and generally have a minimal impact on Library resources and staff time.

Projects of the ESG

The ESG members serve as sustainability experts for the Library and staff. The ESG is made up of green-minded library staff members who have a variety of ideas for projects to work on throughout the year. The ideas are discussed in the monthly meetings, and then the group decides which ideas will be developed and who will take the lead on the project. Each member brings to the group a set of talents and skills that always seem to compliment the others in the group.

One popular idea has been the annual Fruit and Vegetable Exchange that ESG started hosting in 2009. Since many of the library staff, including several ESG members, are prolific gardeners, the ESG created an exchange event for when fruits and veggies are at their peak every summer. The exchange has grown into an exchange of not only fruits and vegetables, but seeds, seedlings, cuttings from plants, flowers and even food that people make from items in their gardens. The group reserves a room in the library, and the exchange is scheduled from approximately 11:30 am -1:30 pm so that staff have a chance to stop by during their lunch hour. This event is open to all library employees, and one does not need to contribute anything to share in order to participate. In 2012, approximately 25 staff attended the exchange, and many staff members have asked that the exchange be held two or three times a year, since many people garden all year in Southern California. In the future, the ESG members have discussed expanding the exchange to invite the student groups who have started community gardens on campus.

The ESG members also regularly contributed a sustainability page to the Library staff newsletter. It featured a different topic every month, such as electric vehicles and composting, new titles in the collection, green events on campus and in the community, and a sustainable craft suggestion. In addition, the group created a Holiday Sustainable/Fair Trade Gift Giving Guide that provides readers with ideas for sustainable gifts to purchase. The guide includes a description of each item and links to the websites where items can be purchased. It also provides information about sustainability events in the local area, a link to a list of thrift stores, gift-wrapping and other sustainable suggestions for cleaning up after the holidays (for example, a link to where to recycle your tree in the city). Each ESG member chose an area of the guide to work on but could also provide content for other sections if they had information to share. The guide was sent out to all library staff via email at the end of November 2012 and also posted on the library's website and on the Environmental Studies Research Guide Lib-guide for library users. The link was also posted to the Library's Facebook and Twitter accounts. The ESG received many positive comments from staff, thanking them for creating the guide. The ESG is currently working on creating a Sustainable Living Guide to provide staff and library users with more information on a variety of sustainability topics.

Yet another low-resource intensive initiative ESG sponsored was in response to a staff suggestion that it would be useful if the Library could provide trash pick-up sticks for individual staff who want to use them to clean up the campus on their breaks and at lunch. The ESG sent a quick email inquiry to the campus Facilities Management department to find out how to go about obtaining some, and Facilities Management responded by providing the Library with four pick-up sticks, as well as trash bags, for free. Working with another department on campus not only helped the ESG avoid having to purchase these materials themselves, but also demonstrated how collaboration can be an impetus for campus-wide sustainability efforts.

Collaborating with Campus Groups

Being involved with various sustainable campus groups helps to increase the visibility of the Library as being a committed partner in furthering the sustainability efforts on campus. By collaborating with campus groups and continuing to network with non-library staff, faculty and student groups on campus, ESG continues to connect with the larger campus and their sustainable efforts. The ESG members have also found that the various campus departments may have resources and items that the Library can use, as with the pick-up sticks the Library received from the Facilities Management department and in working during Earth Week with the Sustainability Resource Center, who help publicize the library events. Good relationships are built and in turn the Library is seen as a sustainability partner on the campus community.

The UC San Diego Procurement & Contracts (P&C) department started a Writing Instrument Brigade (WIB) project to collect defunct pens and markers on campus to keep them from going into the landfill. This department partnered with TerraCycle, and sends the defunct writing instruments off to be up cycled into other products. In return, TerraCycle pays the campus for each pen or marker it receives. The money received goes to the campus Sustainability Resource Center. Initially, ESG's members decided to collect pens and markers in the staff areas of the libraries. The library staff was enthusiastic and departments made their own collection containers. The ESG members collected the pens and markers and requested a free UPS mailing label from the P&C department for sending materials. In 2012, with the support of the Library's Administration and various library departments, the ESG expanded this program to the public areas at both Geisel and the Biomedical Library on campus. For the public areas, ESG decided to purchase containers for a more streamlined look and for consistency, since the containers are located throughout the buildings at many of the service desk areas. The group also wanted to encourage students to recycle and make it easy for them to locate the containers. Initially, when the program was expanded to the public areas of the library, the "Recycle Your Used Pens! Look for the bins and just drop 'em in!" signage on the containers was not explicit enough and some library users thought they could take the recycled pens, not realizing the writing instruments were no longer working. With a suggestion from a staff member, the group re-worded the containers' labels to read "Pen out of ink? Marker dried out? They can be recycled here!" to clarify how the containers were to be used. This change resulted in ESG collecting more defunct pens and markers, and the pens are no longer being taken out of the containers. One member of the group created images to display on the digital signs at both the Geisel and Biomedical libraries to inform students about the WIB, and one of the outreach librarians blasted the information on Facebook and Twitter at the beginning of fall quarter and continues to do so periodically throughout the year. This program has been a success in both the staff and public areas. The library sends a shipment of defunct pens and markers to TerraCycle approximately 6 times a year. More importantly, in the 2011/2012 school year the entire campus kept approximately 5,000 pens and markers out of the landfill. A new goal was set for 2012/2013 and the Library will continue to contribute writing instruments and help build awareness of what can be recycled (Writing Instrument Brigade, 2013).

The Campus Earth Week Celebration

A member of the ESG has participated on the campus Earth Week planning committee since the ESG's inception. This planning committee is organized by the Sustainability Resource Center and hosts the Earth Week celebration on campus each year. The group consists of staff, students, and members of community organizations. Over the years, members of the ESG have been active in helping to organize various educational events during the celebration. One year they helped to plan an educational resource fair that included student sustainability groups and community sustainability organizations. In 2012, the Library hosted a display of the environmental features of the Geisel and Biomedical libraries. The group also created an environmental book display of materials in the various library collections. Throughout the month, the Library's digital signs displayed factoids about water and energy conservation.

In 2013, ESG showed the movie *Bag It*, which explains the impact plastic bags have on our lives and on the environment. To help increase the awareness of reusable products that are available, the group displayed items such as reusable sandwich bags and veggie bags before and after the movie and then raffled them off to attendees. At the Biomedical Library, the ESG partnered with the student group for Roger's Garden (one of the community gardens on campus) and San Diego Coastkeeper (a community water protection group) to create a display in the library. This display had three components: one area highlighting readily-available reusable products that can be substituted for one-time-use items; a second area displaying items that can be recycled on campus; and a third illustrating the effects plastics have on our environment to compliment the *Bag It* screening. Environmental factoids were displayed on the digital signs throughout the month of April at both libraries.

Future Plans for Projects

The ESG members are always considering ways to promote and support the sustainable initiatives on campus. Many of the students would like to reduce or entirely eliminate bottled water on campus, and one way to accomplish this is to provide free filtered water so members of the campus community can refill their reusable containers. Some buildings on campus have already installed separate bottle filling capabilities in their drinking fountains. The ESG has already spoken to our Administration Team liaison to recommend the installation of these stations in the public areas of the library and note that they will compliment not only the students' goals of elimination of disposable water bottles but ESG's as well. (Group Moves Forward Plastic Water Bottle Ban, 2011) The group has also investigated the costs of equipment and plumbing work involved with retrofitting a drinking fountain for a water bottle filling station and then laid the groundwork for future action by bringing the options to the attention of the head of Library Facilities.

The Library is also on the list for the campus-wide Green Office Certification assessment process. The Library staff is already diligent about recycling, and keep recycling and trash bins at their desks, but there are other areas that staff can work on to improve sustainability at the libraries. Working with the campus Sustainability Resource Center and other library staff members, the ESG wants to continue to work towards greening departments within the library.

Lessons Learned

Not all projects that ESG has worked on have been implemented in the Library. Some of the original ESG members wanted to attain Leading Energy and Efficiency Design for Existing Buildings (LEED-EB) certification for the Geisel Library. After months of ESG members researching this initiative and talking with the campus Facilities Management department, who were very supportive of the idea, Library Administration decided at this time, they did not want to devote the resources to pursue this project. All of the research and planning that went into LEED-EB, however, was not wasted. The notes and meeting minutes were saved and will be used as a building block if the library ever decides to go forward with this idea in the future. Additionally, with their new knowledge of LEED standards, the ESG members continue to work on smaller scale projects that will enhance the building's efficiency and its occupants' comfort now and possibly help the Library attain LEED points should it pursue formal certification in the future. Researching LEED-EB also helped the Library and ESG lay the groundwork with campus Facilities Management so they know the Library is interested in LEED-EB certification should campus funding become available.

Since the UC San Diego campus is so actively involved in sustainability, it is important that the Library, as "the intellectual heart of the campus," (Give to the UC San Diego Library, 2010) supports these ideals and values. By creating a group specifically tasked with sustainability projects, the Library's Administration team actively demonstrates its support of these campus efforts and the Library's commitment to serving our campus community's needs and interests. By networking with the various sustainability groups on campus, the ESG members have expanded their support system and increased their awareness of practical resources that can benefit the Library. The group also continues to make allies both on campus and off when it comes to sustainability issues.

ESG's members are library staff interested in sustainability in both their personal and professional lives, and they seek to encourage others to be green at work as well. The group provides members with an outlet for their sustainability actions. The group's activities also benefit the work-lives of the individual staff who are more engaged with their daily work when they can also work on the various sustainability projects and share their expertise with their colleagues. Sustainable activities within the library buildings save the campus and Library's resources and money.

Conclusion

Support for sustainability can be found across all levels of higher education. As Tom Kimmerer, executive director of the AASHE, stated:

"There's leadership from the top: college presidents and university chancellors. Then, leadership from the middle – the operations people are practical folks, many of them well educated in sustainability – who often see that LEED-certified buildings or better lighting have a short [economic] payback. And then there's leadership from the bottom, where student and faculty engagement are linked to one another. The most successful sustainability gains occur when all three levels of leadership work in concert." (Buttenwieser, 2008)

As the hub of their campus communities, libraries are well positioned to lead from the middle. UC San Diego Library's ESG and groups like it (see Appendix II) have a prime opportunity to educate library staff and users about sustainable best practices as well as developing their own for library public and workspaces.

For library staff who dream of greening their libraries, the first thing to do is to determine how to obtain the resources (people, space, funding, etc.) to make those dreams a reality. Each institution has its own particular quirks, between organizational structure, staffing, funding, and space availability, and a successful program will take those local limitations into account. Likewise, a successful program will build on local strengths, needs, and interests, whether it is the role the library plays in campus life or natural institutional partnerships.

References

Alternative transportation. (2013). University of California, San Diego SustainUCSD. Retrieved from http://sustainability.ucsd.edu/initiatives/transportation-alternatives.html

American Library Association Social Responsibilities Round Table. (2013). *Task Force on the Environment.* Retrieved from http://www.ala.org/srrt/tfoe/taskforceenvironment

American Library Association. *Sustainability Round Table.* (2013). Retrieved from http://www.ala.org/sustainrt/

Antonelli, M. (2008). The green library movement: An overview and beyond. *Electronic Green Journal, 1*(27). Retrieved from http://www.escholarship.org/uc/item/39d3v236

Buttenwieser, S. W. (2008). Greening the ivory tower. *Earth Island Journal, 22*(4), 34-38. Retrieved from http://www.earthisland.org/journal/index.php/eij/article/greening_the_ivory_tower/

Campus profile. (2011). University of California, San Diego University Communications and Public Affairs. Retrieved from http://ucsdnews.ucsd.edu/campus_profile

Clean energy. (2013). University of California, San Diego SustainUCSD. Retrieved from http://sustainability.ucsd.edu/initiatives/energy-production.html

Energy Conservation and Sustainability Working Group charge. (2009). University of Illinois at Urbana-Champaign Library. Retrieved from http://www.library.illinois.edu/committee/energy

Galbraith, K. (2009). *Ranking universities by 'Greenness'* [Web log post]. Retrieved from http://green.blogs.nytimes.com/2009/08/20/ranking-universities-by-greenness/

Give to the UC San Diego Library. (2010). University of California, San Diego Library. Retrieved from http://libraries.ucsd.edu/about/give/

Graham, R. (2011). *UC San Diego first California University to achieve 'Gold' STARS sustainability rating.* University of California, San Diego News Center. Retrieved from http://ucsdnews.ucsd.edu/newsrel/general/05-20-11GoldStars.asp

Green Task Force. (2012). East Carolina University Libraries. Retrieved from http://libguides.ecu.edu/content.php?pid=158647&sid=1344540

Group moves forward plastic water bottle ban. (2011). *The Guardian.* Retrieved from http://www.ucsdguardian.org

Jankowska, M. A., & Marcum, J. W. (2010). Sustainability challenge for academic libraries: Planning for the future. *College & Research Libraries*, 71(2), 160-170. Retrieved from http://crl.acrl.org/content/71/2/160.short

A message from the University Librarian. (2010). University of California, San Diego Library. Retrieved from http://libraries.ucsd.edu/about/ul-office/index.html

Michigan State University Libraries. The Michigan State University Library Environmental Committee. (2012). *About us*. Retrieved from http://lec-wiki.lib.msu.edu/index.php/About_Us

Our heritage of sustainability. (2013). University of California, San Diego SustainUCSD. Retrieved from http://sustainability.ucsd.edu/about/heritage.html

Presidents' Climate Commitment. (2013a). *Mission and history*. Retrieved from http://www.presidentsclimatecommitment.org/about/mission-history

Presidents' Climate Commitment. (2013b). *Signatory list by institution name*. Retrieved from http://www.presidentsclimatecommitment.org/signatories/list

Princeton Review's guide to 311 green colleges. (2011). Retrieved from http://www.scribd.com/doc/65197711/Princeton-Review-s-Guide-to-Green-Colleges

Sustainability at Bobst Library. (2012). New York University Libraries. Retrieved from http://nyu.libguides.com/sustainability

Sustainability Tracking, Assessment & Rating System. (2011). *AASHE STARS scorecard: University of California, San Diego*. Retrieved from https://stars.aashe.org/institutions/university-of-California-san-diego-ca/report/2011-05-18/

UC San Diego sustainability. (2013). University of California, San Diego SustainUCSD. Retrieved from http://sustainability.ucsd.edu/

UC San Diego Sustainability Resource Center. (2013). University of California, San Diego SustainUCSD. Retrieved from http://aps-web.ucsd.edu/src/

University of California, San Diego Library. *About the UC San Diego Library*. (2010). Retrieved from http://libraries.ucsd.edu/about/index.html

University of California, San Diego Blink. (2013). *Writing instrument brigade*. Retrieved from http://blink.ucsd.edu/buy-pay/responsible/environment/wri

Appendix I: Advice on Creating Sustainability Group at Your Library

While every institution is different, here are some suggestions based on the ESG's experience:

- Find out whether the college or university has signed on to the American College and University President's Climate Commitment.
  - If yes, has the campus created a climate action plan? It may be easier to build support for sustainability activities from the library's administration if one can demonstrate that establishing a group within the library will help further the campus initiatives.
- Determine whether there is a sustainability champion in the library's administration who might be supportive of these ideas and would work with staff to create the group.
- Once the internal support is established, define the charge for the group and decide if specific departments should be represented on the committee or if a general request will go out for volunteers. By recruiting volunteers, the group will consist of staff passionate about sustainability instead of someone who has merely been assigned to be on the committee and does not have any interest in the subject. Decide how the group will be structured. Does the group have a formal place in the library's organizational structure? To whom does the group report? Will serving on the group be an official part of anyone's job description? If not, how will the members ensure that they have the allotted time they need to work on projects? How often will the group meet? Will public minutes be recorded and posted?
- At the first group meeting, ask members to talk about why they wanted to be on the group and what ideas they would like to work on in the upcoming year.
- Select a few projects and decide how to divide the work. Start small at first and build on local strengths. Try to start with projects that will get the most buy-in or require the least effort on the part of the target audience. (In other words, make it easy to recycle items or fun to learn about reusable products.)
- Seek out other people on campus who are involved in sustainability efforts to create allies and possibly partner on future projects. Serving on any campus-wide groups is extremely useful for networking.

Appendix II: Sustainability Committees in Other Libraries

Many libraries have Sustainability Committees that work on various issues related to sustainability. Some examples are:

New York University Libraries - Sustainability at Bobst Library http:// nyu.libguides.com/content.php?pid=56666&sid=415112

This guide has a wealth of information for both students and staff such as information about purchasing recycled-content supplies for the office and suggestions for reusing various items that libraries often throw away (e.g., acquisitions can give the bubble wrap they receive with books to ILL for shipping).

University Library University of Illinois at Urbana-Champaign : The Energy Conservation and Sustainability Working Group (ECS)
http://www.library.illinois.edu/committee/energy/charge.html

This group is charged with leading the University Library's efforts at achieving a more energy efficient and environmentally sustainable workplace. Through a combination of collaboration, direct action, and advocacy, the ECS seeks to identify and promote policies and practices that will help minimize the Library's environmental impact, reduce energy consumption, and promote a more sustainable library. Outcomes may include:

- Increased use of energy efficient, refillable, reusable, recycled, and recyclable supplies and equipment
- Reduced use of plastics
- Reduced paper consumption
- Decreased resource consumption
- Increased level of recycling
- Promoting and achieving more energy efficient meetings, travel, and personal transportation
- Advocacy for more sustainable practices among our users
- Increased collaboration with campus and university bodies promoting conservation and sustainability (Energy Conservation and Sustainability Working Group Charge, 2009).

The Michigan State University - Library Environmental Committee
http://www.lib.msu.edu/lec

This committee focuses on the Libraries' use of natural resources with an eye toward sustainability, while maintaining and improving their overall working and learning environment. The categories of resources include such items as paper, printing and copier use; energy--lighting, PC's, heating and cooling; cleaning supplies and chemicals; office supplies; recycling and waste reduction; parking and transportation; noise; and general design issues that have an ecological impact. The committee has these functions: 1) Advise library administration and staff; 2) Provide educational information and programming; 3) Maintain resources related to these issues; 4) Act as liaison with the Office of Campus Sustainability and the MSU Surplus Store and Recycling Center; and 5) Contact other units as required and approved (The Michigan State University Library Environmental Committee, 2012).

East Carolina University - Joyner Library Green Task Force
http://libguides.ecu.edu/content.php?pid=158647&sid=1344540
Mission:

1) To research, propose, implement, and promote green education and sustainable environmental practices in the university library environment
2) To raise awareness of green initiatives in Joyner Library, other libraries in the ECU system, and the local community (Green Task Force, 2012).

Sustainability: Putting Principles into Practice at a Catholic University Library

Ted Bergfelt and Allison B. Brungard

Abstract

As a Spiritan institution, Duquesne University's mission embodies the principles of Catholic Social Thought. Sustainability is a natural extension of those principles, two of which are the Common Good and the Stewardship of Creation. These and the related issues of peace and justice are deeply rooted in the curriculum and guide University practice. This chapter examines Duquesne University sustainability initiatives and programs and the Gumberg Library's (GL) role in them, relating these to the larger context of Catholic Social Thought. In support of the University's sustainability efforts, librarians have collaborated with faculty, developed collections, participated in programs, and provided instruction and online research guides on accessing sustainability resources.

Introduction

It is no surprise that Duquesne University (DU) of the Holy Spirit, being "a Catholic university in the Spiritan tradition" would value and foster the idea of sustainability. Both of these adjectives, "Catholic" and "Spiritan" make this essential. As a Catholic institution, the influence of Catholic Social Thought (CST) has and will continue to exert a formative influence. The Spiritans, more formally known as the Congregation of the Holy Spirit, are the religious congregation, which founded and continues to sponsor DU. For the last few decades, the Spiritans, as aspects of their spirituality and ministry, have concerned themselves with the related concepts of "justice, peace, and the integrity of creation" (Kilcrann, 2007), concepts which echo and flow from the principles of CST.

Catholic social thought is based on the teachings of Christian scripture and tradition as they have been applied through the centuries to every aspect of the life of humans in community. It has especially been promulgated in the last century in the encyclicals on social matters by various popes. Among the basic principles of CST are two that are especially relevant to discussions of sustainability: the "common good" and the "stewardship of creation" (http://cctwincities.org/document.doc?id=13).

According to the *Catechism of the Catholic Church*, quoting the 1965 Vatican II document *Gaudium et spes* ("Pastoral Constitution of the Church in the Modern World"), the *common good* is defined as "the sum total of social conditions which allow people, either as groups or as individuals, to reach their fulfillment more fully and more easily" and this document goes on to state that it "concerns the life of all," requiring the prudence of every person (p.465). The *stewardship of creation*, according to the Catholic bishops of the Columbia Watershed region, "is the traditional Christian expression of the role of people in relation to creation. Stewards, as caretakers for the things of God, are called to use wisely and distribute justly the good of God's earth to meet the needs of God's children" (George, 2012, p. 356). While not explicitly employing the phrase "common good," there is no doubt that this is what the bishops had in mind when they speak of wisely and justly distributing the "good of God's earth to meet the needs of God's children." In an even more authoritative statement, the *Catechism of the Catholic Church* links common good and stewardship of creation, alluding to the concept of sustainability without explicitly mentioning it, when it requires of human beings concern not only for one's neighbor's quality of life in the present, but also that of "generations to come." This concern is to be realized by "a religious respect for the integrity of creation" (p.580)

While some secular writers employ the term "environmental stewardship" to describe human responsibility toward the natural world, CST presents this world as something more highly exalted. Human beings, made in the image of God have been given the responsibility, privilege, and honor, to care for and nurture, not only an *environment* and the things in it that are the results of a fortuitous conjunction of random processes, but of a *creation*, a cosmos planned and lovingly fashioned by a transcendent and potent intelligence (George, 2012, p. 356). This stewardship of creation, for the good of all in the present and future, to preserve a world that speaks of the glory of God, is such a serious matter that the United States Conference of Catholic Bishops (2005) has called it, "a requirement of the faith."

It is natural, with the formative influences of Catholic Social Thought and the Spiritan charism, that DU would state, as one of the overarching goals of its 2010-2015 Strategic Plan: "[r]espect for the environment will shape both academic and business decisions." (Planning for, 2010). The Princeton Review's *Guide to Green Colleges* (Princeton Review) has acknowledged Duquesne's commitment to sustainability, and this is also evidenced by other awards that have been earned by the University. Since the related issues of respect for the environment, social justice, and sustainability are important to the University, they are also important to the GL, which supports University initiatives, academic programs, and student and faculty research.

University Academic Sustainability Initiatives

In putting its principles into practice, Duquesne's earliest initiative regarding environmental and sustainability issues dates from 1992, when it began a two-year Master of Science program in Environmental Sciences and Management (ESM). Duquesne was one of the first colleges in the U.S. to offer a master's degree program like this which offered training to professionals in the management of environmental issues. The program was designed with input from the Pennsylvania Director of Environmental Resources and an industry advisory board. Incoming students were required to have a bachelor's degree in biology, chemistry, physics, or engineering. Course content included environmental science concepts, communications, conflict resolution, and national and international environmental public policy. Students were required to do an internship with a regulatory agency or with a private company. Though there was no newspaper or television coverage regarding the new graduate program, the university quickly received 200 inquiries (Rishel, 1997). This program continues today and has graduated over 400 environmental professionals (Duquesne Environmental Science, 2012).

Two years later, DU formed a new school for the natural sciences, the Bayer School. The importance of environmental issues at Duquesne was highlighted in that environmental sciences were included among the programs offered by the new school, now called the Bayer School of Natural and Environmental Sciences (BSNES). The two-year old Master of Science in Environmental Studies found a new home here.

In 1997, within the Bayer School, a new center, the Center for Environmental Research and Education (CERE) was formed to lead the environmental programs of the school. CERE strives to remain in the forefront of environmental education, continually changing the ESM program to keep it fresh by dealing with emerging environmental and sustainability issues. Another source of currency for the program are adjunct professors who bring their real-world environmental expertise from the field into the classroom (20 Years, 2013). CERE has become one of the University's main avenues for environmental and sustainability outreach beyond the classroom, taking part in local environmental studies and reclamation efforts and international cooperative projects. One of the specific ways CERE promotes sustainability is through the publication of a *Greenhouse Gas Emissions Inventory* that reports on the University's carbon footprint and is seen as a model for other regional universities. According to CERE: "The University's carbon footprint, which is based upon all gases emitted, is substantially the smallest of all Atlantic 10 Conference schools completing similar surveys in the past two years" (CERE, 2012).

Another academic program is the Master of Business Administration in Sustainability (SMBA). Flowing out of Catholic Social Teaching, the ethical dimensions of business have always been stressed at Duquesne's Palumbo-Donahue School of Business. It was only natural when the idea of sustainability became prevalent at Duquesne, that a graduate business program incorporating these ideas would be established. Started in 2007, the SMBA program was created to, "meet the growing demand for next-generation leaders who understand that planned growth, ethics, community and the environment all impact business strategy, value creation and shareholder return" (http://mba.sustainability.duq.edu/why-mba-sustainability/index.asp). The curriculum integrates the multiple dimensions of sustainability across all business disciplines. Duquesne's SMBA program is the highest ranked program of its type in Pennsylvania, and has made the top ten in the Aspen Institute's biennial rankings for the last six years (R. Sroufe, personal communication, March 12, 2013).

Along with CERE and the SMBA program, the University supports sustainability programmatically in other ways:

- The Center for Green Industries and Sustainable Business Growth is funded by the U.S. Economic Development Administration. The center offers no-cost confidential consulting services for small businesses within sustainable business sectors and to traditional businesses seeking to increase sustainability in their operations while increasing profitability.
- The Institute for Energy and Environment was established in 2001. The Institute brings together researchers with a shared interest in energy and its impact on global and local communities in the environment. This is

a collaborative effort between the liberal arts, business, law, and science schools in the University as well as experts from outside of Duquesne.

- The Beard Institute, part of the Palumbo Donahue School of Business, advances the management profession through business ethics, sustainability and responsible financial management. The Beard Institute continually supports and hosts an array of sustainability-purposed conferences, including an annual Sustainability Symposium. The most recent conference was *100 Years of Sustainability.*

- The Palumbo Donahue School of Business' recently appointed director of entrepreneurial studies places an emphasis on sustainability and ethics, fostering the continuity of these ideals throughout the other programs in the school.

One other essential way that Duquesne supports green living, environmental awareness, and sustainable community is through service learning venues for service learning by students, faculty, and staff. It includes charities, social and human service agencies, public safety, education, wellness programs, neighborhood beautification, and small business development programs. Students regularly clean up neighborhoods bordering the University campus. Each semester, the SMBA students do case studies of corporate and non-profit partners to determine how sustainable their business practices are, with an eye on suggesting improvements. The partner organizations that the SMBA students work include Alcoa, Westinghouse Nuclear, Bayer Corp., the PPG Pittsburgh Zoo and Aquarium, Carnegie Museum of Pittsburgh, and the Pennsylvania Environmental Council. Altogether, 8,000 Duquesne affiliates perform 209,800 hours of service learning and other sorts of voluntarism each year.

Other University-Wide Sustainability Initiatives

At Duquesne, the concept of sustainability is not just an idea presented in the classroom, but is being practiced in nuts-and-bolts ways. A Facilities Management document, "Greening an Urban Campus," summarizes many of these efforts:

- DU generates most of its own electricity. A natural gas co-generation plant located on campus has produced approximately 85 percent of Duquesne's power for the last decade. Duquesne has also purchased 13 million hours of renewable energy credits. This, coupled with its clean-burning power plant, means that the University relies 100% on clean energy.

- Duquesne has made the switch to using mostly green cleaning products in its maintenance methods. The paints used on campus are VOC free and are the most environmentally friendly products that can be found. A green clause in all requests for proposals by vendors asks that they provide pertinent and verifiable information on the post-consumer recycled content in their products.
- All new building projects and renovation of existing structures are carried out according to LEED green building guidelines, including recent renovations projects in the library itself. It is noteworthy to mention that the GL is housed in a former parking garage built in the 1920s. The garage was repurposed for a library in 1978. (Times, 2008) Environmentally friendly renovations will continue for the next few years.
- While recycling has a long history at Duquesne, with the GL being the first department on campus to adopt the use of paper recycling bins, a further development has been the recycling of 100% of its cooking oil from the many food service facilities on the campus.

Gumberg Library Support for Sustainability

As the concept of sustainability began to be incorporated in various University documents, becoming enshrined in academic programs, initiatives, and the University Strategic Plan, the library took a proactive approach through building the reference collection. The library purchased a set of twelve electronic reference works produced by Sage on a range of green topics (including titles like *Green Culture: An A to Z Guide* and *Green Technology: An A to Z Guide*) as well as an array of other reference materials on environmental subjects, with the e-Book version of the ten-volume *Berkshire Encyclopedia of Sustainability* being the latest acquisition.

As academic departments placed an increased emphasis on environment and global concerns, the librarians recognized a need for additional online resources highlighting environmental and sustainability issues. The *GreenFILE* and *Global Socrates* databases were acquired. *GreenFILE* is freely available through EBSCOhost and provides scholarly, government, and industry information on the environmental effects of individuals, corporations and local and national governments, and what can be done at each level to minimize these effects. *GreenFILE* particularly focuses on global warming, green building, pollution, sustainable agriculture, renewables, and recycling. *Global Socrates* provides information on the environmental, social, and governance performance of the top 4,000 global companies. Companies are evaluated on things such as their environmental and climate change policies, renewable energy, greenhouse gas emissions, hazardous waste and discharges to water.

In 2009, under the leadership of environmental science faculty, a committee was formed including interested faculty from the Bayer school and the nine other schools of DU. It was called the University Academic Sustainability Committee (UASC). The purpose of the UASC would be to integrate sustainability concepts into the educational experience through sustainability courses and course components and through research and service learning opportunities (http://www.duq.edu/about/sustainability/academic-committee). Library support for university sustainability initiatives came about through the passion and determination of one of the reference and instruction librarians. The natural sciences librarian attended the initial UASC committee meeting and highlighted library support for sustainability. She set up a small booth at the program venue, with a poster to draw attention, and spoke to all who were interested on the library's collection building efforts. She proposed that the UASC add a new member representing GL. The UASC chair agreed and since that time a faculty librarian has been actively involved in the UASC membership.

Due to its representation on the UASC, the library has had continuous opportunities to support sustainability efforts at the course level. Recognizing that library support for student research would be critical, UASC members team teaching the class asked the librarian on UASC to help direct students to the growing number of library resources related to sustainability. They created online research guides for the courses and highlighted and linked to those items the students would find most useful for their work. The online course guide produced for "Imagining a Sustainable World" has a separate tab for each module, and through these tabs students can access assorted resources that support each module. The guide for Green Building includes URL lists, reference works, books (through links that perform subject searches in the catalog), periodical databases, vetted websites, and embedded videos. Links to these guides have been placed on the respective class pages in the University's course management system.

There are other ways that the Library supports the sustainability-focused entities at Duquesne. At the beginning of each academic year, a librarian provides an overview of sustainability resources and then more specialized instruction based on a research assignment that the students need to complete. This sustainability LibGuide (http://guides.library.duq.edu/sustainable-business) showcases these resources and, based on feedback, the students are most grateful for the help.

Supporting Sustainability through Practice

The library is an integral part of the university's sustainability initiatives, programs, and curriculum. In support of these efforts, librarians have collaborated with faculty, participated in programs, and provided resources and instruction as mentioned. Librarians also facilitate greening the library, with an emphasis on developing and maintaining digital collections combined with reducing waste and energy use while increasing usable space. More study space has consistently been a student desire reflected in many surveys. Other library sustainability activities include in-house recycling programs, environmentally sound renovation of the building, and space redesign. Task forces are in place to execute and accomplish these goals that have been identified as strategic priorities.

The library partners with the University's Computers and Technology Services department (CTS) to reduce consumption and waste and to save energy. Recently the systems librarian decommissioned the server room and now all servers run on a cloud using socially responsibly VMware and Solaris Logical Domains (LDOM). One very specific (and long-discussed) initiative which the GL has a starring role in finally implementing is a recently imposed printing quota for students. The idea of the "paperless office" has long been seen as a lame joke by CTS and the GL, with Internet and database use actually spurring the over-consumption of paper. For years the library has been the main place that students come to on campus for their printing needs. While many of the things printed, such as papers and lecture notes, are educationally important, at the same time the amount of waste that wholesale and thoughtless printing has generated is phenomenal. More gentle efforts at user education did not have much of an effect. So, to save money as well as resources, CTS determined to institute a print quota during the spring 2013 semester. As part of the implementation of this quota, the library created a LibGuide to help explain the quota and the reasons for it. One further step in the implementation will involve faculty. In a survey of over 600 respondents, it was reported that faculty often require students to print and bring to class their lecture notes or PowerPoint presentations. CTS and the library hope to educate faculty on the amount of waste that needless printing generates (not to mention the cost to students and the University). As on other campuses, the majority of students now use some sort of mobile device with wireless access. Since class notes and PowerPoint slides can easily be viewed on these, printing is not necessary and the hope is that the printing requirement can soon be eliminated.

In concurrence with printing reduction efforts, another reference librarian initiated a collaborative Earth Day project that will be based in the library. She met with the student group Evergreen and the Student Government Association to begin work on a sculpture of recycled material. While recycling is not a novel idea, it has long been championed by the library, which was the first building on campus to get large, user-friendly recycle bins. To further illustrate support for the university's green initiatives, in one year alone, the library recycled over 27 tons of co-mingled products (Gumberg Library, 2008).

Conclusion

DU aspires to be a leader in sustainability because of its commitment to Catholic social teaching. The library is an extension of the university and now, and in the future, will continue to support sustainability efforts, through collection building, instruction, committee service, and classroom and research support, always seeking new ways to supply users with needed resources on sustainable practices. Sustainability is not a self-generating phenomenon. Sustainability requires action. It is more than a way of thinking; it is a collection of activities that necessitate engagement and commitment from the campus community, including the GL. The Catholic tradition of peace, justice, and respect for the integrity of creation embraces these core values and motivates its adherents to serious commitment regarding them. A Catholic institution that is truly sustainable will contribute -- at the institutional, departmental, and personal levels -- to peace, harmony and an overall quality of life in service of its faith commitment.

References

Aspen Institute Center for Business Education. (2012). *Beyond grey pinstripes, 2011-2012: Top 100 MBA programs.* Retrieved from http://www.aspeninstitute.org/sites/default/files/content/docs/pubs/BGP%202011-2012%20Global%20Report-small.pdf

Catholic Charities of St. Paul and Minneapolis, Office of Social Justice. (n.d.). *Key principles of catholic social teaching.* Retrieved from http://cctwincities.org/document.doc?id=13

Catholic Church. (1997). *Catechism of the Catholic Church (2nd, rev. in accordance with the official Latin text promulgated by Pope John Paul II ed.).* Vatican City: Libreria Editrice Vaticana.

CERE: Over the past 20 years. (2012). Retrieved from http://www.duq.edu/academics/schools/natural-and-environmental-sciences/academic-programs/environmental-science-and-management/historical-milestones

Duquesne University. (2013) *20 years of preparing environmental professionals.* Retrieved from http://www.duq.edu/academics/schools/natural-and-environmental-sciences/academic-programs/environmental-science-and-management

Duquesne University. (2012) *Duquesne environmental science and management master's: Pioneering for 20 years.* Retrieved from http://www.duq.edu/academics/schools/natural-and-environmental-sciences/academic-programs/environmental-science-and-management

George, M. I. (2012). Stewardship of creation. In M. L. Coulter, R. S. Myers & J. A. Vacrelli (Eds.), *Encyclopedia of Catholic social thought, social science, and social policy, vol. 3.* Lanham: Scarecrow Press.

IHP 203:62 imagining a sustainable world [course syllabus]. (2012). Unpublished manuscript.

Kilcrann, J. (2007). Constructing a Spiritan spirituality of justice, peace, and the integrity of creation. *Spiritan Horizons, (2).*

Now free from diesel fumes, Gumberg enjoys the sweet smell of success. (2008, May). *Duquesne University Times,* pp. 8.

Planning for the future. (2010, Winter). *Duquesne University Magazine.*

Princeton Review's guide to 322 green colleges. (2012, April 17). Retrieved from http://www.princetonreview.com/green-schools-full-list.aspx

Rishel, J. F. (1997). *The Spirit that gives life: The history of Duquesne University, 1878-1996.* Pittsburgh, PA: Duquesne University Press.

United States Conference of Catholic Bishops. (2005). *Seven themes of Catholic social teaching*. Retrieved from http://www.usccb.org/beliefs-and-teachings/what-we-believe/catholic-social-teaching/seven-themes-of-catholic-social-teaching.cfm

White, T. (2013). *Business from a higher perspective: 100 years of the Duquesne University School of Business*. Pittsburgh: Duquesne University, Palumbo-Donahue School of Business.

Seed Libraries: Growing a New Library Service

René Tanner

Abstract

The author describes the efforts made by libraries as well as various institutions to preserve seed diversity and encourage gardening. The decision made by some libraries to cultivate their own "seed library" programs, offer a unique opportunity for additional services and encourage more sustainable living in their respective communities. The chapter also delves into the main reasons why seed preservation is important and the benefits seed libraries can have to promote diverse food ecosystems.

"In a handful of wild seeds taken from any one natural community, there is hidden the distillation of millions of years of coevolution of plants and animals"... (Nabhan, 1989, p. xix).

Introduction

A number of public libraries in the United States have begun to provide a new service: seed-lending libraries. The service enables patrons to "borrow" seeds, plant and harvest a crop, let a few plants go to seed, and then return new seeds for the next gardener. This idea originated in California and has spread to an additional 25 states to date. There are also seed libraries in Canada and Europe (Richmond Grows Seed Lending Library, n.d.b). What would we do without seeds? Seeds are the ultimate renewable resource. Seeds are alive, and their genetic material changes and adapts to the climatic conditions of the environment (moisture, temperature, days of sunlight) in which they are grown. Their adaptations have been a boon for humankind, as we rely on crops to maintain large populations and a modern lifestyle.

Seed diversity, however, is under attack. That may sound like the title of a B movie, but unfortunately it is not an exaggeration. Seed diversity, the very foundation of our food system, is disappearing at an alarming rate, and it is not due to an alien invasion. In many cases it is due to the success of monoculture crops (which have squeezed other species out of the commercial market), government policies, or because the people who traditionally grew them have left an agrarian lifestyle (Flower and Mooney, 1990; Nabhan and Reichhardt, 1983).

Domestic crops originated from wild species. However, these primitive varieties or landraces have not fared well. They face pressure and extinction due to habitat loss, market forces and the desire for high-yield crops. In addition many have been impacted by the flow of genetic material from domesticated crops into the wild populations (Joshi et al., 2004). The variety of genetic material within landraces has helped humankind combat many agricultural crises, including the potato blight *Phytophtora infestans*. This blight destroyed Ireland's potato crops in the 1840s, and in conjunction with British policies that prevented aid to the poor due to the belief that they would become dependent, led to a devastating famine. Resistant potatoes were eventually found in the Andes and Mexico (Flower and Mooney, 1990). The importance of genetic resources becomes apparent when one ponders the following facts: 1) fewer than 20 plant species produce most of the world's food, and 2) most of the world's population is dependent on four main crops: wheat, corn, rice, and potatoes (Smithsonian National Museum of Natural History, n.d.).

Genebanks

There have been many responses to the loss of crop diversity. One has been to form ex situ or doomsday seed banks such as the Svalbard Global Seed Vault, carved within a permafrost mountain off the coast of Norway; it holds a consistent temperature of 18 degrees Celsius. The project was the idea of Cary Fowler, a U.S. agriculturalist. The Svalbard Global Seed Vault is a joint venture between the Norwegian government and the Global Crop Diversity Trust. The project encourages countries to deposit seeds with the guarantee that they will be permitted to withdraw them at any time (Myklebust, 2013). There are now

725,000 different seeds in portions of 500 each stored in the Svalbard Global Seed Vault, which has a total capacity of 2.5 to three million seeds and has been labelled the Noah's Ark of seeds, or a "doomsday vault" (Myklebust, 2013).

According to the website for the Millennium Seed Bank Partnership they are the largest *ex situ* plant conservation effort in the world and plan to bank seeds from 25% of the world's wild plant species by 2020. Other efforts include the U.S. Government genebank, the Plant Germplasm Preservation Research Unit (PGPRU) whose mission is to improve ex situ genebanks and expand the use of genebanked samples to make genetic improvements in plants. The preservation of genetic diversity within plants may prove to be an invaluable resource as we face climate change and other threats to our crops.

Seed Libraries

The narrowing of crop diversity has led to a renewed interest in heirloom seeds and the formation of cooperatives and libraries organized around the concept of sharing knowledge and rare seeds. The Native Seeds/SEARCH (NS/S) in Tucson, Arizona, offers seeds and other related items for sale in addition to a seed library where locally adapted seeds can be borrowed and returned.

The NS/S began in 1983 as a result of a project to establish gardens on Tohono O'odham land. Co-founders Gary Nabham and Mahina Drees presented broccoli and radish seeds as potential crops and were asked by tribal leaders if they had seeds for crops that their tribal grandparents had grown. With this request, the NS/S was established to preserve traditional endangered seeds. Nearly 2,000 arid-adapted seed varieties are preserved in their seed bank, and over 500 varieties are grown in their conservation farm and offered for sale. The NS/S promotes ancient crops and their wild relatives by distributing seeds worldwide (Native Seeds/SEARCH, 2011). As NS/S co-founder Barney Burns remarked, "*If we went out today to gather the seeds in our collection, we couldn't do it. They're not there*" (Native Seeds/SEARCH, 2011).

Seed libraries are both a new and an old concept. Humankind has been sowing and sharing seeds since the dawn of the agricultural age approximately 12,000 years ago. However, the development of an organized seed library is a fairly new concept that started with Sascha DuBrul, who got the idea after volunteering with a community sustainable agriculture group (CSA) in British Columbia. During this experience he witnessed the impact of crop genetics when domestic crops were intermingled with their wild relatives. He noticed how these crossings could improve the health of the domesticated crop. The opportunity presented itself for a seed library when a large collection of seeds became available at UC Berkeley after the on-campus CSA farm was evicted to make room for trials of genetically modified corn by Novartis (McDorman and Thomas, 2012). With his seed-sharing idea and the seeds, he began to organize seed-saving workshops and founded the Bay Area Seed Interchange Library (BASIL) in 1999. In 2003, DuBrul was working in upstate New York on another farm when he visited the local Gardiner Public Library. There, he met Ken Greene, a librarian who after meeting DuBrul started a seed library as part of Gardiner Public Library. Building on its success, Greene began farming, and in 2008 he took the seeds out of the library and made them available online. Greene's Hudson Valley Seed Library is now an online library with a paid membership structure to make it financially sustainable (McDorman and Thomas, 2012).

In 2010, Rebecca Newburn, a graduate of the Seed School run by Bill McDorman, started the Richmond Grows Seed Lending Library at the main branch of the Richmond Public Library in California's East Bay. The seeds for the collection are stored in a re-purposed card catalog cabinet with drawers labeled "Super Easy," "Easy" and "Difficult" (McDorman and Thomas, 2012). Richmond Grows hosts seed-saving workshops and events, and even has a demonstration garden on site. They also focus on nurturing the efforts of other seed libraries. They host a "Create a Seed Library" webpage complete with step-by-step instructions and sample fliers, signage and brochures that can be freely downloaded and customized for other non-profit projects. As Rebecca Newburn is quoted: "We're seeing the rebirth of seed saving as an essential part of home gardening and local resilience. My vision is that more and more communities will have seed libraries and systems for sharing locally grown seeds" (McDorman and Thomas, 2012.)

In 2011, librarian and Seed School graduate Justine Hernandez spread the idea to the Pima County Library System in Tucson, Ariz., and now five branches there are starting seed libraries. Word continues to spread; a recent article in *American Libraries* notes the rise of seed libraries (Landgraf, 2011). "Our community has really embraced it," said Justine Hernandez of the Pima County Public Library. "It's really about people nurturing these plants and then sharing them with their neighbors and friends." Hernandez estimates that the library has circulated 7,000 seed packets of more than 433 varieties (Toppo, 2013).

A Facebook page for the University Seed Libraries Association (USLA) has recently been created. The USLA page is a place where students can gather online and share information about starting a lending library and preserving heirloom varieties. The potential for academic libraries to be successful offering this service is likely, given the growing adoption of sustainability efforts on academic campuses. For example, Arizona State University (ASU) is committed to fostering and increasing sustainability efforts and is one of the first universities to have a School of Sustainability. As a result, many sustainability efforts have been initiated, including a Campus Harvest organization. Harvests involve collecting oranges, dates, pecans, olives, figs, pomegranates and peaches from plants on campus and working with the university dining service and local charities to ensure the foods are consumed and not sent to landfills. In addition to local fruit and nuts, an organic herb garden is located on campus, and the entire campus grounds are cared for without pesticides. Approximately 12 tons of green waste (tree trimmings, etc.) per month is delivered to a local farm for composting and then reused on campus. The Campus Harvest organization has even created a gardening manual complete with harvesting guidelines and recipes (ASU, n.d.).

Many efforts have been spearheaded by ASU's School of Sustainability, including lectures open to the public. Lecture topics have included informational sessions by master gardeners, professors, policy makers, climate scientists and historians. In that spirit, the ASU Science Library invited Bill McDorman, the director of Native Seeds/SEARCH, to present a lecture in October of 2012 on the importance of seeds and heirloom varieties. In conjunction with the presentation, a collection of desert-adapted seeds and botanical books was curated.

Steps to Create a Library

There are many resources to guide and support individuals who want to start a seed library. Richmond Grows is a non-profit seed-lending library located within the Richmond Public Library. They generously share their experience and expertise with anyone who would like to start a seed library, and have outlined the seven basic steps needed to start a library (Richmond Grows a Seed Lending Library, n.d.). The steps are summarized below:

- Organize and contact your natural supporters (permaculture clubs, etc.).
- Locate a space that is highly used and visible.
- Acquire needed library materials.
- Create signage for your library.
- Create a brochure.
- Launch your seed library.
- Provide library orientations.

Conclusion

Libraries have seen their patrons' needs change as well as the formats of the content they provide those patrons. While books are still the brand of libraries, seed lending may be another service that helps libraries retain their place in the community (Runyon, 2013). Libraries have an opportunity to build non-book services, which add value to the community while they continue to support traditional services such as book collections (Haefele, 2011).

Seeds are a building block for our food. Starting a seed library at your public or university library is one way to reach out to the local community, while supporting campus sustainability efforts and providing a valuable ecological service. As the focus on sustainability and local foods increases, so too will seed lending on university campuses. By planting heirloom seeds as well as those partial to the local climate, library patrons can help preserve genetic diversity for future generations.

References

Arizona State University, Ground Services, Arboretum. (n.d.). *Guide to harvesting produce at ASU*. Retrieved from http://www.asu.edu/fm/documents/arboretum/CampusHarvest.pdf

Fowler, C., & Mooney, P. R. (1990). *Shattering: food, politics, and the loss of genetic diversity*. Tucson: University of Arizona Press.

Haefele, C. (2011). The case for home-grown, sustainable, next generation library services. *Public Services Quarterly, 7*(3-4), 158-168.

Joshi, B. K., Upadhyay, M. P., Gauchan, D., Sthapit, B. R., & Joshi, K. D. (2004). Red listing of agricultural crop species, varieties and landraces. *Nepal Agricultural Research Journal, 5*, 73-80.

Landgraf, G. (2011). Seed lending libraries bloom. *American Libraries*. Retrieved from http://americanlibrariesmagazine.org/green-your-library/seed-lending-libraries-bloom

McDorman, B. and Thomas, S. (2012). Sowing revolution: Seed libraries offer hope for freedom of Food. *Acres, 42*(1). Retrieved from http://www.nativeseeds.org/pdf/Jan2012_McDormanThomas.pdf

Millennium Seed Bank. (n.d.). *About the millennium seed bank partnership*. Retrieved from http://www.kew.org/science-conservation/save-seed-prosper/millennium-seed-bank/index.htm

Myklebust, J. P. (2013, January 19). Rich research pickings from world's largest seed bank. *University World News*. Retrieved from http://www.universityworldnews.com/article.php?story=2013011714064150

Nabhan, G. P. (1989). *Enduring seeds: Native American agriculture and wild plant conservation*. Tucson: University of Arizona Press.

Nabhan, G.P. and Karen L. Reichhardt. (1983). Hopi protection of helianthus anomalus, a rare sunflower. *The Southwestern Naturalist, 28*(2), 231-235. Retrieved from http://www.jstor.org/stable/3671392

Native Seeds/SEARCH. (2011). *History and mission*. Retrieved from http://www.nativeseeds.org/index.php/about-us/historymission

Richmond Grows Seed Lending Library. (n.d. a) *Create a library*. Retrieved from http://www.richmondgrowsseeds.org/create-a-library.html

Richmond Grows Seed Lending Library. (n.d. b) *Sister seed lending libraries*. Retrieved from http://www.richmondgrowsseeds.org/sister-libraries.html

Runyon, L. (2013, February 2). How to save a public library: Make it a seed bank. *National Public Radio*. Podcast retrieved from http://www.npr.org/blogs/thesalt/2013/02/02/170846948/how-to-save-a-public-library-make-it-a-seed-bank

Smith, B. (2012, October 24). Libraries help to grow gardening interest: Valley permaculture provides seeds on loan. *The Republic*. Retrieved from http://www.azcentral.com/community/phoenix/articles/20121024libraries-help-grow-gardening-interest.html

Smithsonian National Museum of Natural History. (n.d.). *What does it mean to be human?* Retrieved from http://humanorigins.si.edu/human-characteristics/change

Toppo, G. (2013, March 6). Libraries offer weird things to draw new borrowers. *USA Today*. Retrieved from http://www.usatoday.com/story/news/nation/2013/03/06/public-libraries-loaning/1962011/

U.S. Department of Agriculture. (2011). Agricultural Research Services. *Plant germplasm preservation research unit*. Retrieved from http://www.ars.usda.gov/

Sustainability and the Increasing Energy Demand to Access Library Resources

Mara M. J. Egherman

Abstract

One constant in academic librarianship is change; particularly in the ways librarians perform their work. How do librarians serve their stated missions while approaching new technologies in an environmentally responsible fashion? This chapter reports on how librarians in higher education are taking a leadership role in reducing energy demands to access library resources.

Introduction

Award-winning journalist Timothy Egan praised environmental initiatives within the higher education sector in *The New York Times.* He stated that the sustainability movement ". . . seems to have the greatest resonance on college campuses, always a home for new thinking" (2006). History professor James Farrell also thought about the environment and the college campus publishing *The Nature of College* (2010), an eye-opening view to the resources used on a residential campus each day, from where a campus gets its water supply to the staggering amount of energy required to support universities' daily technology habits. The authors of a 2012 *Encyclopedia of Sustainability,* a law professor and a sustainability researcher, asserted that "[a]s centers for advanced learning and education, colleges and universities are places for leadership in environmental policy. This is also true in the area of sustainability" (Collin, p. 126).

In a recent *Chronicle of Higher Education* editorial, the sustainability director at a large university argued that the push for campus sustainability is at its peak and that we must take additional action at this key point in order to continue to progress toward greener campuses (Newport, 2012).

Broad global awareness of sustainability issues to include climate change may in fact *depend* on the education and higher education communities according to the United Nations Environment Program. Their *Greening Universities Toolkit,* 2013, states:

> "Education has been described as humanity's best hope and most effective means in the quest to achieve sustainable development. In this context, universities have a special responsibility to help define and also to *exemplify* best practice. …Universities are coming under increasing pressure to engage with and respond to climate change and other sustainable development issues and the associated risks and challenges. They are expected to be the engines and innovation centers for sustainable development through teaching and learning, research and knowledge transfer." (United Nations Environment Program, p. 5)

The liberal arts and sustainability are natural partners, because beyond needing scholars in the hard sciences, this effort requires the ethics, values and cultural knowledge of humanists (Weissman, 2012, pp. 6-13). When research and keeping records of cultural knowledge are considered, libraries are an obvious place to start.

Academic Librarians' Initiatives

In light of current sustainability discussions in and about academia, a small group of eco-minded librarians working at various universities throughout the nation were concerned about what appeared to be dwindling interest in the two-decades-old Task Force on the Environment (TFOE) of the American Library Association (ALA)'s Social Responsibility Roundtable (SRRT). Chief among these were Madeleine Charney of the University of Massachusetts, Beth Filar-Williams of the University of North Carolina at Greensboro, and Bonnie Smith of the University of Florida. It was reported by the editor of this volume and a longtime leader of that group that TFOE attendance at the ALA midwinter meeting in 2011 had stagnated and the ["y]ear of 2011 was not fruitful on environmental fronts for the Task Force and ALA" (Jankowska, 2011, p. 15). Several academic librarians active in the work of the Association for the Advancement of Sustainability in Higher Education (AASHE) thought that an official group under the auspices of ALA was critical to maintain. In winter 2012, the concerned librarians initiated a yearlong series of webinars (Libraries for Sustainability Webinar, 2012) to brainstorm about reinvigorating the TFOE group.

Dozens of librarians, library workers, and LIS graduate students attended the webinars. At ALA midwinter 2013, the group had the opportunity to act quickly on what had become the consensus during the webinar series: proposing a new ALA Sustainability Round Table (SustainRT). SustainRT would move one level higher than TFOE in the ALA hierarchy, hopefully drawing more librarians and others in, to include those from academic, school, public and special libraries. Webinar organizers had posted an online petition to gain the 100 required signatures for such an initiative, and in a very few weeks had more than the needed number. New leaders had emerged via the webinars. Aided by mentor Jonathan Betz-Zall from the SRRT, librarian Ashley Jones of Miami University in Ohio brought the petition to the ALA Committee on Organization. It was briefly discussed, approved, and sent on for the final seal by ALA Council. The Council approved it on 28 January 2013 (ALA Council, 2013). Leighann Wood of ALA kept the group informed of its official ALA status and aided in forming a new listserv. Newcomer Joseph Fox of Indianapolis Public Library organized a SustainRT cultural walk along the canal in Indianapolis during the Association for College and Research Libraries (ACRL) conference (Filar Williams, 2013). The first official SustainRT ALA session was held in July 2013 in Chicago. Currently the group is crafting bylaws and establishing a social media presence. The round table defines sustainability broadly in its mission statement (http://www.ala.org/sustainrt/home).

Why the Time for Action is Now

On a global scale, few deny that there has been significant, human-created change influencing the environment. In March 2012, *Time* magazine listed "the ten ideas that are changing your life" to include the assertion, "Nature is over" (Walsh, pp. 82-3). The accompanying photo was a stark double page landscape of a city devoid of all plant or animal life, and sans human activity from the camera's viewpoint.

Prompt action is needed because the library profession, too, is seeing a lot of change. Sometimes change seems to be the only constant in the current state of librarianship. Users constantly demand increasing amounts of information at their fingertips. Institutions are flocking to cloud-based storage. People buy more and more electronic devices to access all of the data on the cloud. The result puts further pressure on limited planetary resources. Gobinda Chowdhury declared:

"Information retrieval, which was once of interest and concern for a select few, especially those who were engaged in knowledge-intensive activities like education and research, has now become an integral part of our everyday activities . . . [w]e conduct billions of searches every month to find information on the web, library catalogs and databases, digital libraries, institutional repositories, e-books, e-journals, and so on." (2012, pp. 1067-1068)

Tony Horava, in his article about managing library collections in the digital age, also summed it up well: "The blurring of traditional boundaries has become a hallmark of our age. The interconnections between our services and collections are a consequence of the technological, social, economic and educational climate in which we work" (2010, p. 146). The demand for electric power and the emission of carbon increases while providers (Lefevre & Orgerie, 2010) and policy-makers try to keep up (Ruth, 2011). At this point, the energy supply is simply not keeping up with demand (Vale & Vale, 2009, pp. 216-225).

In terms of hardware, the average estimated lifespan of computers in 2005 was only two years (Francis, 2011, p. 145). A business writer in 2009 anticipated that as laptops were being shipped in high volume compared to desktops, that their lifespans were even shorter ". . . more likely to be disposed of on an annual basis" (Salkever, 2009). Peoples' desire for frequently upgraded versions of laptops, notebook computers, and smartphones continues to outpace the efforts of those companies that have begun to green the supporting power grid. The American population has not rejected "planned obsolescence" as a sales strategy for the many electronic gadgets and other consumer goods that are advertised to them at every turn. Moreover, manufacturers have not been careful about using sustainable and safe methods for built-up goods or managing waste. There are close to 2 billion laptops and PCs in use worldwide (Ruth, 2011, p. 210). "Ecodesign has not become a natural part of the electronics business" (Francis, 2011, p. 145). "In the United States, at least 3 million tons of computers end up in landfills annually. There they very slowly decompose and leach over 70 known hazardous chemicals into the environment" (Collin & Collin, 2010, p. 140). The U.S. ranked 45th globally in sustainability efforts in 2005 because our greenhouse gas emissions are so high and we generate far too much waste (Bureau of National Affairs, Inc, 2005).

The convenient, latest-model devices are powered with electricity and each Internet search contributes an additional energy demand. Chowdhury (2012) estimated that a single Google search generated nearly 1.4 g of carbon dioxide (p. 1070). Though many professions have seen large shifts from paper to digital documents and increases in use of data and metadata, academic librarians have a particular leadership opportunity in this area. They are trained in the organization and dissemination of information. Librarians are in a position to educate themselves, their colleagues and their users on sustainability.

Use of Technology Helps Librarians and Libraries

"Technology makes libraries more relevant and useful," argued keynote speaker Michael Porter of Library Renewal at a recent Midwest state academic library conference (2012). Most academic libraries began serving their patron base via chat a few years ago, so that students and faculty did not need to cross the campus to the physical library for reference help (Devine, Paladino & Davis, 2011). Others have evolved to serve distance education courses with library support and resources. More recently, reference and research consultation has been also offered via text, as students and faculty have migrated toward mobile communication (Vecchione & Ruppel, 2012, pp. 355-372).

The opportunities for shared online resources (Golden, 2008) have huge implications for academia. Cloud computing allows individual users to have a great amount of power and capacity at their fingertips (Jaeger, 2009). Instead of applications that reside and run on a user's computer, users can work on a network that thousands may access simultaneously (Chu-Carroll, 2011). Finally, preservation and disaster recovery for special collections and valuable archives was hugely improved with cloud technology (Breeding, 2013).

Unfortunately, it is simultaneously true that, "technology is a waste creator on several levels. Even if the new technology has a lower environmental impact, decisions about what to do with the old technology need to be considered for sustainability purposes" (Collin & Collin, 2010, p. 140). Farrell asserted that people are not only connected to their servers and the cloud, "but to coal and uranium mines and to natural gas fields. . .The immateriality of computing "rests on a very material base" (2010, p. 147) .

Dialogues around best practices for energy efficiency of electronics and educating the academic community and the general public about energy sources, energy use, design and creation of electronics, and the disposal of e-waste have begun within the information science (IS) and information technology (IT) communities. The traditional library community needs to work to catch up. Though many graduate institutions now refer to our field as library and information science (LIS), the fields of library science and information science have not merged with regard to sustainability research about our online, cloud-based workplaces.

What Can Librarians Do To Save Energy?

Librarians and library workers may begin by taking it on as part of their jobs to teach themselves, their colleagues, and their users about energy use in their work. They should begin by looking to places where things are being done more sustainably already. For example, most sources the author used for this essay pointed to the European Union as having more sustainability policies in place than anywhere else. Many library professionals know where to look for resources from ALA or ACRL. The International Federation of Library Associations (IFLA), also has a regular sustainability agenda at their meetings, and has a special interest group on Environmental Sustainability in Libraries—librarians may look to their publications for guidance.

Academic librarians can team up with student life programs when they have dormitory competitions for least energy usage, publicizing a resource guide as a useful tool to aid in active student learning. They may partner with campus food services when they try going trayless or incorporating local food into their on campus meal plans by advertising books and other resources the library has on that subject. Libraries can invite other departments' projects to their physical or virtual spaces. For example, coordinating with one of the science departments, an interactive display might be designed in the library where solar or pedal-power charges users' mobile devices. Physics and engineering students could demonstrate their work in the library regarding energy use or energy savings. Librarians may bring in speakers or authors whose focus is sustainability. A visit or book reading by a green building architect, a local food advocate, or a prose writer or poet incorporating environmental themes into their work can inspire green innovation and entrepreneurship.

Signs on printers, scanners, and computers may educate users about the power needed for each piece of equipment. Thin clients, desktops, laptops and notebooks could be compared for efficiency. Just as paper towel dispensers say, "these come from trees," labels on computers and scanners might say "powered by coal" or "this machine uses half the energy of that machine to do the same task." A discussion whether it is ultimately greener to acquire a print book or an e-book could also start discussion. Ideas about data curation and storage may ensue, including what value is attributed to the 24/7 access and text searchability of an e-book. This versus the economic and environmental cost, longevity of the device used to access the e-book, and branding may be debated. One may pose the question about what a print book equals in a carbon offset. Vale and Vale, co-authors of the provocatively titled book *Time to eat the dog? The real guide to sustainable living*, offered a very detailed argument for the carbon offset a person would need to purchase, or something that you would give up in order to make up for buying their paperback, 384 page book. Among their solutions are that one could give up two pints of beer or one 100 gram bar of chocolate (2009, p. 290). Maybe your library users could come up with additional equivalents.

Conclusion

The work done in libraries has changed and will continue to change. Librarians and library workers need to keep abreast of how what they do and how they do it affects the world around them, from global energy consumption to the toxic components used in the technology industry and electronic waste. Librarians and library workers should educate themselves, demonstrate role-model sustainable behaviors, and reach out to their communities to promote sustainable practices.

References

ALA Council. (2013, January 28). *Actions of the Council--ALA Council II*. Retrieved from http://www.ala.org/aboutala/sites/ala.org.aboutala/files/content/Actions%20-%202013%20ALA%20Midwinter%20Meeting_0.pdf

Breeding, M. (2013, March). Digitial archiving in the age of cloud computing. *Computers in Libraries, 33*(2), 22-26.

Bureau of National Affairs, Inc. (2005, January 31). U.S. Sustainability Efforts Rank 45th Among Countries. *Environmental Compliance, 12*(3), pp. 33-48.

Chowdhury, G. (2012). An agenda for green information retrieval research. *Information Processing and Management, 48*, 1067-1077.

Chu-Carroll, M. C. (2011). *Code in the cloud: Programming Google App Engine*. Raleigh, NC: Pragmatic Bookshelf.

Collin, R. M. & Collin, R. W. (2010). *Encyclopedia of sustainability*. (Vols. 1-3). Santa Barbara, CA: Greenwood Press.

Devine, C., Paladino, E. B., & Davis, J. A. (2011). Chat reference training after one decade: The results of a national survey of academic libraries. *Journal of Academic Librarianship*, 37, 197-206.

Egan, T. (2006, January 8). The greening of America's campuses. *New York Times*. Retrieved from http://www.nytimes.com/2006/01/08/education/edlife/egan_environment.html?pagewanted=1&_r=0&ei=5070&en=4e18 8a755c0efb02&ex=1138770000

Farrell, J. (2010). *The nature of college: How a new understanding of campus life can change the world*. Minneapolis: Milkweed Editions.

Filar Williams, B. (2013). Canal Walk with SustainRT. *ACRL 2013 Conference Photos* . Indianapolis. Retrieved from http://www.flickr.com/photos/filarwilliams/8648512602/

Francis, S. (2011). Eco-Electronics. In D. Mulvaney (Ed.), *Green technology: An A-Z guide* (pp. 143-148). Los Angeles: Sage.

Golden, C. (2008). On being green. *Educause Review, 43*(3), 88.

Horava, IFLA: International Federation of Library Associations and Institutions. (2011). *Environmental Sustainability and Libraries Special Interest Group*. Retrieved from http://www.ifla.org/en/environmental-sustainability-and-libraries

Jaeger, P. T., Lin, J., & Simmons, S. N. (2009). Where is the cloud? Geography, economics, environment, and jurisdiction in cloud computing. *First Monday, 14*(5), 1-16.

Jankowska, M. A. (2011). Going beyond environmental programs and green practices at the American Library Association. *Electronic Green Journal, 1*(32), 1-17. Retrieved from http://www.escholarship.org/uc/item/1zs6k7m2

Lefevre, L., & Orgerie, A.-C. (2010, March). Designing and evaluating an energy efficient cloud. *Journal of Supercomputing,* 352-373.

Libraries for Sustainability Webinar Series (2012). Call to Action and Collaboration, held 28 February, 24 April, 12 June and 28 August 2012.

Newport, D. (2012, April 1). Campus sustainability: It's about people. *Chronicle of Higher Education.* Retrieved from http://chronicle.com/article/Campus-Sustainability-Its/131370/

Porter, M. (2012, March 25) *Build on our strengths: Design for our future.* Iowa Library Association/Association for College and Research Libraries Conference. Decorah, Iowa.

Ruth, S. (2011). Reducing ICT-related carbon emissions: An exemplar for global energy policy? *IETE Technical Review,* 207-211.

Salkever, A. (2009, August 10). How green is your laptop? Eco-electronics registry now global. *DailyFinance.com.* Retrieved from http://www.dailyfinance.com/2009/08/10/how-green-is-your-laptop-eco-electronics-registry-now-global

United Nations Environment Program. (2013). *Greening Universities Toolkit (draft).* Retrieved from http://www.unep.org/training/publications/Rio+20/Greening_unis_toolkit%20120326.pdf

Vale, R., & Vale, B. (2009). *Time to eat the dog?: The real guide to sustainable living.* London: Thames and Hudson.

Vecchione, A., & Ruppel, M. (2012). Reference is neither here nor there: A snapshot of SMS reference services. *Reference Librarian,* 53(4). doi:10.108 0/02763877.2012.704569.

Walsh, B. (2012, March 12). Nature is over. *Time.*

Weissman, N. (2012, Fall). Sustainability and liberal education: Partners by nature. *Liberal Education.*

About Contributing Authors

Introduction

Maria Anna Jankowska <majankowska@library.ucla.edu> has a Ph.D. in economics from Poznan University of Economics in Poland and MLIS degree from the University of California in Berkeley. Currently she is a Social Sciences Librarian at the Charles E. Young Research Library, University of California at Los Angeles. Maria represents the library in the UCLA Academic Sustainability Committee and works closely with the UCLA Office on Sustainability. She is a funder and general editor of the *Electronic Green Journal* and a long-time active member of the American Library Association's Task Force on the Environment, and more recently the Association for the Advancement of Sustainability in Higher Education. She co-authored with Bonnie Smith from University of Florida Libraries and Marianne Buehler from the University of Nevada Libraries an article "Engagement of academic libraries and information science schools in creating curriculum for sustainability: An exploratory study" to be published in *The Journal of Academic Librarianship*.

Section 1

Legitimizing the Local: Integrating Sustainability into Information Literacy Instruction and First-Year Composition

Kathleen J. Ryan <kathleen.ryan3@msu.montana.edu> is a new professor of Rhetoric and Composition at Montana State University and formerly directed the Composition Program at the University of Montana. She teaches courses in composition pedagogy and rhetorical studies, and her research focuses on feminist rhetorical studies and writing program administration. She coedited *Walking and Talking Feminist Rhetoric* with Lindal Buchanan and is one of the coauthors of *GenAdmin: Theorizing WPA Identities in the Twenty-First Century.*

Megan Stark <megan.stark@umontana.edu> is the Undergraduate Services Librarian and Assistant Professor at the University of Montana. She teaches in the first-year curriculum and coordinates the library's information literacy instruction program at the undergraduate level. She studies sustainability, civic engagement and place-based research within the context of information literacy and academic libraries.

Three for One: Teaching Sustainable Education, Information Literacy, and Visual Literacy with the Inventory Compilation Assignment

Alessia Zanin-Yost <azaniny@wcu.edu> is the Research and Instruction Librarian/Visual and Performing Arts Liaison at Western Carolina University, North Carolina. She holds an MA in art history from UC Davis and her MLIS is from San Jose State University. Her field of research is teaching and assessment of visual and information literacy, the intersection of how information/visual literacy skills affect lifelong skills and curriculum planning. She has presented nationally and internationally on these topics. Her writings have appeared in a variety of scholarly journals and books. Alessia is actively involved with ACRL.

Sustainability Literacy and Information Literacy: Leveraging Librarian Expertise

Toni M. Carter < tcarter@auburn.edu> received a MLIS and MA in History from the University of Alabama and has twelve years of experience in academic and special libraries. Her research interests include information literacy instruction and assessment. Toni serves as an Instruction/Reference Librarian and liaison to the College of Human Sciences at Auburn University.

Greg Schmidt <schmigr@auburn.edu> is the Special Collections Librarian for Auburn University and serves as liaison to the Academic Sustainability Program and the Department of Sociology, Anthropology and Social Work. He received his MLIS from the University of Alabama in 2007. Prior to his MLIS, he earned a Masters in Rural Sociology from Auburn University with a research focus on social capital and community opposition to chemical weapons incineration in Alabama.

Teaching Sustainable Information Literacy: A Collaborative Endeavor in the Humanities

Amy Pajewski < apajewski@wtamu.edu> is a Reference & Instruction Librarian at West Texas A&M University where she provides leadership in social media outreach and emerging technologies in the classroom. She is near completion of her MA in English Literature focusing on Western Eco-literature and is a poetry editor for Sundog Lit. Her work has appeared in numerous literary journals and she serves on the editorial committee for Open Library of Humanities. Amy holds an MS in Library Science from Clarion University of Pennsylvania as well as a BA in English from Millersville University. She is also a graduate from the Harvard Graduate School's Leadership Institute for Academic Librarians class of 2013.

Making Research Real: Focusing on Community-Based Sustainability

Laura Burt-Nicholas <burt-nicholasl@cod.edu> is a Reference Librarian and Assistant Professor at the College of DuPage. She serves as Science Liaison, managing the print and electronic resources in the physical and natural sciences, and working with faculty to infuse information literacy into the science curriculum.

She studies sustainability, civic engagement and place-based research within the context of information literacy and academic libraries.

Teaching by Doing: Sustainability Education and Practice in a Student-Services Program

Mary G. Scanlon <scanlomg@wfu.edu> is the Research and Instruction Librarian for Business & Economics in the Z. Smith Reynolds Library at Wake Forest University. She earned her M.B.A at the Weatherhead School of Management at Case Western University and her M.L.I.S at Kent State University. She serves as a founding member of the ZSR Sustainability Committee; the library's Green Team Co-Captain - a liaison to the university's Office of Sustainability; and a regular volunteer at the Piedmont Triad Earth Day Fair. Her most recent publication is *The Entrepreneurial Librarian: Essays on the Infusion of Private-Business Dynamism* into Professional Service from McFarland, Inc.

Peter Romanov <romanopa@wfu.edu> is a Library Specialist III at the Z. Smith Reynolds Library at Wake Forest University. He earned his Bachelor of Arts in English at High Point University and his Master of Arts in Liberal Studies at Wake Forest University. He serves as the Chair and founding member of the ZSR Sustainability Committee and serves as the library's Green Team Co-Captain - a liaison to the university's Office of Sustainability.

Mary Beth Lock <lockmb@wfu.edu> is the Director of Access Services at the Z. Smith Reynolds Library at Wake Forest University in Winston Salem, North Carolina. She earned her B.S. degree in biology from Wayne State University and her M.L.S degree from North Carolina Central University. She served on both steering committees, in 2009 and 2011, which planned and executed The Entrepreneurial Librarian Conference. A recent publication is a chapter, "Ethical Uses of Information: the Good, the Bad, the Confusing" for an open-source information literacy textbook. She has been an environmental activist all of her adult life and continually works to implement more sustainable practices into her home and work.

Library Showcase: Modeling Sustainability across Campus

Dawn Emsellem <dawn.emsellem@salve.edu> is an Outreach and Instruction Librarian at Salve Regina University. She earned a BA in Political Science from

Barnard College and a Master's in Library and Information Science from University of Illinois. She has done research on grassroots environmental justice activism in New York City, filmed a documentary about a city-planning and environmental activist in Newport, RI, and observed the corporate perspective of environmental issues while working for a lobbyist with waste management and short line railroad clients at New York's City Hall. She also earned a certificate in sustainable village design and building techniques at the Farm Ecovillage in Summertown, Tennessee. At Salve Regina University, she formed the staff/faculty environmental group and acted as facilitator for the first year, and formed and facilitated the library's building-wide environmental group.

Jameson F. Chace <jameson.chace@salve.edu> is an Associate Professor of Biology and coordinator of the Environmental Studies program at Salve Regina University. He earned his BS-Biology from Eastern Connecticut State University, MA and PhD in Ecology from the University of Colorado-Boulder. During his post-doctoral fellowship at Villanova University he helped establish a university sustainability policy, and did the same at Salve Regina University in 2006. He and his students conduct research on water quality, sustainable agriculture, seabird responses to climate change and landscape effects on avian communities and populations.

Section 2

Building an Academic Library Collection to Support Sustainability

Amy Brunvand <amy.brunvand@utah.edu> is the Associate Librarian in the University of Utah J. Willard Marriott Library Digital Scholarship Lab. She serves as librarian liaison for Environmental and Sustainability Studies, and Environmental Humanities programs at the University of Utah. She writes a monthly column for *Catalyst* magazine in Salt Lake City focusing on local environmental issues.

Alison Regan <alison.regan@utah.edu> is the Associate Librarian and Head of Scholarship and Education Services at the University of Utah J. Willard Marriott Library and Adjunct Associate Professor in the University of Utah, Department of Communication University Writing Program. She serves as liaison for the Honors College and for a decade was the liaison to Gender Studies. From

1994-1999, she was Assistant Professor of English at the University of Hawaii-Manoa.

Joshua Lenart <joshua.lenart@utah.edu> recently defended his dissertation *Wilderness and Wildlife in the American West: Confronting Rhetoric in the Mule Deer Debate* and completed his Ph.D. in English Studies at the University of Utah. In Fall 2013, he will begin an adjunct teaching position at Westminister College in Salt Lake City.

Jessica Breiman <jessica.breiman@utah.edu> is a Multi-Media Archivist in the University of Utah J. Willard Marriott Library Special Collections Department, and is completing an MLS at Emporia State University. She has expertise in Art and Art History and in information visualization.

Emily Bullough <emily.bullough@utah.edu> works in the University of Utah J. Willard Marriott Library Acquisitions department. She recently finished her MSLS at the University of North Texas. She has been a long-standing member of the Marriott Library Green Team. She is liaison to the Ethnic Studies Program and teaches extensively for the Education Services Team.

Interdisciplinary Collaboration for Collection Development in Sustainability: Starting from Scratch

Greg Schmidt <schmigr@auburn.edu> is the Special Collections Librarian for Auburn University and serves as liaison to the Academic Sustainability Program and the Department of Sociology, Anthropology and Social Work. He received his MLIS from the University of Alabama in 2007. Prior to his MLIS, he earned a Masters in Rural Sociology from Auburn University with a research focus on social capital and community opposition to chemical weapons incineration in Alabama.

Kasia Leousis <ksl0008@auburn.edu> is the Architecture and Art Librarian at Auburn University and serves as liaison to the College of Architecture, Design and Construction and the Department of Art. She received her Master's in Art History and MSLS from the University of North Carolina at Chapel Hill.

Section 3

Connecting Journal Articles with Their Underlying Data: Encouraging Sustainable Scholarship through the PKP-Dataverse Integration Project

Eleni Castro <ecastro@fas.harvard.edu> is a Research Coordinator for the Data Science team at Harvard University's Institute for Quantitative Social Science (IQSS). She previously worked in various roles in library related settings (in Canada and the USA) with an emphasis on technology and improving public access to information. She has an MLIS from McGill University.

Library Publishing Services for Sustainability

Barbara DeFelice <Barbara.DeFelice@dartmouth.edu> is the Director of the Digital Resources and Scholarly Communication Programs at the Dartmouth College Library, and works on digital publishing, copyright, and open access issues. She serves as the liaison librarian to Dartmouth's Environmental Studies Program. She holds a Master in Science in Library Science from Simmons College and a Masters in Arts in Liberal Studies from Dartmouth College. She recently completed work on the ACRL White Paper "Intersections of Scholarly Communication and Information Literacy: Creating Strategic Collaborations for a Changing Academic Environment".

Community Archiving and Sustainability: Denison University's Homestead

Joshua Finnell <finnellj@denison.edu> is the Humanities Librarian at William Howard Doane Library at Denison University and a visiting lecturer in the Library Science Program at McNeese State University. For the last four years, he has served on the advisory board for the Denison University Homestead. His work has appeared in *Library Philosophy and Practice*, *Journal for the Study of Radicalism*, and *New Library World*.

Section 4

The Triple Bottom Line: Portable Applications and Best Practices for Sustainability in Academic Libraries

Anne Marie Casey <caseya3@erau.edu> is Director of the Hunt Library at Embry-Riddle Aeronautical University. Prior to this she worked at the libraries of Central Michigan University, National University, the University of Louisiana at Lafayette, and the Springfield (MA) City Library. She holds a PhD in Managerial Leadership in the Information Professions from Simmons College, an AMLS from the University of Michigan, an MA in Medieval Studies from the Catholic University of America, and a BA in Classics from UMass-Amherst. Anne Marie is the 2007 recipient of the ACRL Distance Learning Section Award.

Jon E. Cawthorne serves as the Associate Dean for Public Services and Assessment at Florida State University Libraries (FSUL). Before joining FSUL, Jon worked as the Associate University Librarian for Public Services at Boston College and held positions of increasing leadership responsibility at San Diego State University, Detroit Public Library, University of Oregon and Ohio State University. Jon earned a PhD in Managerial Leadership in the Information Professions from Simmons College in Boston, an MLS from the University of Maryland at College Park and a BA from the Evergreen State College. Jon attended leadership institutes at Snowbird, Frye and Senior Fellows and his research focuses on leadership, human resources and organizational culture.

Kathleen De Long is Associate University Librarian (Human Resources and Teaching/Learning), University of Alberta Libraries. As well as her MLIS, Kathleen has a Master's in Public Management from the University of Alberta, and recently completed her doctorate in Managerial Leadership in the Information Professions at Simmons College in Boston. Her current research focuses upon investigating leadership within the library profession. In 2003, Kathleen was awarded the Miles Blackwell Award for Outstanding Academic Librarian by the Canadian Association of College and University Libraries.

Irene M.H. Herold is the University Librarian at the University of Hawaii at Manoa. Previously she served as the Dean of the Library at Keene State College in New Hampshire. She holds a Masters in history from Western Illinois University as well as her B.A. and M.L.S. from the University of Washington in Seattle. In 2012, she completed her doctorate in Managerial Leadership in the Information Professions at Simmons College in Boston. Herold is currently editing a forthcoming volume on academic library leadership development programs.

Adriene Lim is the Dean of University Libraries at Oakland University in Michigan. Previously she served in several positions at Portland State University and Wayne State University. Lim earned her Ph.D. in Managerial Leadership in the Information Professions at Simmons College in Boston in 2012. She holds an MLIS and a bachelor's degree in Fine Arts from Wayne State University. Lim received the Loleta D. Fyan Award for creative library service from the Michigan Library Association in 2004 and the Butler Award for excellence in faculty service at Portland State in 2007.

Becoming Sustainability Leaders: A Professional Development Experience for Librarians

Madeleine Charney <mcharney@library.umass.edu> is the Sustainability Studies Librarian at the University of Massachusetts Amherst. She holds an MLS from the University of Rhode Island and an MALD from the Conway School of Landscape Design. Her areas of expertise include food systems, small farms, and perm culture design.

Academic Libraries as Sustainability Leaders

Karren Nichols <karren.nichols@utah.edu> is the Administrative and Sustainability Coordinator at the J. Willard Marriott Library, University of Utah. She is dedicated to the expansion of green teams and believes the most successful way to implement a sustainability project is through student, staff, and faculty collaboration.

Greening the Mothership: Growing the Environmental Sustainability Group at the UC San Diego Library

Kim Kane <kmkane@ucsd.edu> is the Government Information Acquisitions Specialist at UC San Diego. She earned her MLS at Southern Connecticut State

University. She serves as the Chair of the UC San Diego Library Environmental Sustainability Group and as a Staff Representative on the UC San Diego Advisory Committee on Sustainability.

Annelise Sklar <asklar@ucsd.edu> is the Librarian for Political Science, Environmental Policy, Law & Society, International Government Information, and Social Sciences Data at UC San Diego. She previously worked at the University of New Mexico and has an MSLS from the University of North Carolina at Chapel Hill, where she also served as a library intern at the Environmental Protection Agency Research Triangle Park campus.

Sustainability: Putting Principles into Practice at a Catholic University Library

Ted Bergfelt <bergfeltt@duq.edu> has a BA in English Literature and a Master's degree in library science, both from the University of Pittsburgh. He was coordinator of Public Services at Carlow University for over a decade before coming to Duquesne. He is currently a Reference and Instruction Librarian at Gumberg Library, where he serves as liaison to the departments of English, Philosophy, Theology, and the Center for Health Care Ethics. Since the Gumberg Library's adoption of the LibGuides content management system for the creation of library-related webpages, Ted has become one of its most experienced users and takes great pleasure in creating guides that point users in his subject areas to all useful resources.

Allison Brungard <brungard@duq.edu> is a Reference and Instruction Librarian at the Gumberg Library at Duquesne University. She earned a Bachelor of Arts degree from Youngstown State University and a Masters of Library and Information Science degree from the University of Pittsburgh. Allison has more than 13 years of experience in academic libraries and currently serves as Liaison to the Biology, Chemistry and Biochemistry, Environmental Science, Forensics, and Physics Departments. She is an instructor of Research and information Skills, a core curriculum course, and a member of the university's Academic Sustainability Committee and the library's Web Committee. Allison participated in ACRL's Institute for Information Literacy and is currently a member of the Western Pennsylvania/West Virginia Chapter of ACRL and the Special Libraries Association, Academic Libraries Division.

Seed Libraries: Growing a New Library Service

René Tanner <rene.tanner@asu.edu> is the Life Sciences Librarian and a library liaison to the School of Sustainability at Arizona State University in Tempe, Arizona. Previously, she was the Agricultural Sciences Librarian at Montana State University in Bozeman, Montana. She has an MA in Library Science and an MS in Soil and Water Science from the University of Arizona.

Sustainability and the Increasing Energy Demand to Access Library Resources

Mara M. J. Egherman <eghermanm@central.edu> is the collection management librarian at Central College in Pella, Iowa. She holds a B.A. in women's studies from the University of Wisconsin–Madison, an interdisciplinary M.A. from San Diego State University, and M.L.I.S. from the University of Iowa. She helped facilitate the Libraries for Sustainability Webinar series in 2012 and was fortunate to witness the resulting birth of the ALA Sustainability Round Table (SustainRT) at the ALA Midwinter 2013 conference in Seattle. Mara is a prairie gardener and a vegetarian. She carpools to work, unplugs her workstation every evening, hangs her laundry out to dry outdoors and in, and has recently reduced the urban heat island effect in her own little corner of the Midwest by depaving her driveway.

Index

formation can be obtained at www.ICGtesting.com
the USA
2209280214
5LV00004B/1030/P

CPSIA in
Printed in
LVOW08
3755